SCHOLASTIC

Jumbo Book of Fun for Kids

This book belongs to:

Editor: Ourania Papacharalambous
Design: Mina Chen
Production: Radames Espinoza, Michelle H. Kim
Cover illustration: Eric Barclay

Interior images: ©: 7: OlenaKlymenok/iStockphoto; 12: Dean Macadam; 17 top right: Askold Romanov/iStockphoto; 31: nayro2008/iStockphoto; 42: Paige Keiser; 44: peanutpie/iStockphoto; 51: vectorbomb/iStockphoto; 75: Garry Colby; 82 top right, bottom left: TopVectors/iStockphoto; 90: natixa/iStockphoto; 96: dedMazay/iStockphoto; 97: Peter Pahl; 105 top left: xenia_ok/iStockphoto; 107 hamster: photohampster/iStockphoto; 107 guinea pig: Refluo/iStockphoto; 118: Michelle Barbera; 130 cupcakes: 4x6/iStockphoto; 137: Bigmouse108/iStockphoto; 140 top right: kathykonkle/iStockphoto; 149 top left: Savaryn/iStockphoto; 161: TAW4/iStockphoto; 162 bottom right: Kubkoo/iStockphoto; 165: Michelle Barbera; 201: Michelle Barbera; 215: Jobalou/iStockphoto; 230: James Madsen; 239: A-Digit/iStockphoto; 242: mariaflaya/iStockphoto; 253: Maggie Swanson; 256 top left: Saenko/iStockphoto; 256 top right: askmenow/iStockphoto; 256 center top left, center bottom right: -ALINA-/iStockphoto; 256 center top: arbuza/iStockphoto; 256 center top right: Tigatelu/iStockphoto; 256 center left, bottom center right: Sapunkele/iStockphoto; 256 bottom left: kunst-mp/iStockphoto; 256 center bottom left: carol_woodcock/iStockphoto; 256 bottom center left: tintin75/iStockphoto; 256 bottom right: Magnilion/iStockphoto; 258: adekvat/iStockphoto; 260: johnstiles40/iStockphoto; 266: Bill Mayer; 280 center right: ankomando/iStockphoto; 280 center left: vladwel/iStockphoto; 280 bottom center: pukrufus/iStockphoto; 294: Cathi Mingus; 306: Little_cuckoo/iStockphoto; other images throughout by Maxie Chambliss, Rusty Fletcher, Doug Jones, Kelly Kennedy, Mike Moran, Jim Paillot, and Karen Sevaly.

ISBN: 978-1-338-21834-3

First printing, June 2017.

5 6 7 8 9 10 144 24 23 22 21

Dear Parent:

Congratulations! You have just chosen a wonderful resource for your child. At Scholastic, we know that it is never too early to begin sharpening essential skills—especially when doing so is lots of fun! This book is packed with a variety of playful activities just right for young children.

The *Jumbo Book of Fun for Kids* has more than 300 activity pages that will delight, entertain, and engage your child. You'll find colorfully illustrated mazes, hidden pictures, and spot the difference activity pages as well as word searches, patterns, connect the dots, crosswords, and more! As your child completes each activity, he or she will develop hand-eye coordination, visual discrimination, fine-motor skills, word recognition, and learn to pay attention to detail.

We hope that these activities will bring your child hours and hours of skill-building fun!

Sincerely,

The editors

Connect the dots from 1 to 30. Then color the picture.

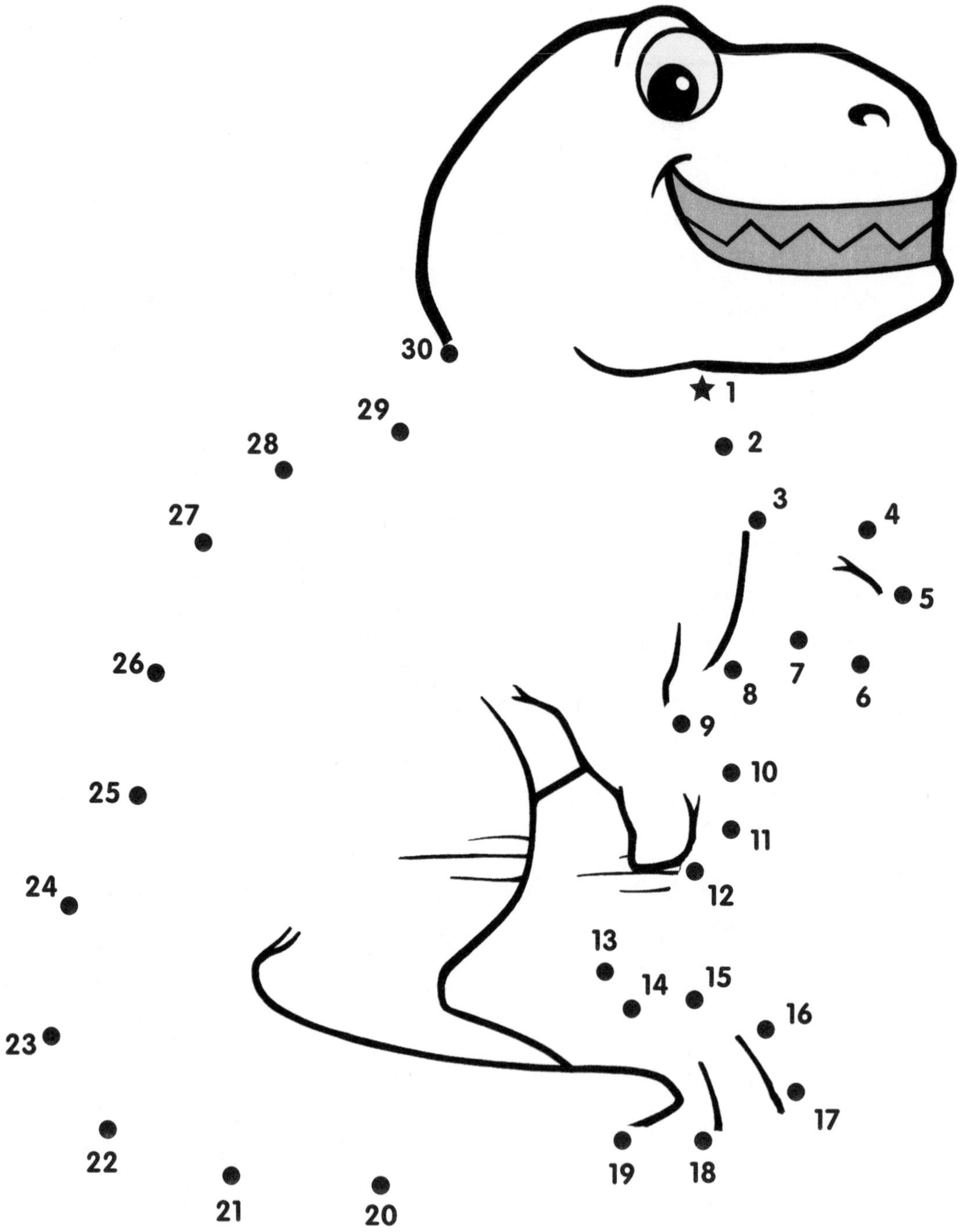

30
29
28
27
26
25
24
23
22
21
20
1
2
3
4
5
6
7
8
9
10
11
12
13
14
15
16
17
18
19

Help the baby ducks find Mama duck.

Draw something you would like to invent.

Read the riddle. The answer is written in code.
Use the decoder to solve the riddle.

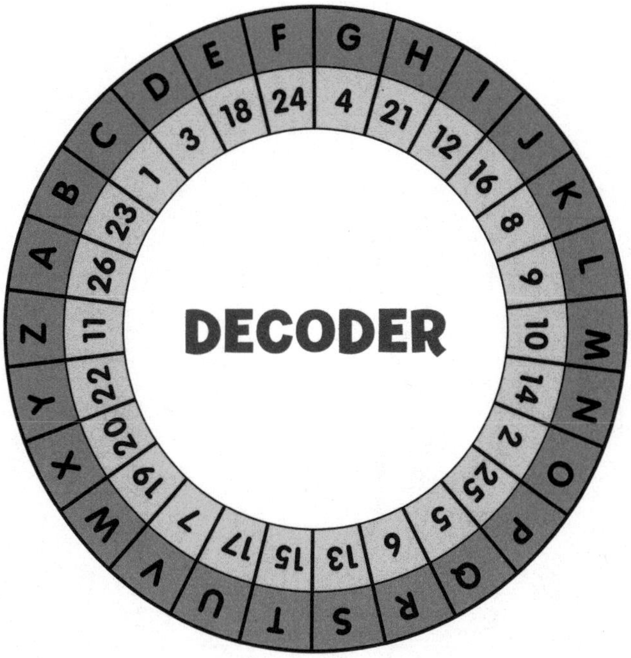
DECODER
A 26
B 23
C 1
D 3
E 18
F 24
G 4
H 21
I 12
J 16
K 8
L 9
M 10
N 14
O 2
P 25
Q 5
R 6
S 13
T 15
U 17
V 7
W 19
X 20
Y 22
Z 11

Why should you stay inside when it is raining cats and dogs?

23 18 1 26 17 13 18   22 2 17   10 12 4 21 15

13 15 18 25   12 14   26   25 2 2 3 9 18 !

JUST 4 DUCK

Circle six differences.

JUST 4 DUCK

Games We Play

Find the words below in the puzzle.
Words are hidden → and ↓.

CARDS	CHECKERS	CHESS	DODGEBALL
FRISBEE	HOPSCOTCH	JACKS	KICKBALL
MARBLES	PUZZLES	SOFTBALL	TAG

H	O	P	S	C	O	T	C	H	M
D	J	A	C	K	S	M	A	C	A
O	W	S	A	I	V	G	E	H	R
D	S	P	R	C	C	H	F	E	B
G	Q	U	D	K	H	A	R	C	L
E	J	Z	S	B	E	K	I	K	E
B	T	Z	E	A	S	L	S	E	S
A	N	L	S	L	S	Y	B	R	L
L	L	E	K	L	R	I	E	S	M
L	J	S	L	T	A	G	E	R	O
Q	S	O	F	T	B	A	L	L	P

Circle the two scarecrows that are the same.

Find and circle each item in the big picture.

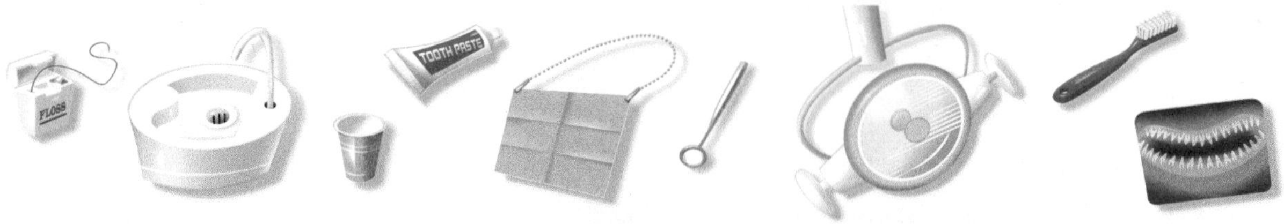
FLOSS
TOOTH PASTE

FLOSS
TOOTH PASTE

How many hidden carrots can you find? ______

How many smaller words can you make using the letters in

government?

1 ______ 16 ______
2 ______ 17 ______
3 ______ 18 ______
4 ______ 19 ______
5 ______ 20 ______
6 ______ 21 ______
7 ______ 22 ______
8 ______ 23 ______
9 ______ 24 ______
10 ______ 25 ______
11 ______ 26 ______
12 ______ 27 ______
13 ______ 28 ______
14 ______ 29 ______
15 ______ 30 ______

government (GUHV-ern-muhnt) n. – a system of rules and laws for a state or country

Connect the dots from a to z. Then color the picture.

a
b
c
d
e
f
g
h
i
j
k
l
m
n
o
p
q
r
s
t
u
v
w
x
y
z

Side by Side

Solve the crossword. Use the words in the Word Box.

Hint The compound word in each clue is missing a part. Find the other part of the word to solve the crossword.

Word Box	
BED	BATH
CAKE	BRUSH
FARM	DOWN
FLOWER	FINGER
HIVE	GROUND
LID	KNOB
SHELF	PLANE

1
2
3
4
5
6
7
8
9
10
11
12
13

Across

4. ______tub
5. ______print
7. eye______
8. air______
9. tooth______
12. sun______
13. cup______

Down

1. book______
2. bee______
3. under______
4. ______time
6. sun______
10. door______
11. ______house

Find each space with as, ask, may, were, and when. Color those spaces gray. Then color the rest of the picture.

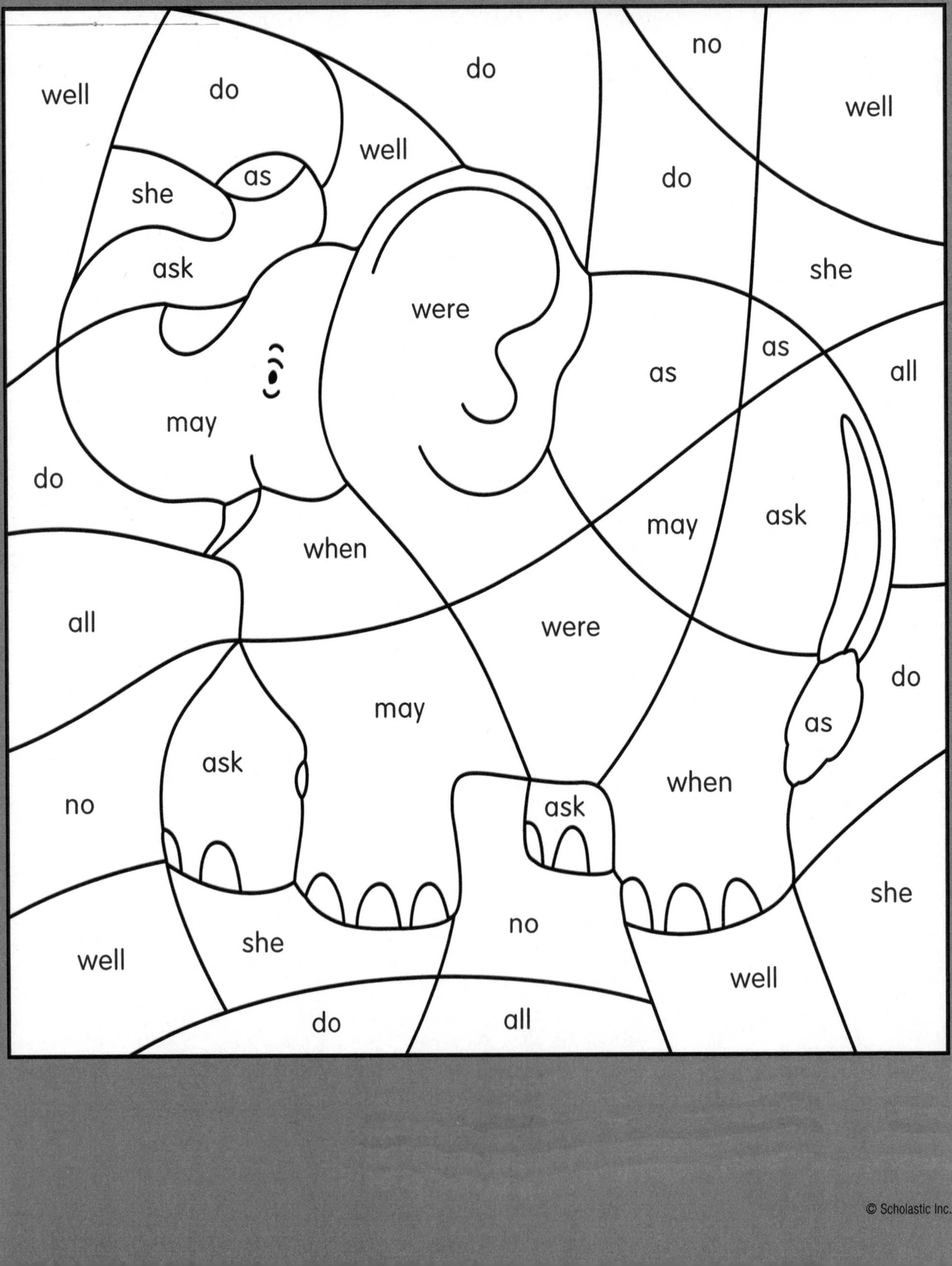

well
do
do
no
well
well
she
as
do
ask
she
were
as
as
all
may
do
may
ask
when
all
were
do
may
as
ask
when
no
ask
she
no
well
she
well
do
all

Summer Days

Read the clues. Write the words.
Start at the bottom and climb to the top.

this is worn on your head
change the last letter

___ ___ ___

a popular pet
change the first letter

___ ___ ___

this is used to hit a baseball
change the first letter

___ ___ ___

wipe your feet on this
change the last letter

___ ___ ___

opposite of *woman*
change the first letter

___ ___ ___

f a n

Label each picture. Use the Word Box.
Match the pictures with words that sound the same.

Word Box							
FLOUR	FLOWER	ONE	RIGHT	WAY	WEIGH	WON	WRITE

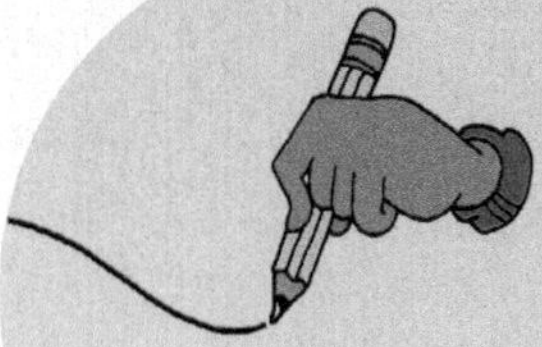

____

1

____

1

____

____

____

____

FLOUR

____

____

Add. Color the picture. Use the color key below.

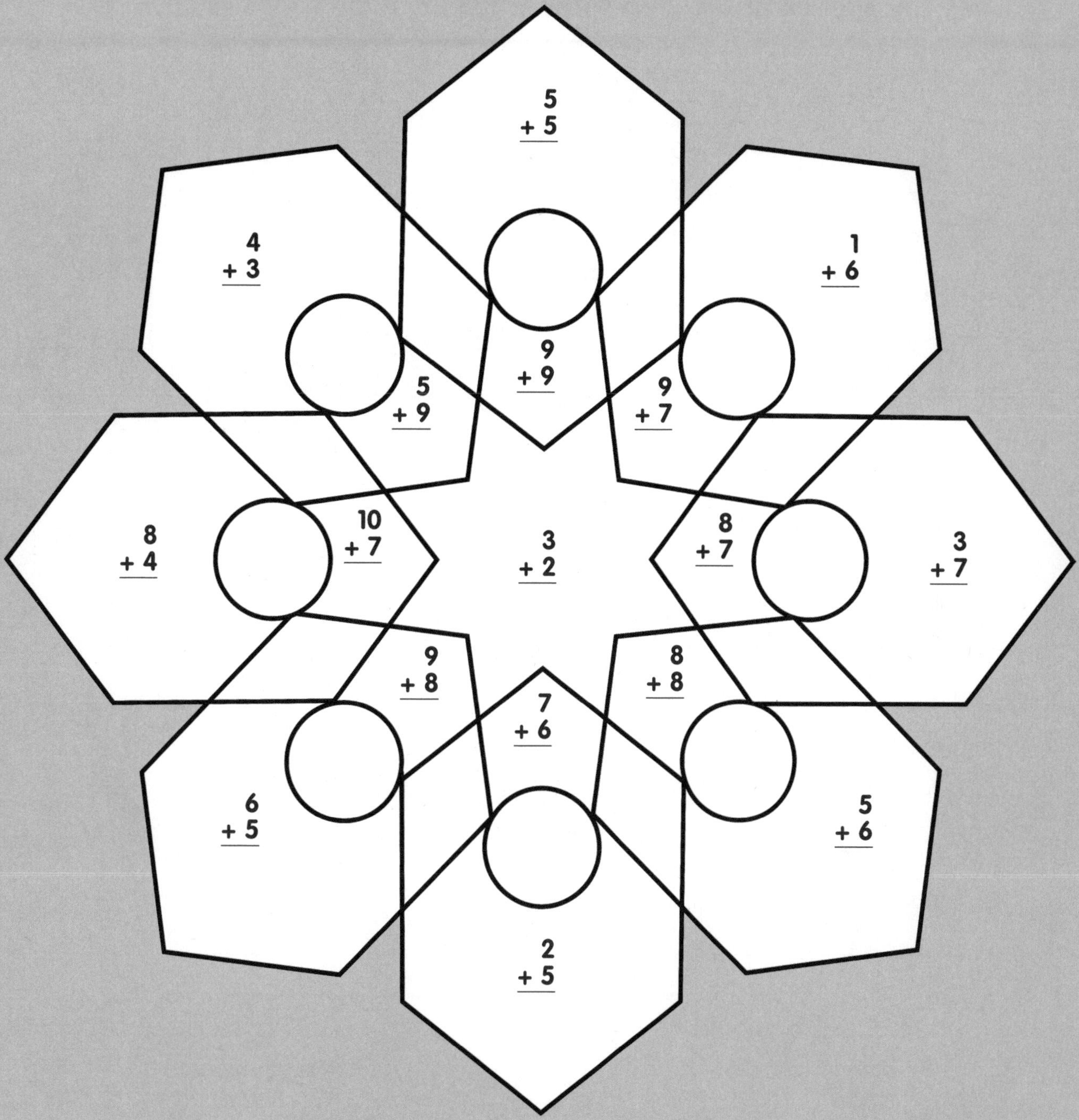

5 + 5
4 + 3
1 + 6
9 + 9
5 + 9
9 + 7
8 + 4
10 + 7
3 + 2
8 + 7
3 + 7
9 + 8
8 + 8
7 + 6
6 + 5
5 + 6
2 + 5

If the sum is between	Color the space
1 and 6	red
7 and 12	purple
13 and 18	blue

Fill in the other spaces with colors of your choice.

Crazy Cartoons

Use the speech bubbles to show what each character is saying.

Brrr! It's cold in the Arctic. I don't need these sunglasses.

Design a shopping bag.

Skip count by 2 to connect the dots. Then color the picture.

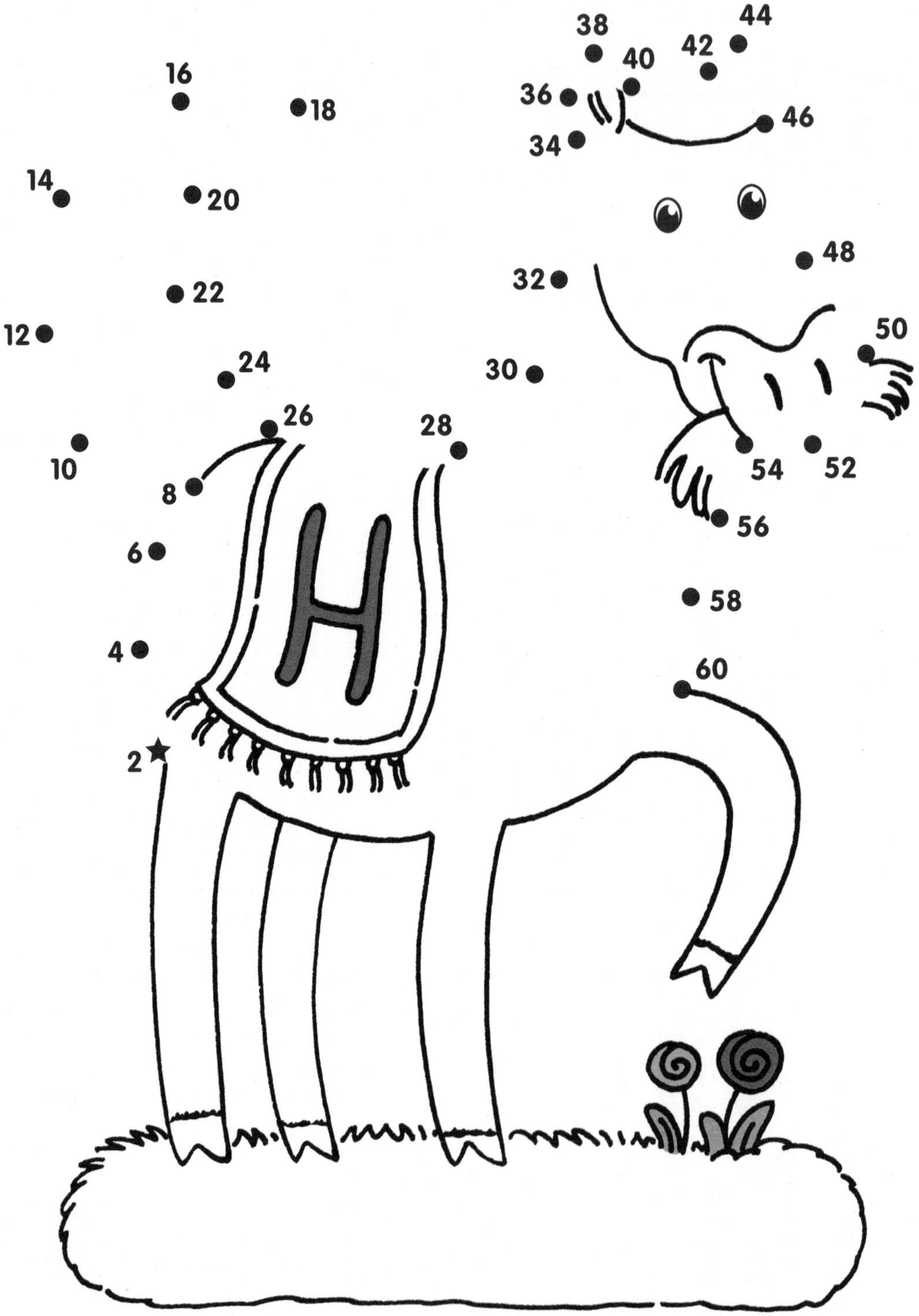

2
4
6
8
10
12
14
16
18
20
22
24
26
28
30
32
34
36
38
40
42
44
46
48
50
52
54
56
58
60
H

Help the school bus get to the school.

SCHOOL BUS

What picture is missing?
Find the sticker on page 321. Add it to the pattern.

Draw your own pattern below.

Color the picture. Use the color key.

If the word begins with a blend like the one in					
Color the space	blue	red	yellow	green	purple

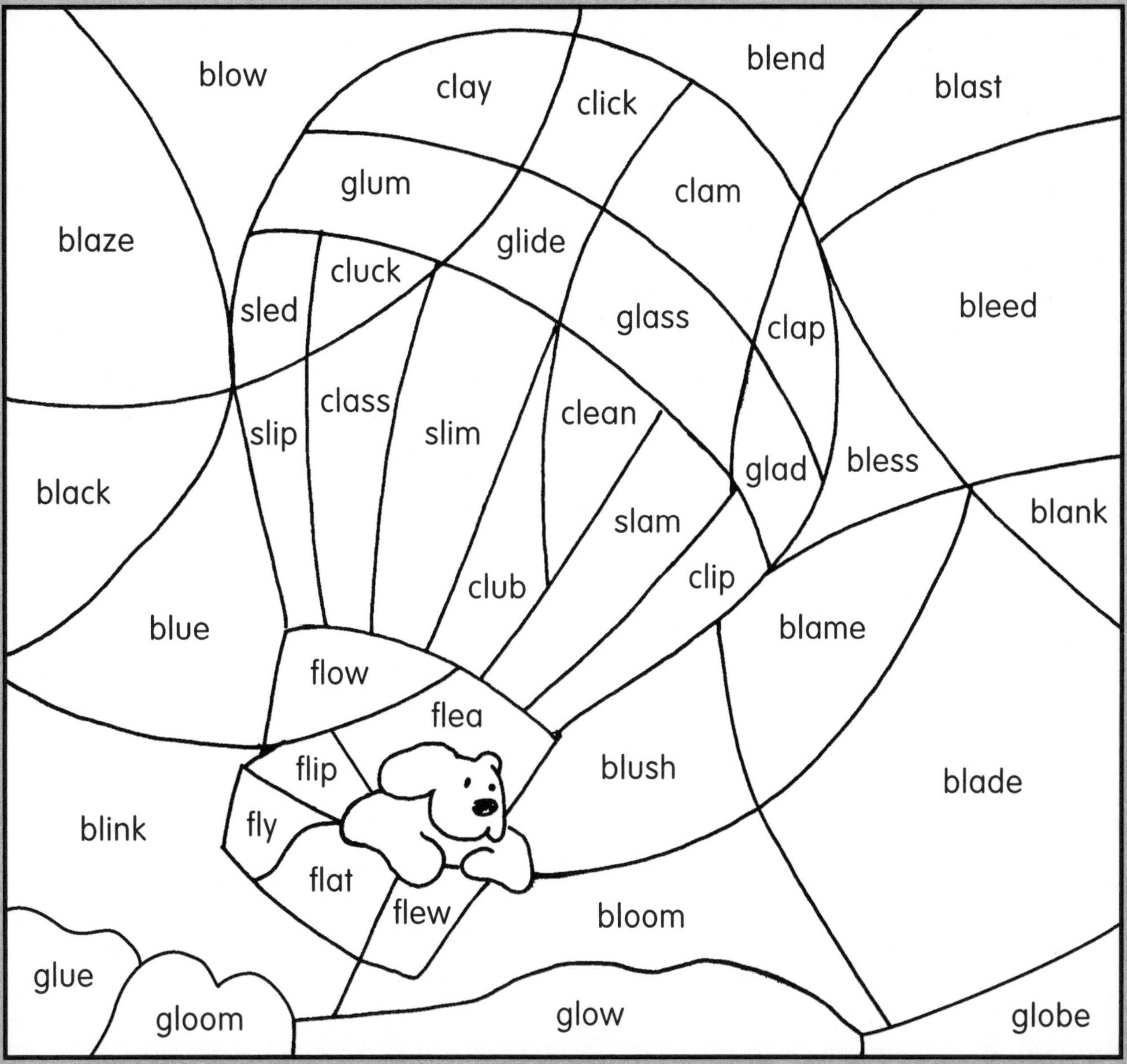
blow
clay
click
blend
blast
glum
clam
blaze
glide
cluck
sled
glass
clap
bleed
class
slip
slim
clean
glad
bless
black
slam
blank
club
clip
blue
blame
flow
flea
flip
blush
blade
blink
fly
flat
flew
bloom
glue
gloom
glow
globe

Draw the items shown to complete the grid.
Each row, column, and minigrid should have one of each item.

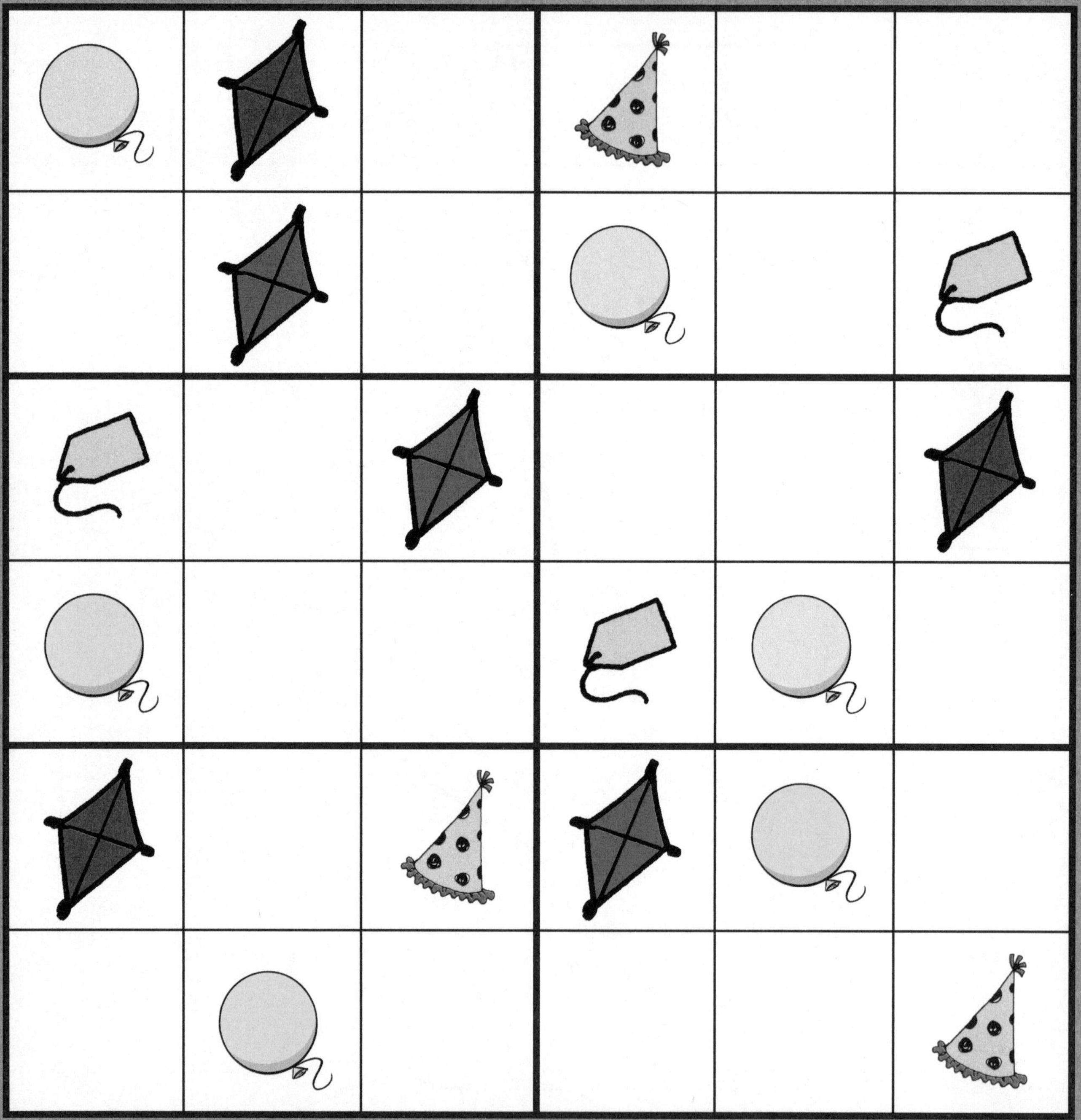

Read the riddle. The answer is written in code.
Use the decoder to solve the riddle.

DECODER			
A	8	N	20
B	9	O	26
C	10	P	23
D	14	Q	1
E	2	R	3
F	25	S	18
G	5	T	24
H	6	U	4
I	13	V	21
J	15	W	12
K	17	X	16
L	7	Y	22
M	19	Z	11

What did the parrot say when he fell in love with the duck?

"____ ____ ____ ____ ____   ____ ____ ____ ____   ____
23 26 7 7 22   12 8 20 24   8

____ ____ ____ ____ ____ ____ ____!"
1 4 8 10 17 2 3

Change man into pie. Use the picture clues and letter tiles. Start at the bottom and climb to the top.

i e n p m a

Add. Color the picture. Use the color key below.

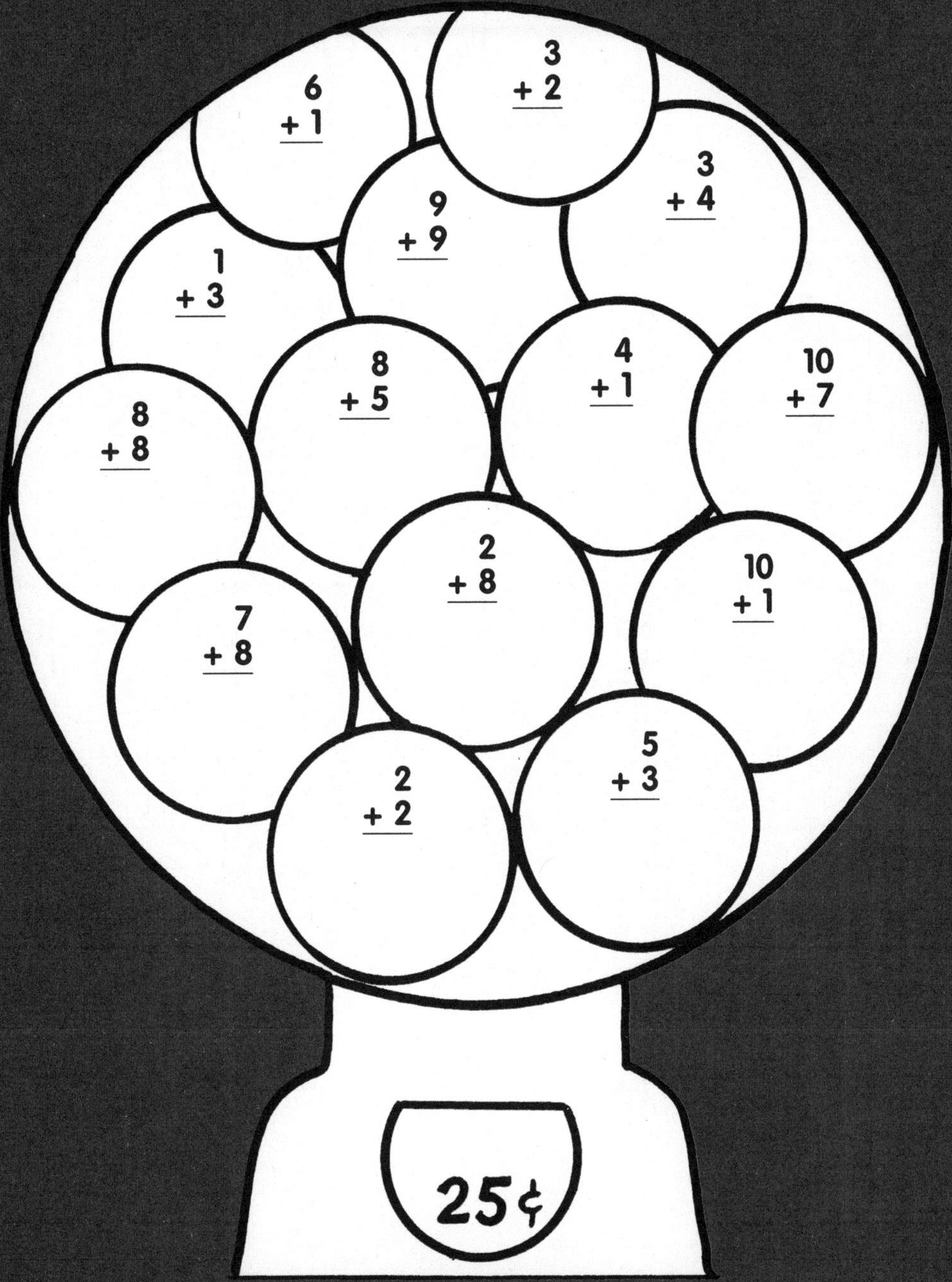

6 + 1
3 + 2
3 + 4
9 + 9
1 + 3
8 + 5
4 + 1
10 + 7
8 + 8
2 + 8
10 + 1
7 + 8
5 + 3
2 + 2
25¢

If the sum is between	Color the space
1 and 5	green
6 and 10	red
11 and 15	yellow
16 and 18	orange

Fill in the other spaces with colors of your choice.

Math Tic-Tac-Toe

Add. Draw a line through the three problems in a row with the same answer. The row can go →, ↓, ↘ or ↗.

8 + 14	9 + 8	16 + 8
20 + 13	12 + 10	21 + 9
15 + 10	9 + 9	7 + 15

18 + 7	20 + 5	14 + 2
19 + 6	16 + 6	12 + 12
14 + 11	16 + 7	21 + 3

9 + 22	34 + 12	22 + 19
18 + 15	16 + 32	28 + 13
22 + 13	19 + 16	21 + 14

42 + 21	25 + 9	29 + 22
39 + 12	48 + 15	36 + 21
38 + 16	18 + 10	19 + 44

Draw the first alien that will visit Earth.

The Mid-Atlantic Scramble

Unscramble the name of each state.

DLEAEWAR

8				1			

MRAYLADN

					2		

WNE REYSEJ

5									

EWN YROK

7					6			

PANSYLNIEVAN

				3						4	

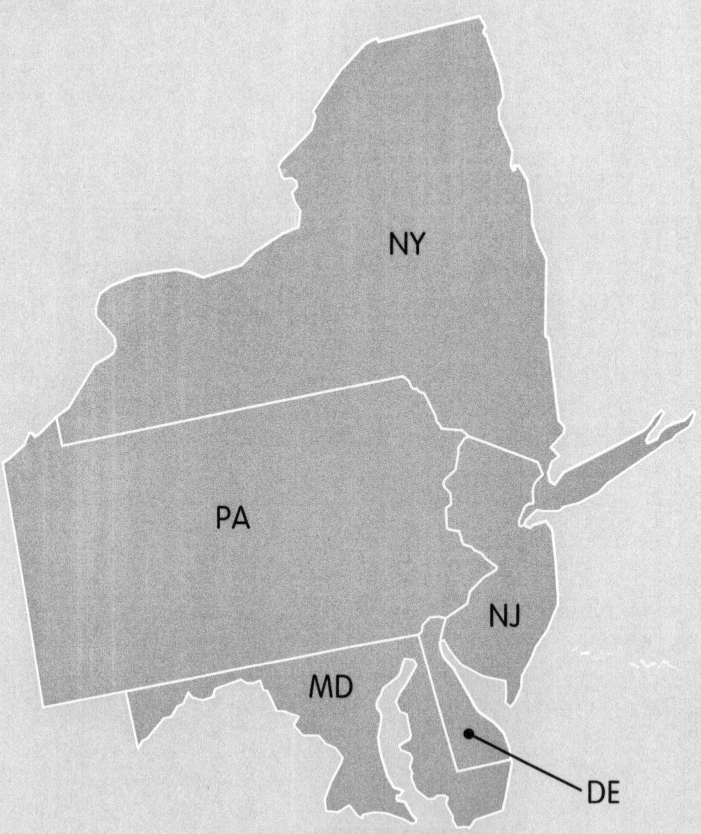
NY
PA
NJ
MD
DE

Copy the letters in the numbered cells to answer the question.

What city in the mid-Atlantic is not part of any state?

			H			G	T				. C	.
1	2	3		4	5			6	7	8		

Connect the dots from 1 to 30. Then color the picture.

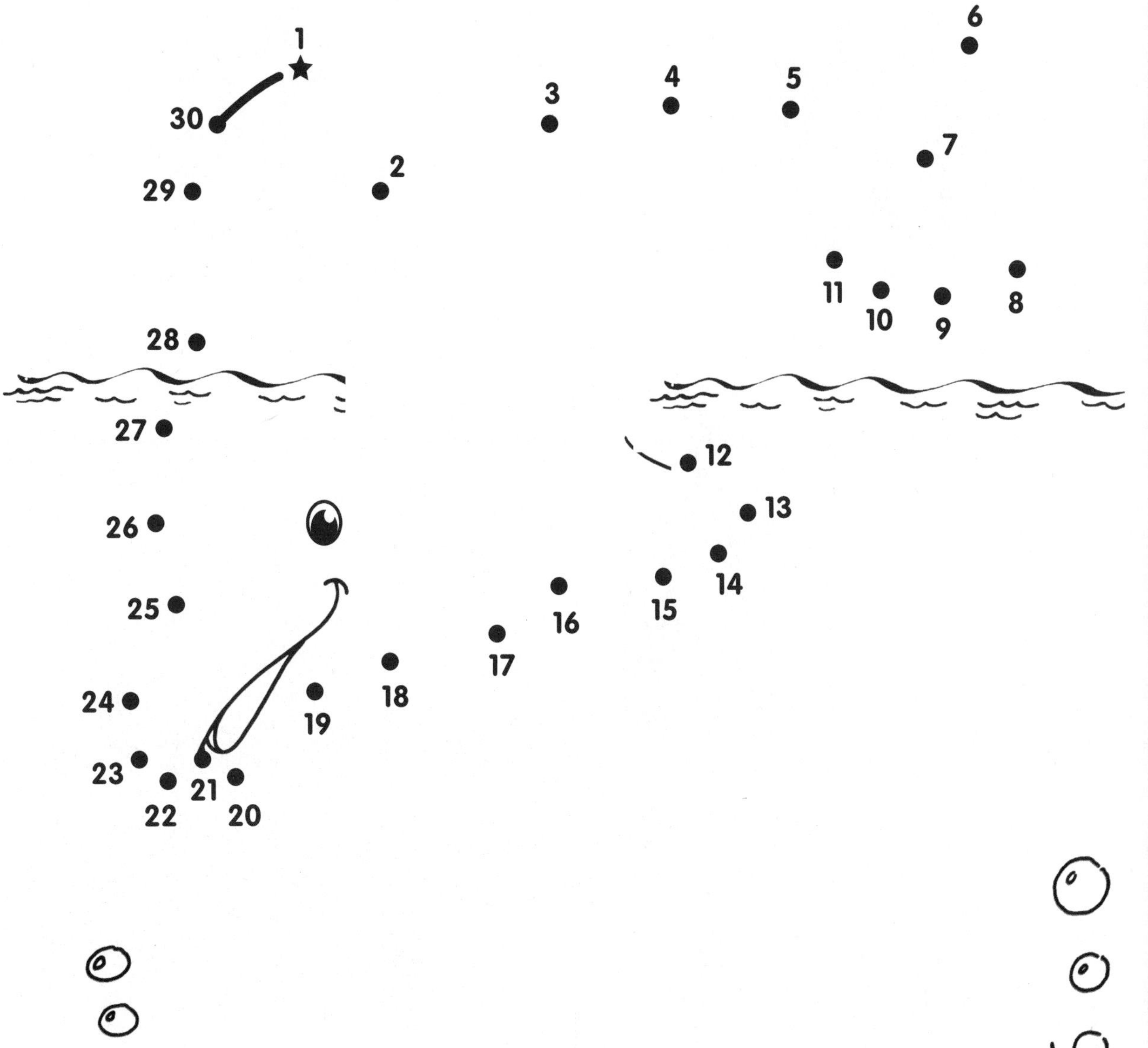
1
2
3
4
5
6
7
8
9
10
11
12
13
14
15
16
17
18
19
20
21
22
23
24
25
26
27
28
29
30

Circle the two monsters that do not have a twin.

Birds of a Feather

Find the words below in the puzzle.
Words are hidden →, ↓, ↘ and ↗.

BLACKBIRD	BLUEBIRD	CROW	DOVE
FINCH	JAY	LARK	LONGSPUR
MEADOWLARK	ROBIN	STARLING	SWALLOW

B	L	A	C	K	B	I	R	D	T	G	Q	S
F	H	B	E	Q	S	S	B	R	K	C	L	K
U	C	V	B	P	T	K	W	V	M	N	A	P
U	O	R	L	H	A	E	U	A	D	M	R	H
D	J	E	U	C	R	S	X	Y	L	L	K	L
W	P	X	E	E	L	K	J	N	S	L	R	S
O	N	T	B	M	I	R	A	U	Y	T	O	D
T	A	P	I	V	N	E	O	I	C	R	O	W
K	X	Z	R	G	G	U	G	B	L	B	E	F
N	T	N	D	A	H	X	I	M	I	D	S	I
L	O	N	G	S	P	U	R	Y	W	N	K	N
S	T	K	Y	Q	M	N	S	A	H	Z	D	C
A	R	I	J	J	U	I	R	L	T	R	A	H
A	O	M	E	A	D	O	W	L	A	R	K	G
M	Y	R	E	Y	K	I	L	O	Q	D	R	T

Color the picture. Use the color key.

If the word has the same vowel sound as		
Color the star	yellow	orange

now
house
brown
coin
joy
count
soil
soy
gown
round
join
toy

How many smaller words can you make using the letters in

dictionary?

1 ______________________
2 ______________________
3 ______________________
4 ______________________
5 ______________________
6 ______________________
7 ______________________
8 ______________________
9 ______________________
10 ______________________
11 ______________________
12 ______________________
13 ______________________
14 ______________________
15 ______________________
16 ______________________
17 ______________________
18 ______________________
19 ______________________
20 ______________________
21 ______________________
22 ______________________
23 ______________________
24 ______________________
25 ______________________
26 ______________________
27 ______________________
28 ______________________
29 ______________________
30 ______________________

R

dictionary (DIK-shun-ner-ee) n. – a book that lists words alphabetically and explains the words' meanings

Circle six differences.

Help the boy catch the fish.

To the Top

Starting at the bottom, add each pair of side-by-side numbers. Write the sum in the box directly above the pair. Continue to add each pair until you reach the top.

Example

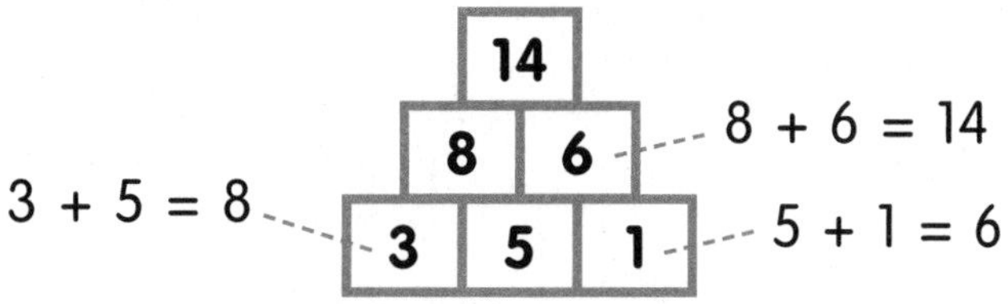
14
8 6
3 5 1
3 + 5 = 8
8 + 6 = 14
5 + 1 = 6

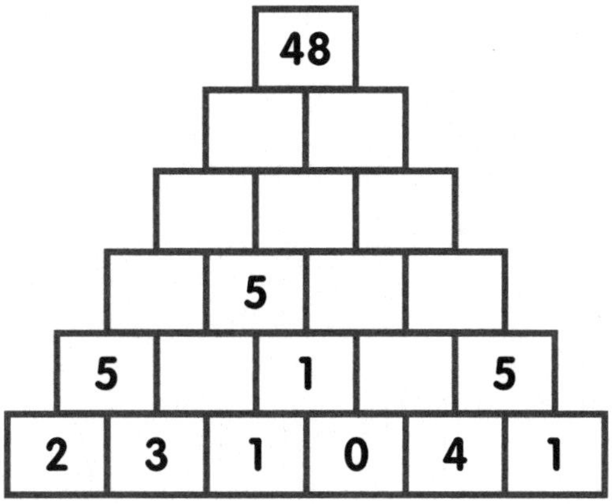
48
5
5 1 5
2 3 1 0 4 1

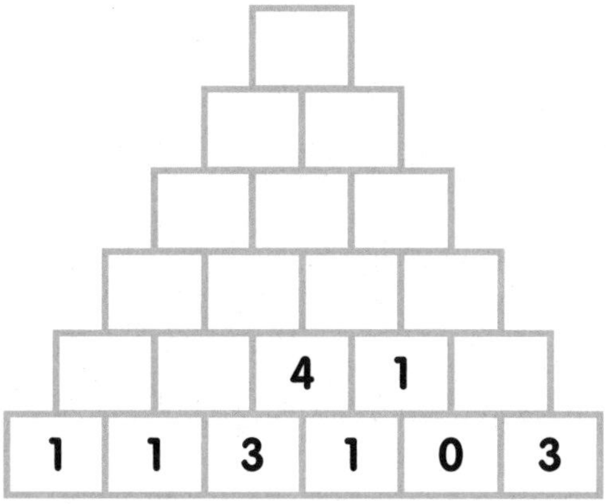
4 1
1 1 3 1 0 3

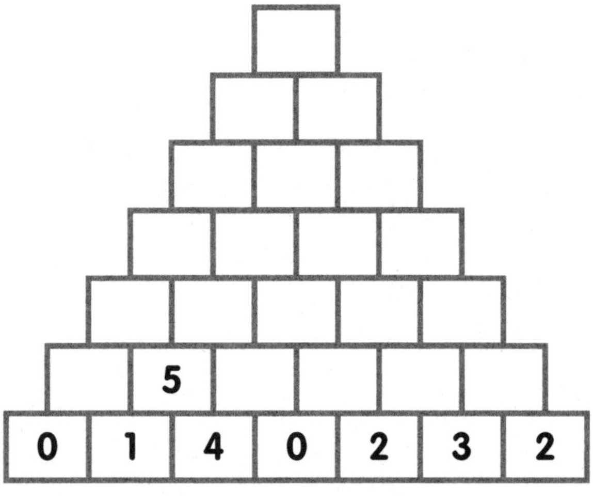
5
0 1 4 0 2 3 2

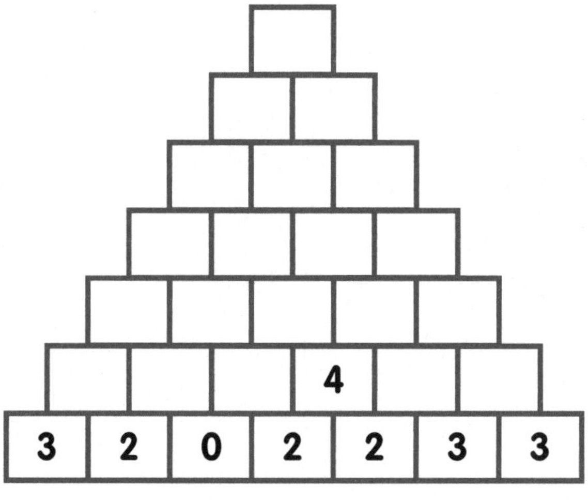
4
3 2 0 2 2 3 3

Find and circle each item in the big picture.

The End of Summer

Read the clues. Write the words.
Start at the bottom and climb to the top.

opposite of *hot*
change the first letter

the past tense of *tell*
change the last letter

a fee charged on bridges
change the vowel

opposite of *short*
change the first letter

f a l l

What picture is missing?
Find the sticker on page 321. Add it to the pattern.

Draw your own pattern below.

Help the rabbit get away from the fox!
Hop →, ↓, and ← into boxes with even numbers.
Draw a line to show the rabbit's path.

	6		3	5	7
9	4	2	8	13	75
47	11	1	44	24	19
21		36	12	17	15
23	43	18		35	27
25	21	32	20	22	26
51	29	27	45	68	53
33	89	37		42	
	31	Home Sweet Home	38	64	59

My Body

Solve the crossword. Use the Word Box and picture clues.

Across

2

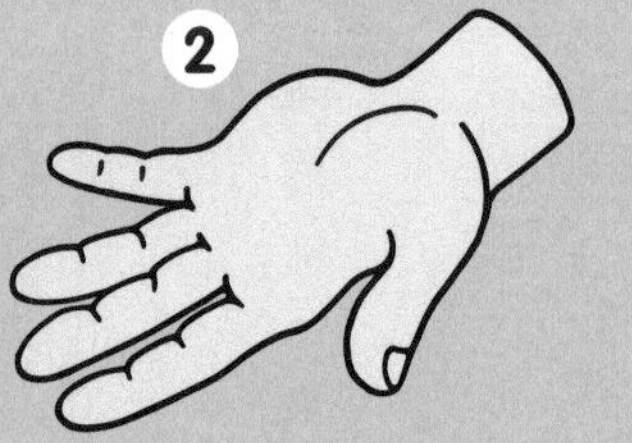

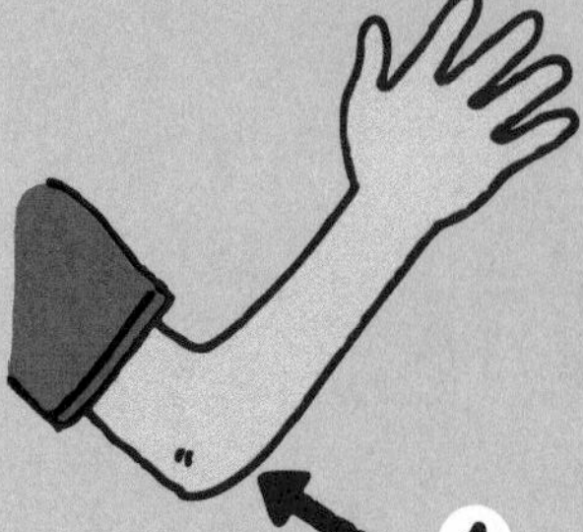

4

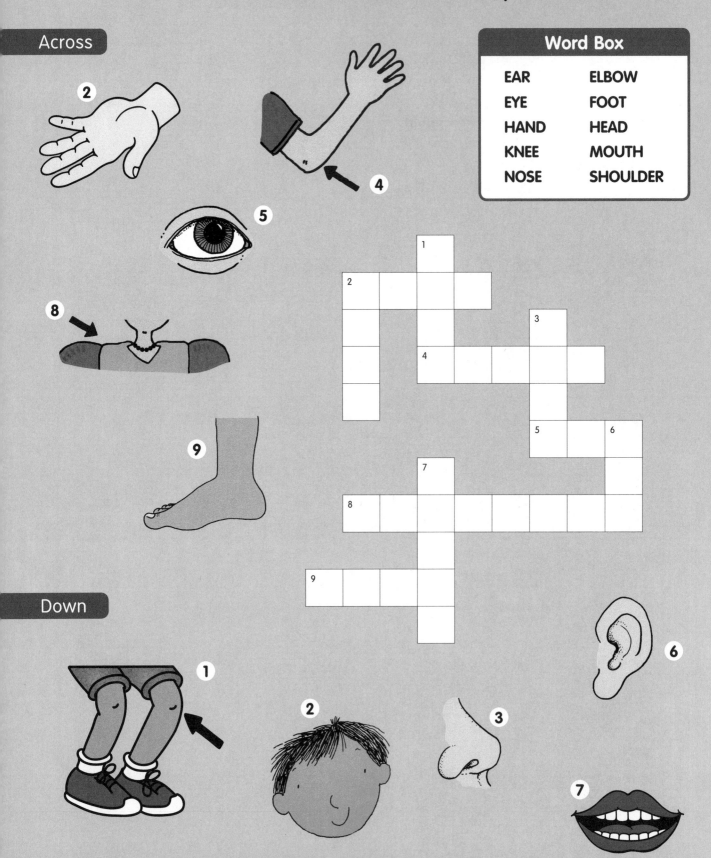

Word Box	
EAR	ELBOW
EYE	FOOT
HAND	HEAD
KNEE	MOUTH
NOSE	SHOULDER

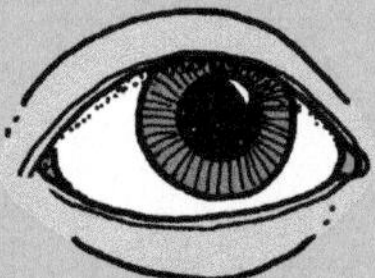

5

8

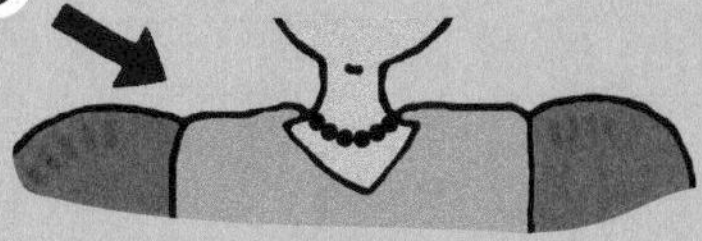

9

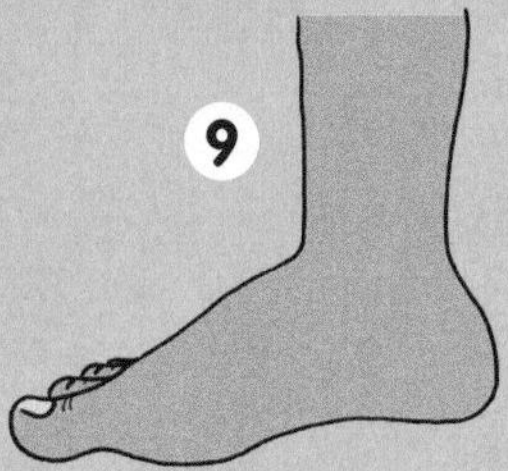

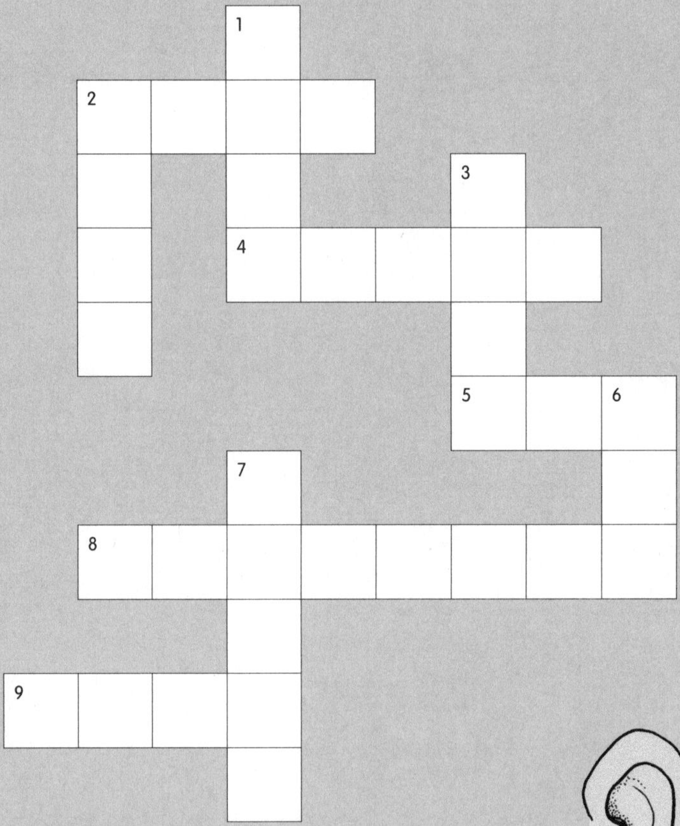
1
2
3
4
5
6
7
8
9

Down

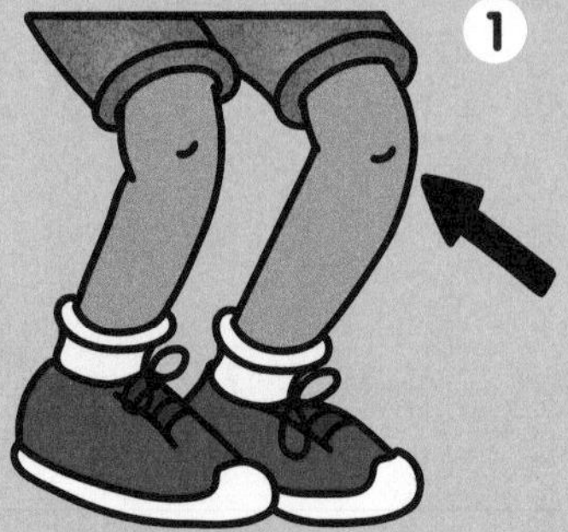

1

6

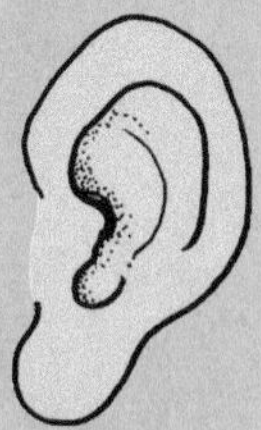

2

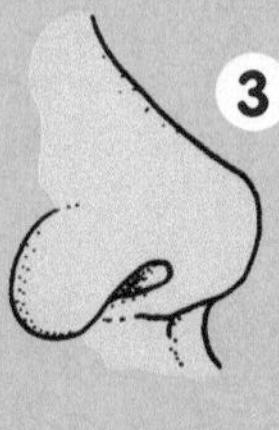

3

7

Change wig into bell. Use the picture clues and letter tiles.
Start at the bottom and climb to the top.

l e i p b g w

Multi
Vita

Find each space with an, again, just, over, and think. Color those spaces orange. Then color the rest of the picture.

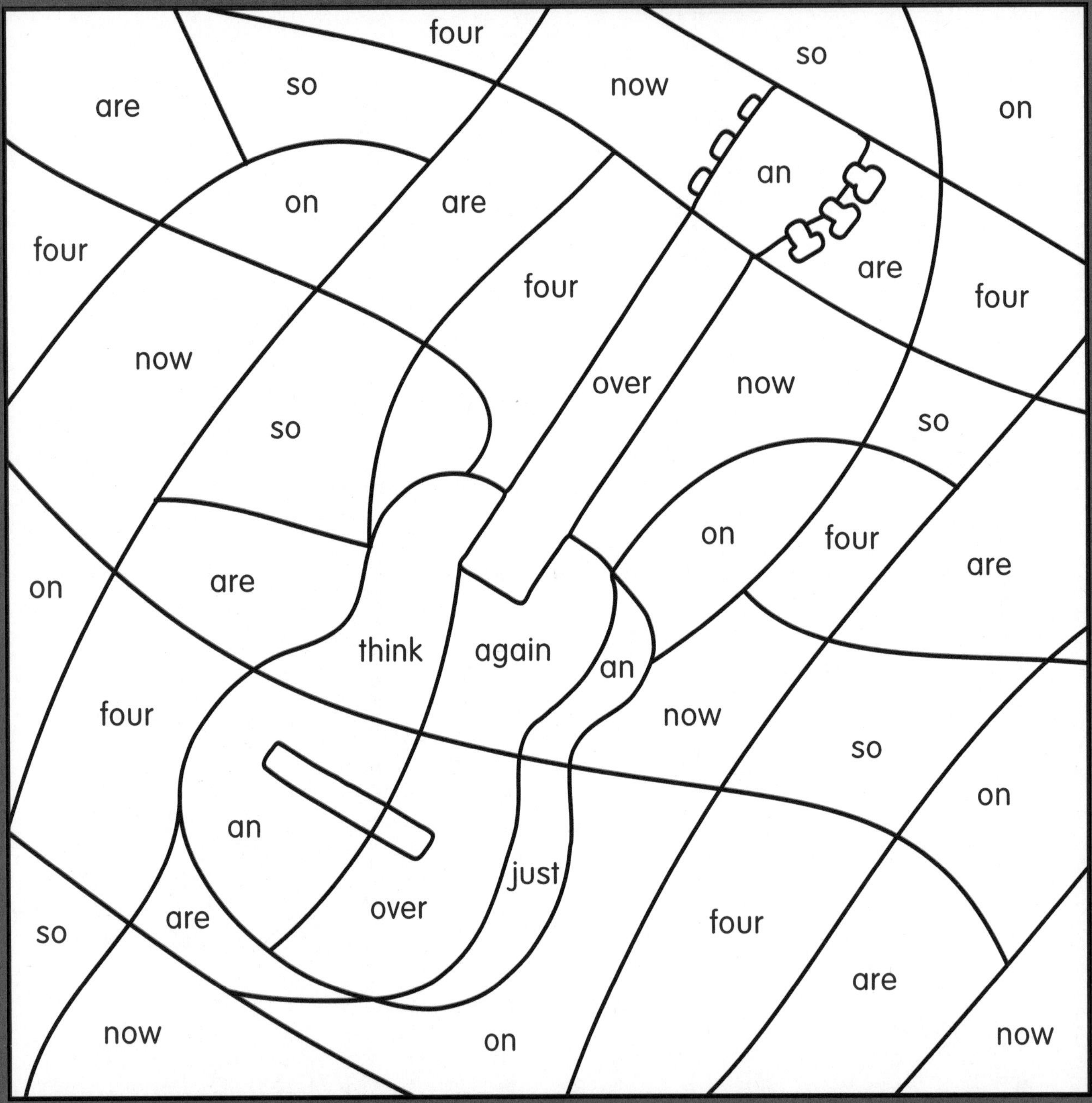
four
so
are
so
now
on
an
on
are
four
are
four
four
now
over
now
so
so
on
four
on
are
are
think
again
an
four
now
so
on
an
just
are
over
four
so
are
now
on
now

Make a Cartoon

Read the sentence below each picture.
In the bubbles, write what each character could be saying.

Mr. Giraffe asked Mr. Zebra why he had stripes. Mr. Zebra didn't know.

Mr. Giraffe said that he should ask Mrs. Owl. Mr. Zebra agreed.

Mr. Zebra asked Mrs. Owl why he had stripes. Mrs. Owl laughed.

Mrs. Owl told Mr. Zebra that the Magic Fairy painted him that way!

Spring Scramble

Unscramble each word. To help you get started, the first and last letter and some vowels are filled in.

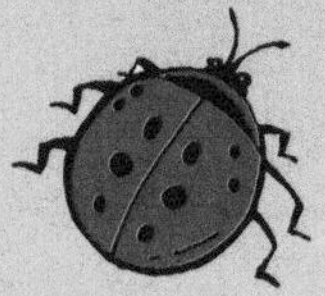

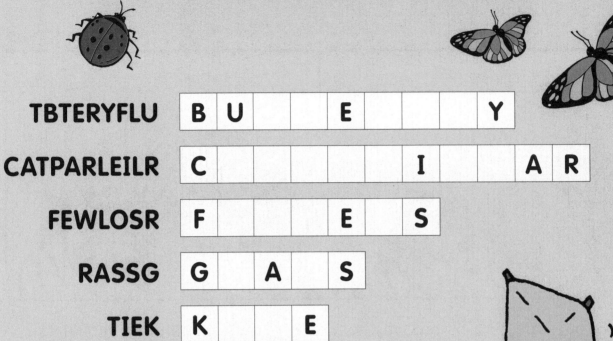

TBTERYFLU	B	U			E				Y		
CATPARLEILR	C						I			A	R
FEWLOSR	F				E		S				
RASSG	G		A		S						
TIEK	K			E							
LYUDABG	L					U	G				
NIRWABO	R	A				O	W				
UMLEARLB	U				E			A			
RANI	R		I	N							

My favorite sport is . . .

Color the picture. Use the color key.

If the word has the same ending sound as					GUM
Color the space	blue	green	gray	red	brown

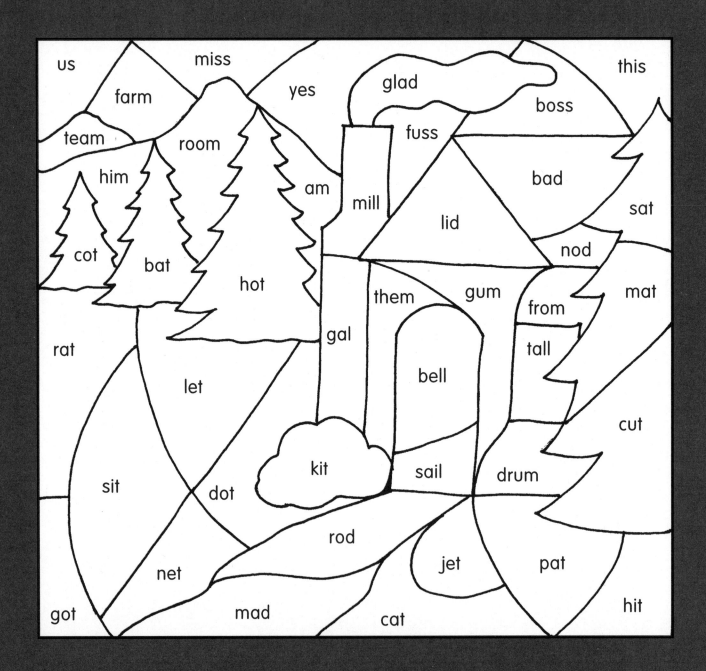

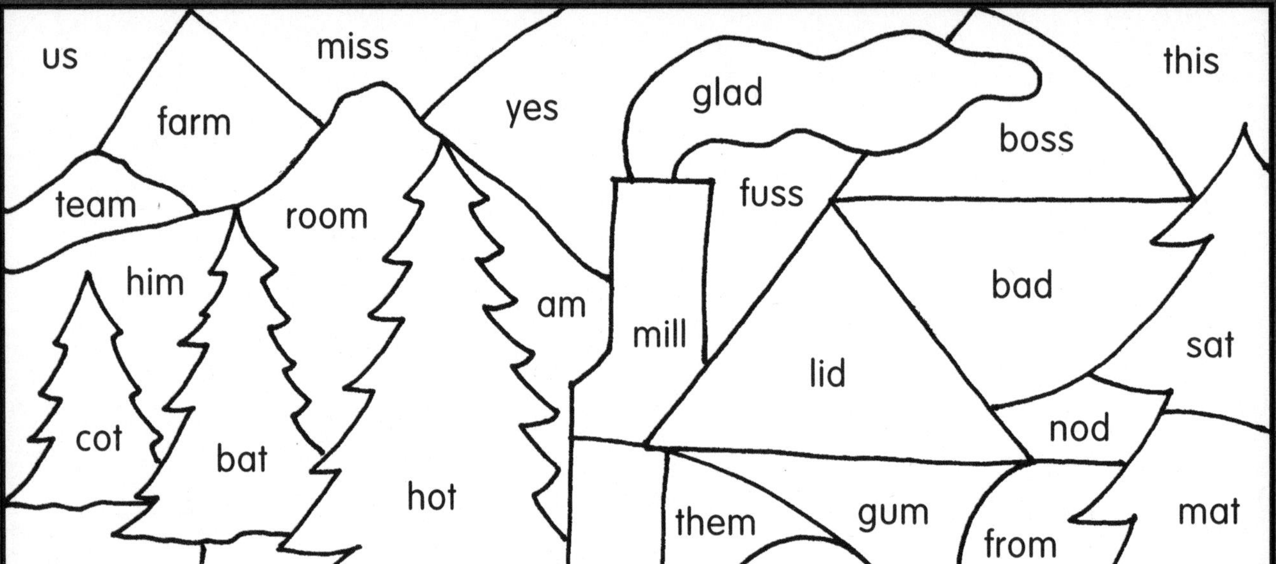
us
miss
farm
yes
glad
this
boss
team
room
fuss
him
bad
am
mill
sat
lid
cot
nod
bat
hot
them
gum
mat
from
gal
rat
tall
let
bell
cut
kit
sail
drum
sit
dot
rod
jet
pat
net
got
mad
cat
hit

Find the missing number.
Match each answer on the left with one on the right.

1. 100, 75, ________ , 25
2. 29, ________ , 37, 41
3. 10, 8, 6, ________
4. 44, 32, 20, ________
5. 15, 30, 45, ________
6. 9, 7, 5, ________

A. 33, 23, 13, ________
B. 11, 22, ________ , 44
C. 30, 40, 50, ________
D. 200, 150, 100, ________
E. 6, 7, ________ , 9
F. 0, ________ , 8, 12

Help the race car get to the trophy.

5
1

Draw vegetables to complete the grid.
Each row, column, and minigrid should have one of each kind.

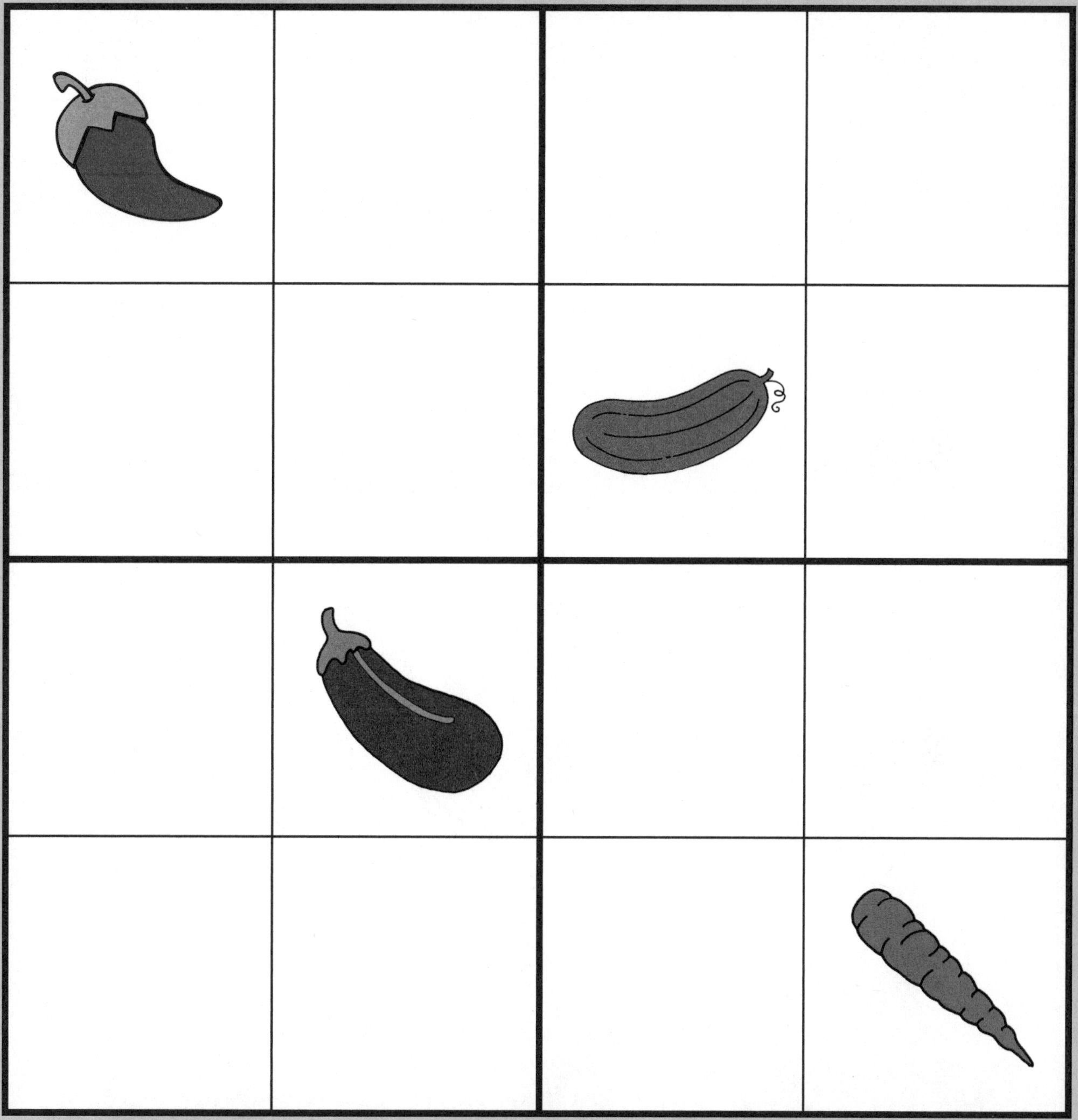

Circle the two hats that are the same.

Find each space with after, fly, how, open, and then. Color those spaces yellow. Then color the rest of the picture.

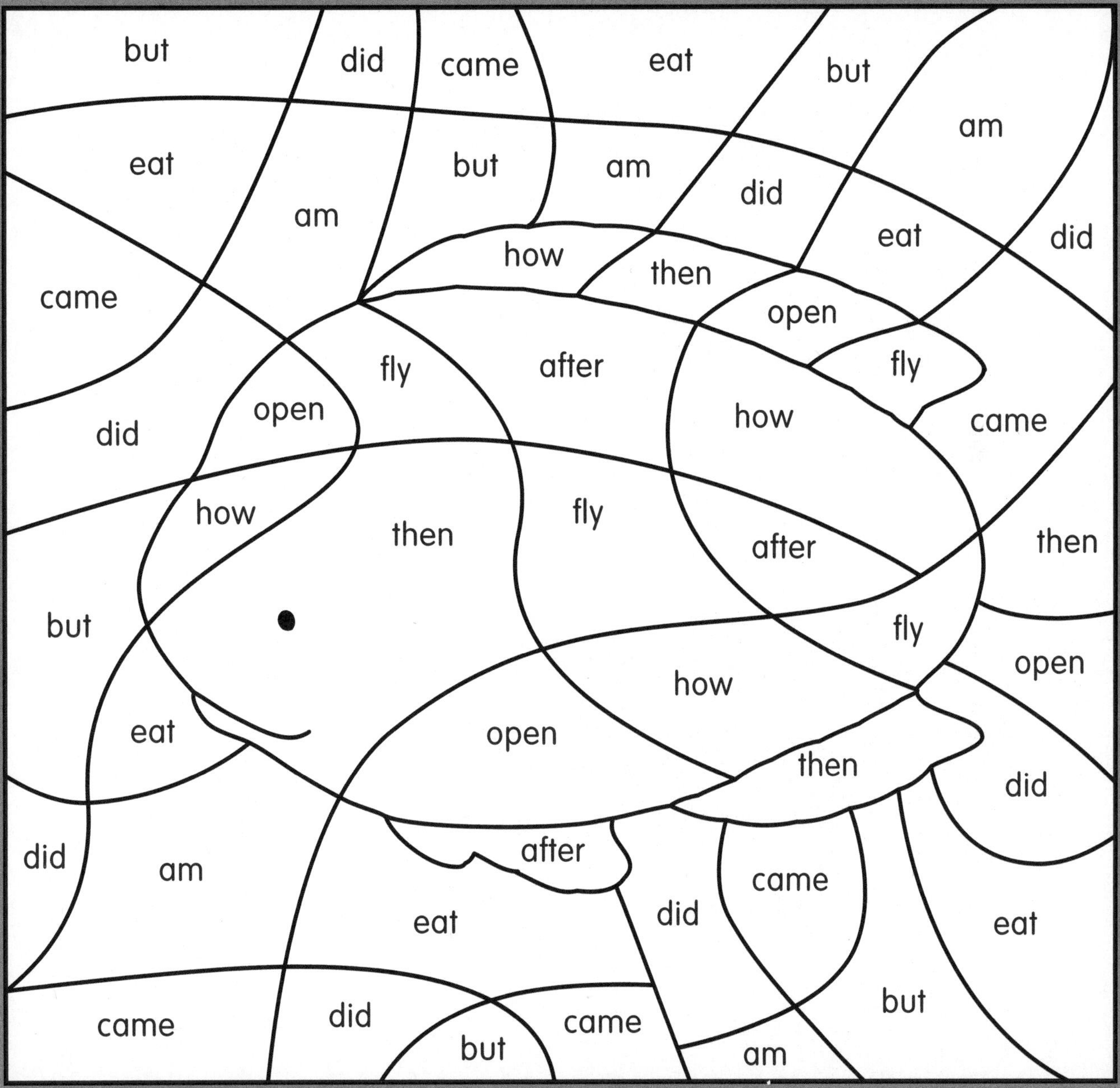
but
did
came
eat
but
am
eat
but
am
did
am
how
then
eat
did
came
open
fly
after
fly
open
how
came
did
how
then
fly
after
then
but
fly
open
how
eat
open
then
did
after
did
am
came
eat
did
eat
but
came
did
but
came
am

In the Desert

Find the words below in the puzzle.
Words are hidden → and ↓.

ARMADILLO	CACTUS	COYOTE	DUNES
IGUANA	JACKRABBIT	ROADRUNNER	SAND
SAGUARO	SCORPION	SPIDER	VULTURE

B	M	S	C	O	R	P	I	O	N
L	R	M	N	T	B	C	L	J	K
A	O	C	A	C	T	U	S	L	H
J	A	C	K	R	A	B	B	I	T
S	D	S	P	I	D	E	R	C	V
A	R	M	A	D	I	L	L	O	U
G	U	F	V	U	G	Z	S	Y	L
U	N	M	D	N	U	L	A	O	T
A	N	X	Y	E	A	L	N	T	U
R	E	Z	K	S	N	U	D	E	R
O	R	R	G	P	A	J	A	Q	E

Skip count by 2 to connect the dots. Then color the picture.

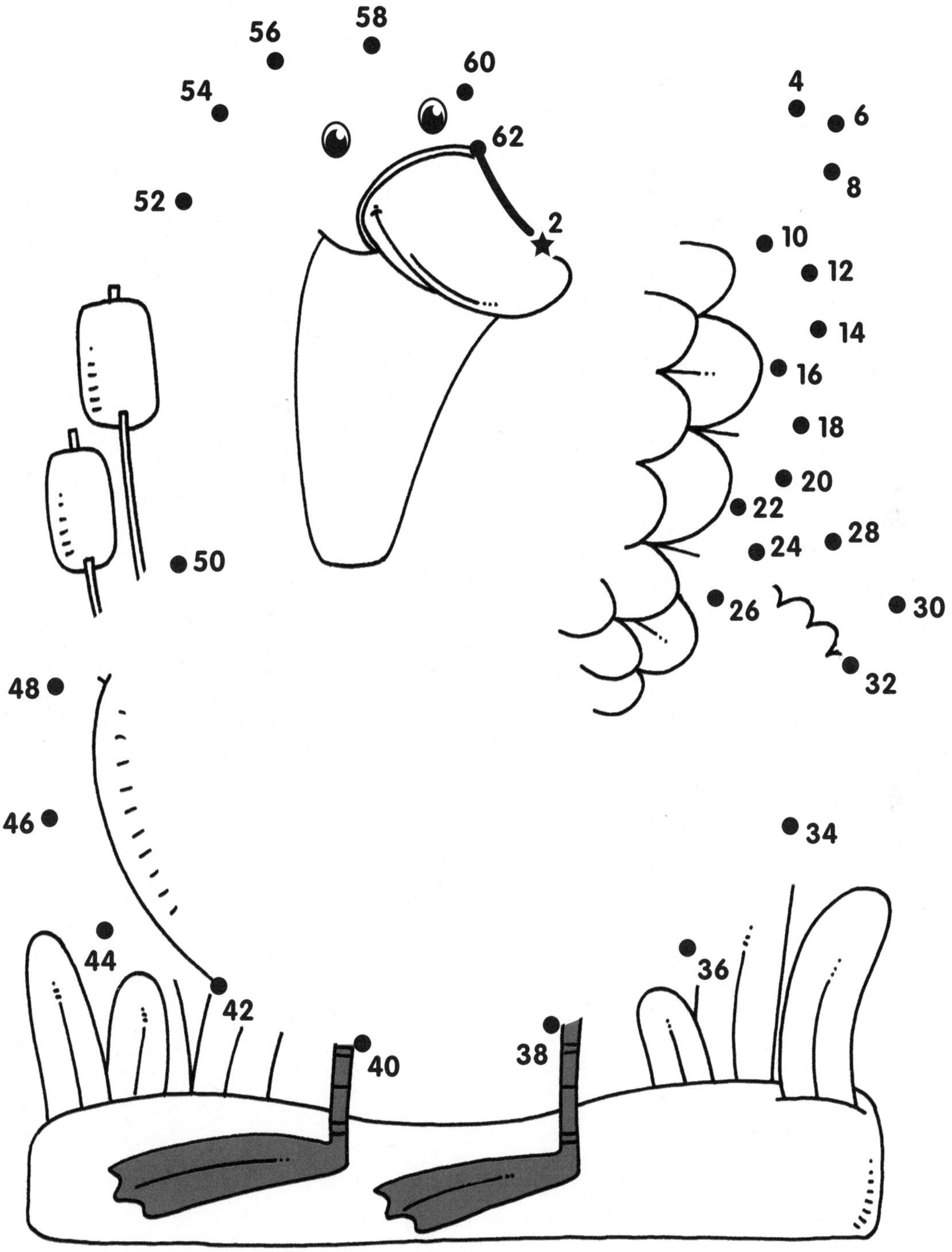

58
56
60
54
4
6
62
8
52
2
10
12
14
16
18
20
22
28
24
50
26
30
32
48
46
34
44
36
42
38
40

The Perfect Pet!

Read the clues. Write the words.
Start at the bottom and climb to the top.

animal similar to a toad
add a letter after the first letter

___ ___ ___ ___

synonym of *mist*
change the first letter

___ ___ ___

a popular pet
change the last letter

___ ___ ___

a small round mark
change the first letter

___ ___ ___

a small bed
change the vowel

___ ___ ___

c a t

Add. Color the picture. Use the color key.

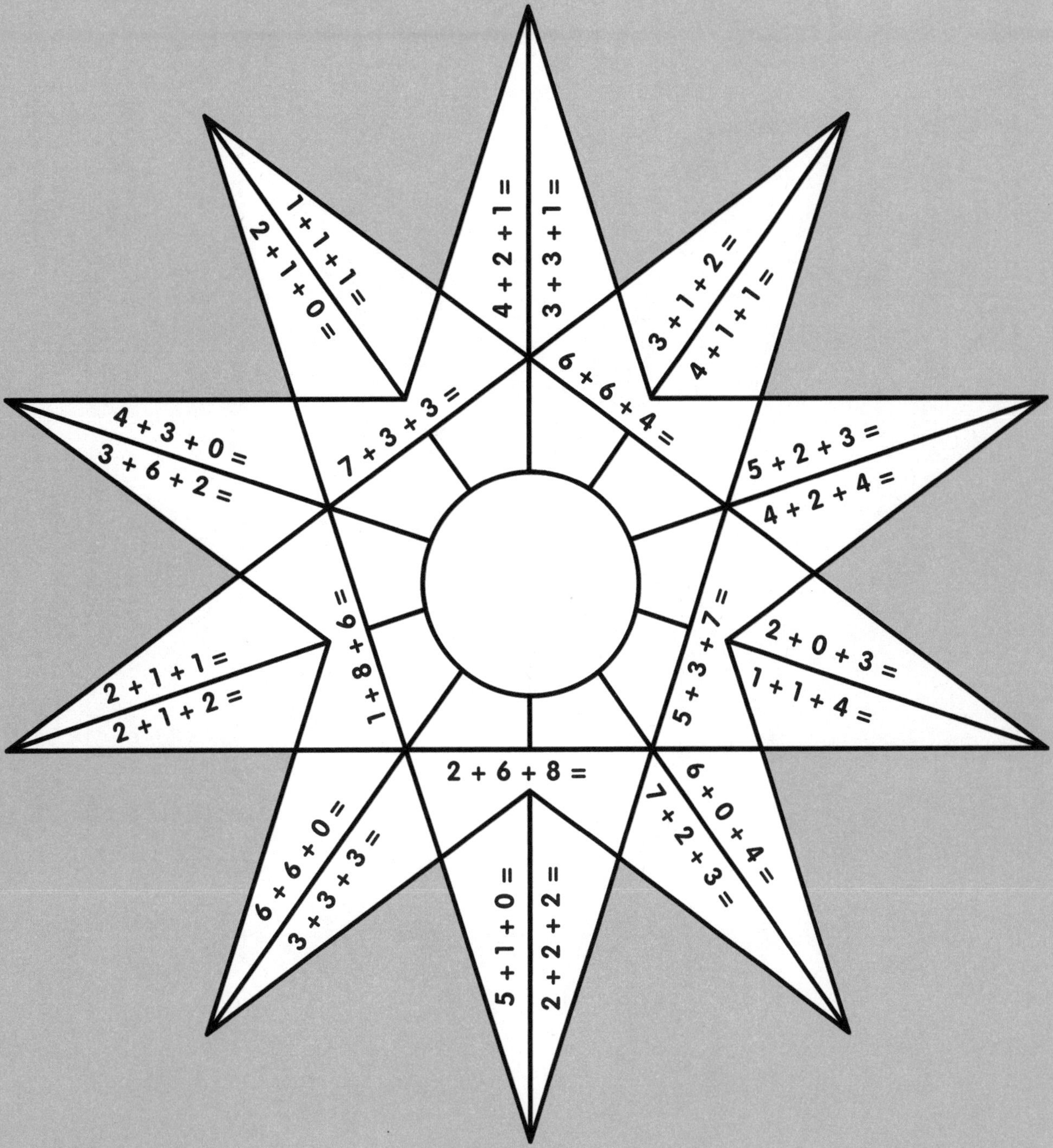
1 + 1 + 1 =
2 + 1 + 0 =
4 + 2 + 1 =
3 + 3 + 1 =
3 + 1 + 2 =
4 + 1 + 1 =
4 + 3 + 0 =
3 + 6 + 2 =
7 + 3 + 3 =
6 + 6 + 4 =
5 + 2 + 3 =
4 + 2 + 4 =
1 + 8 + 6 =
5 + 3 + 7 =
2 + 1 + 1 =
2 + 1 + 2 =
2 + 0 + 3 =
1 + 1 + 4 =
2 + 6 + 8 =
6 + 6 + 0 =
3 + 3 + 3 =
6 + 0 + 4 =
7 + 2 + 3 =
5 + 1 + 0 =
2 + 2 + 2 =

If the sum is between	Color the space
1 and 6	yellow
7 and 12	orange
13 and 18	red

Fill in the other spaces with colors of your choice.

Read the riddle. The answer is written in code.
Use the decoder to solve the riddle.

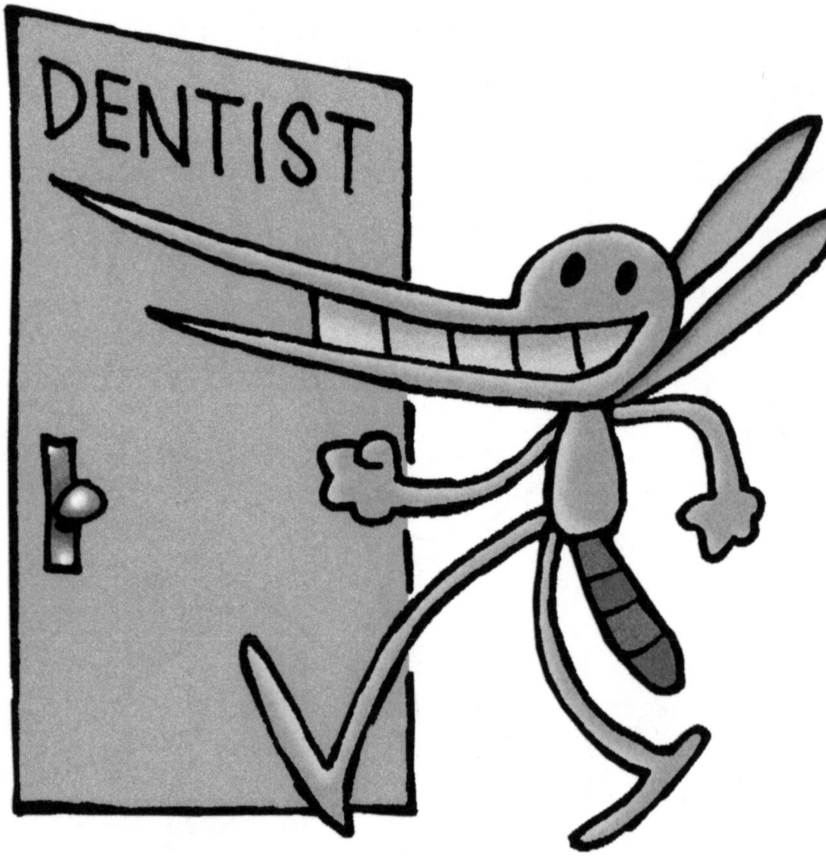
DENTIST

DECODER			
A	☺	N	❒
B	🕓	O	💧
C	⮫	P	❄
D	☆	Q	◆
E	★	R	📫
F	⌛	S	⟐
G	❀	T	😐
H	✋	U	✈
I	✘	V	❖
J	✓	W	☹
K	◯	X	⚑
L	☸	Y	☼
M	⚐	Z	🖱

Why did the mosquito go to see the dentist?

__ __   __ __ __ __ __ __   __ __

✋ ★   ☹ ☺ ❒ 😐 ★ ☆   😐 💧

__ __ __ __ __ __ __   __ __ __   __ __ __ __ !

✘ ⚐ ❄ 📫 💧 ❖ ★   ✋ ✘ ⟐   🕓 ✘ 😐 ★

Help the mole find its way above ground.

Change stop into hill. Use the picture clues and letter tiles. Start at the bottom and climb to the top.

p l i o s h t

STOP

Fun Short-u Words

Solve the crossword. Use the words in the Word Box.

Word Box

BUBBLE	BUG	BULB	BUS	DRUG
DULL	GRUDGE	MUD	MUTT	NUT
RUN	SCRUB	SMUDGE	SUN	TUB

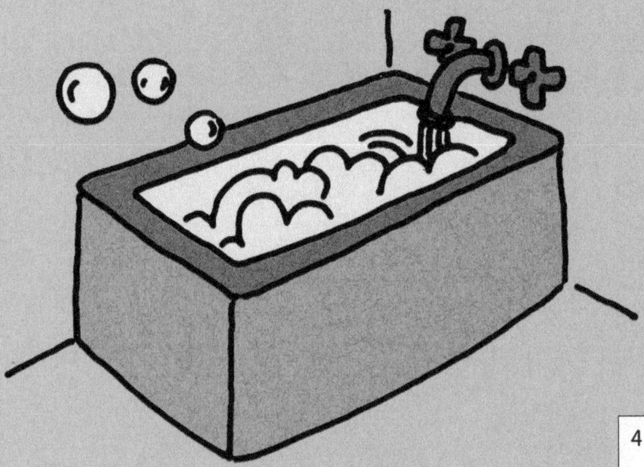

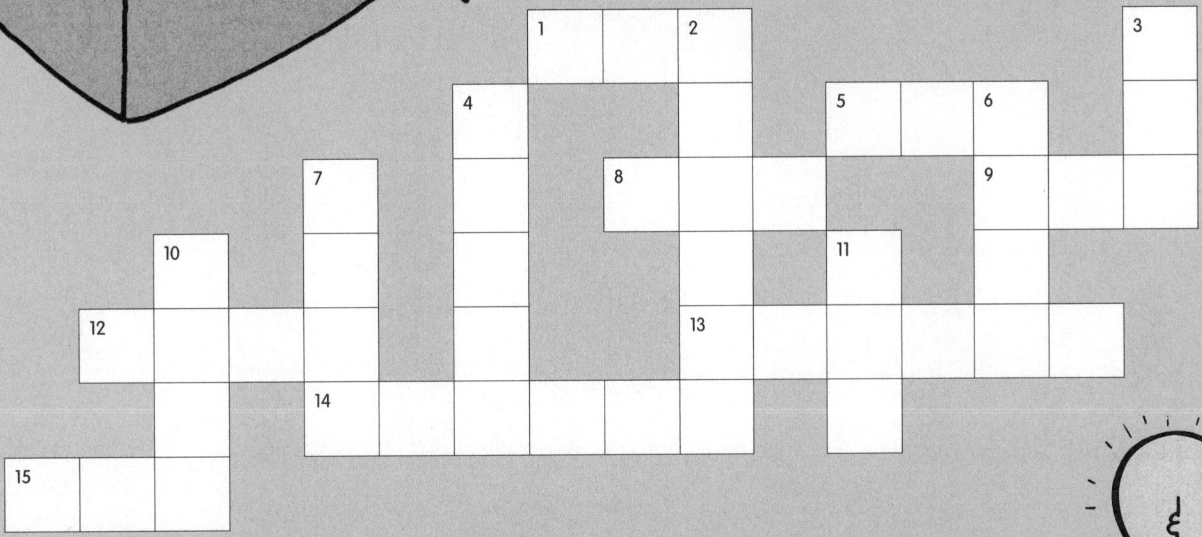

Across

1. transportation to school
5. wet dirt
8. another word for insect
9. to move fast
12. boring
13. stay mad at someone, hold a ____
14. a kind of gum
15. something buried by a squirrel

Down

2. to smear something
3. a source of light on Earth
4. to rub hard to clean well
6. a medicine
7. a light____
10. a mixed breed of dog
11. a place for a bath

Label each picture. Use the Word Box.
Match the pictures with words that sound the same.

Word Box							
BAND	BANNED	PAIR	PEAR	SON	SUN	WAIST	WASTE

____

____

____

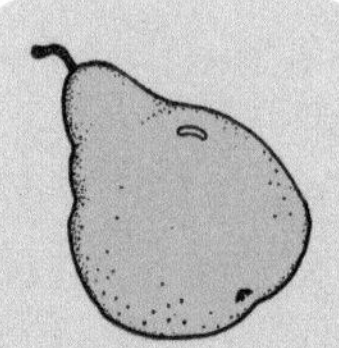

____

____

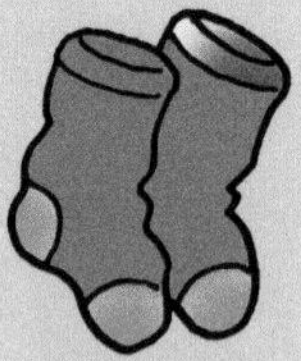

____

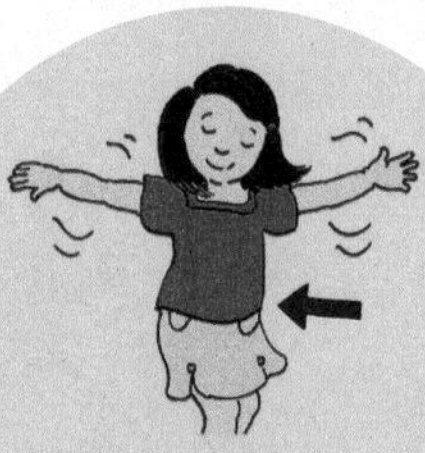

____

____

Design a postage stamp.

Circle six differences.

Connect the dots from a to z. Then color the picture.

s
r
t
u
j
q
x
y
v
p
z
w
k
l
i
m
o
h
g
n
f
e
d
c
b
a

Landforms

Find the words below in the puzzle.
Words are hidden →, ↓, ↘ and ↗.

DESERT	GLACIER	HILL	ISLAND
LAKE	MOUNTAIN	OCEAN	PLAIN
PLATEAU	RIVER	VALLEY	VOLCANO

D	X	L	L	D	P	L	A	I	N	T	R	V
O	X	E	A	S	L	Y	T	E	J	H	C	O
O	G	Z	K	G	A	X	T	E	M	F	L	L
Z	D	Z	E	N	T	T	V	L	C	K	H	C
U	J	E	N	Z	E	R	A	A	O	L	H	A
R	X	J	S	D	A	M	P	A	L	V	K	N
G	T	U	F	E	U	V	L	L	S	L	E	O
L	X	H	B	S	R	F	M	E	A	S	E	U
A	F	I	A	Y	O	T	E	F	O	H	K	Y
C	Y	L	U	H	S	C	I	S	L	A	N	D
I	X	L	Q	R	R	Z	E	X	Y	O	S	M
E	T	X	E	I	M	E	S	A	L	X	Q	D
R	F	V	O	P	A	C	A	O	N	T	B	L
E	I	Z	S	L	M	O	U	N	T	A	I	N
R	O	P	K	U	J	O	Z	Y	I	O	O	N

Magic Squares

In these magic squares, fill in the missing numbers so that every row—vertical, horizontal, and diagonal—adds up to the sum in the star. Use the numbers in each answer box to help you.

Example

18

9	4	5
2	6	10
7	8	3

15

		2
	5	
8		6

Answers
1 4 7 9 3

12

	4	8
7	2	

Answers
1 5 0 6 3

21

	5	6
	7	

Answers
11 4 10 8 9 3

18

5	10	
	6	

Answers
2 3 4 7 8 9

Help the spider reach the center of the web.

A Stormy Day

Read the story. Draw pictures of the things that happened.

Big, black clouds appeared in the sky. Lightning struck the tallest tree. The scared cow cried, "Moo!" It rained hard. Soon there was a mud puddle by the barn door. Hay blew out of the barn window.

Find and circle each item in the big picture.

2+2=4
Paste

Connect the dots from 1 to 33. Then color the picture.

1
2
3
4
5
6
7
8
9
10
11
12
13
14
15
16
17
18
19
20
21
22
23
24
25
26
27
28
29
30
31
32
33

The South Scramble

Unscramble the name of each state.

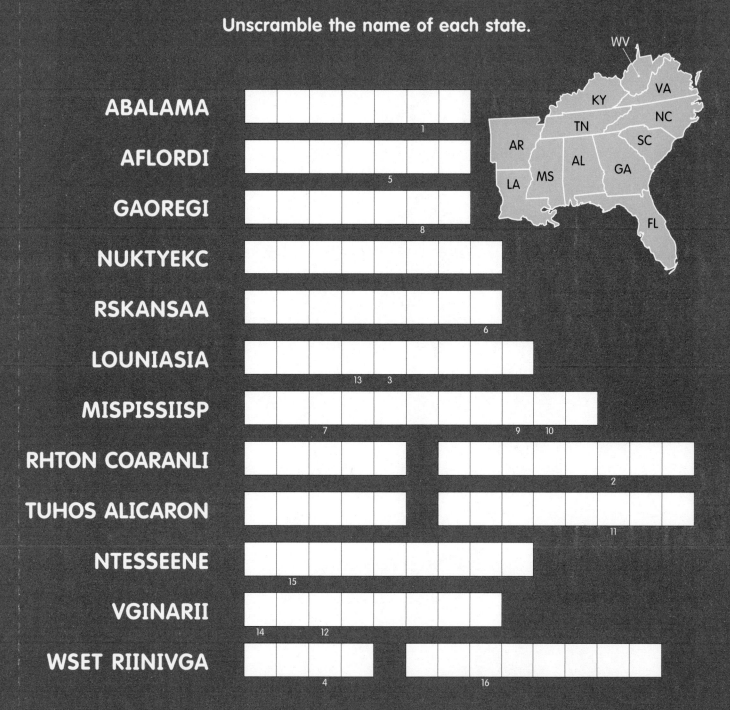

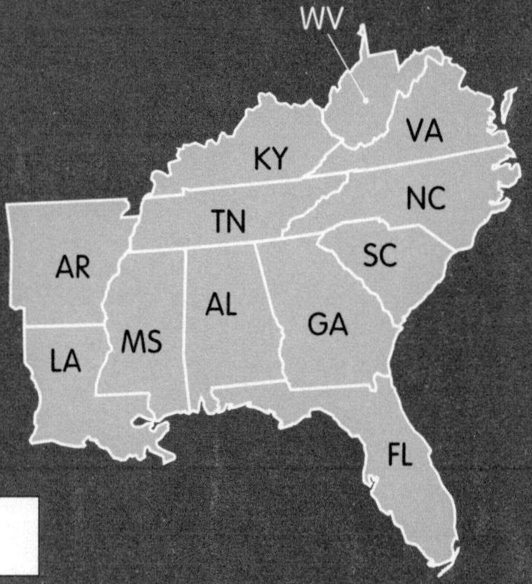

WV
KY
VA
NC
TN
SC
AR
AL
GA
MS
LA
FL

ABALAMA — 1

AFLORDI — 5

GAOREGI — 8

NUKTYEKC

RSKANSAA — 6

LOUNIASIA — 13, 3

MISPISSIISP — 7, 9, 10

RHTON COARANLI — 2

TUHOS ALICARON — 11

NTESSEENE — 15

VGINARII — 14, 12

WSET RIINIVGA — 4, 16

Copy the letters in the numbered cells to answer the question.

What is the second longest river in the United States?

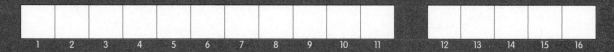

1 2 3 4 5 6 7 8 9 10 11   12 13 14 15 16

RAY

Circle six differences.

RAY

What will people look like in the future? Draw a picture.

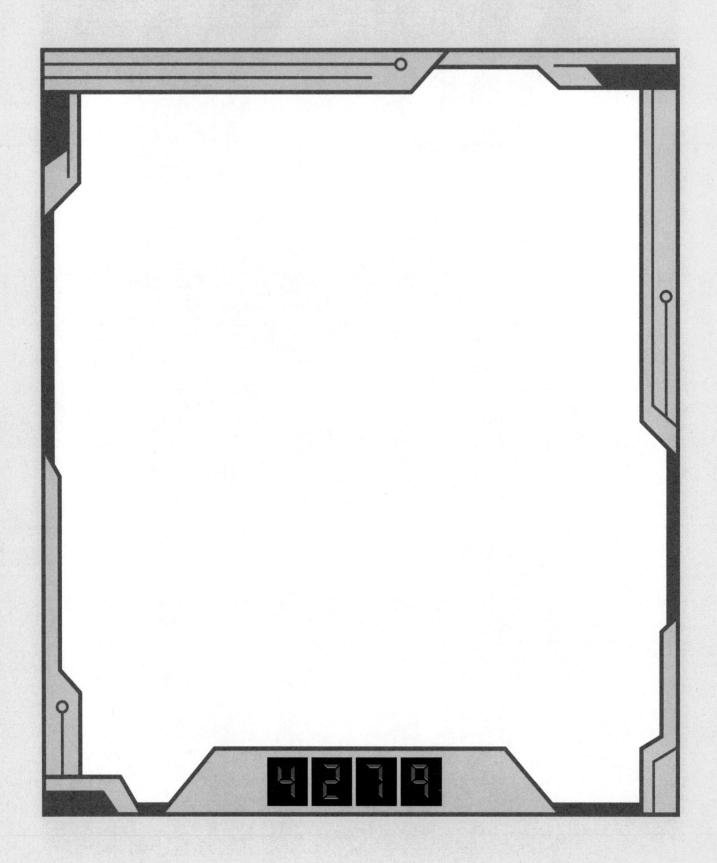

Color the picture. Use the color key.

If the word has the same beginning sound as			
Color the space	purple	red	green

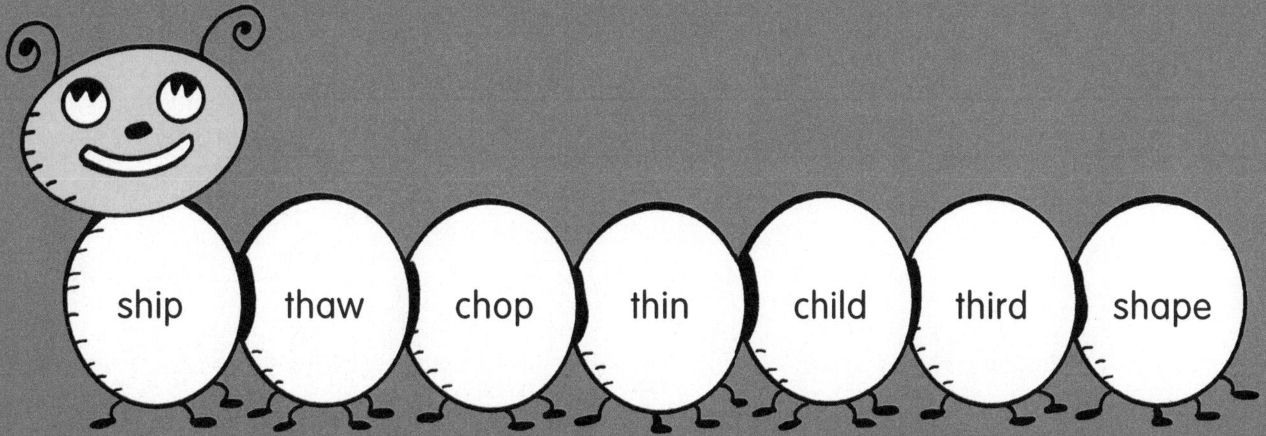
ship
thaw
chop
thin
child
third
shape

thing
thorn
shoe
shade
chin
cheep
thick

chew
chalk
chick
thank
short
shave
shirt

Handmade

Read the clues. Write the words.
Start at the bottom and climb to the top.

synonym of *created*
change the first letter

to disappear gradually
change the third letter

some call it luck
change the first letter

opposite of *early*
change the third letter

a narrow road or path
change the last letter

opposite of *sea*
change the first letter

h a n d

Add. Color the picture. Use the color key below.

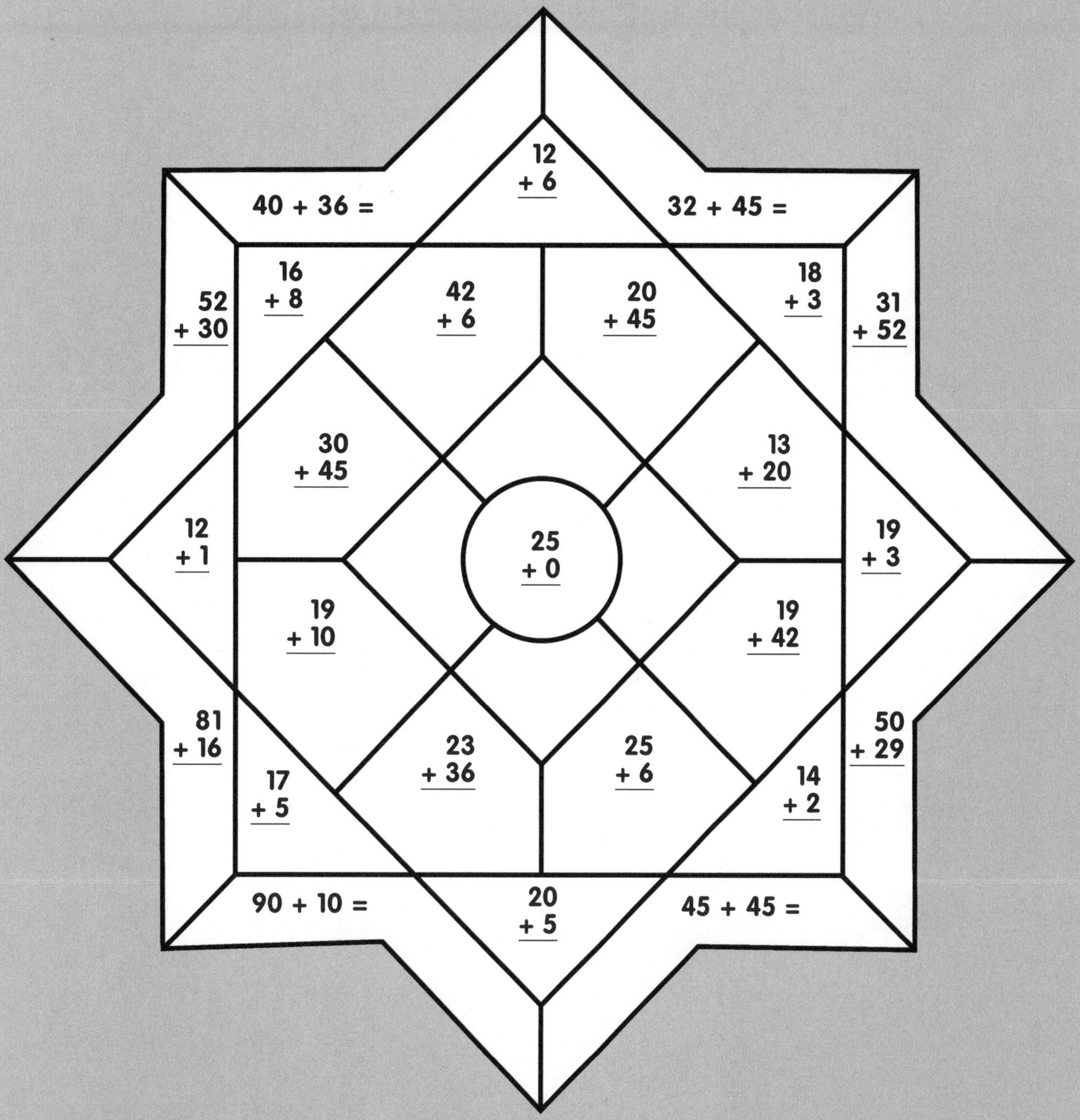

12 + 6
40 + 36 =
32 + 45 =
16 + 8
42 + 6
20 + 45
18 + 3
52 + 30
31 + 52
30 + 45
13 + 20
12 + 1
25 + 0
19 + 3
19 + 10
19 + 42
81 + 16
50 + 29
17 + 5
23 + 36
25 + 6
14 + 2
90 + 10 =
20 + 5
45 + 45 =

If the sum is between	Color the space
1 and 25	blue
26 and 50	orange
51 and 75	purple
76 and 100	red

Fill in the other spaces with colors of your choice.

Change jar into crane. Use the picture clues and letter tiles. Start at the bottom and climb to the top.

j c e n r a

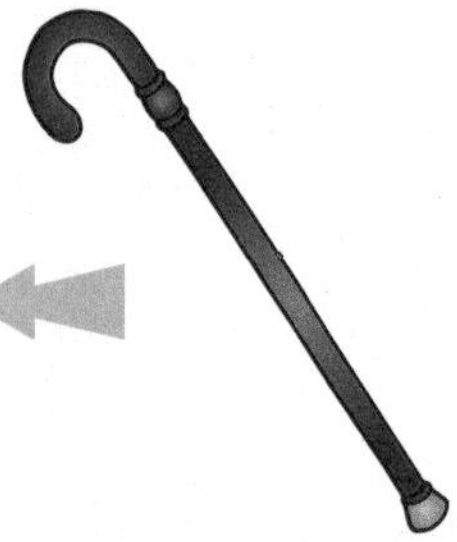

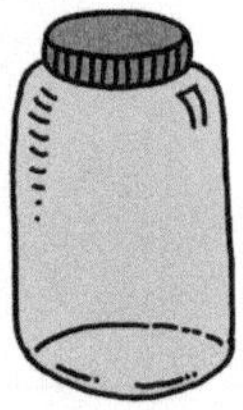

Color the picture. Use the color key.

If the word has a	Long-*a* sound	Long-*i* sound	Long-*o* sound	Long-*u* sound
Color the space	**blue**	**green**	**purple**	**red**

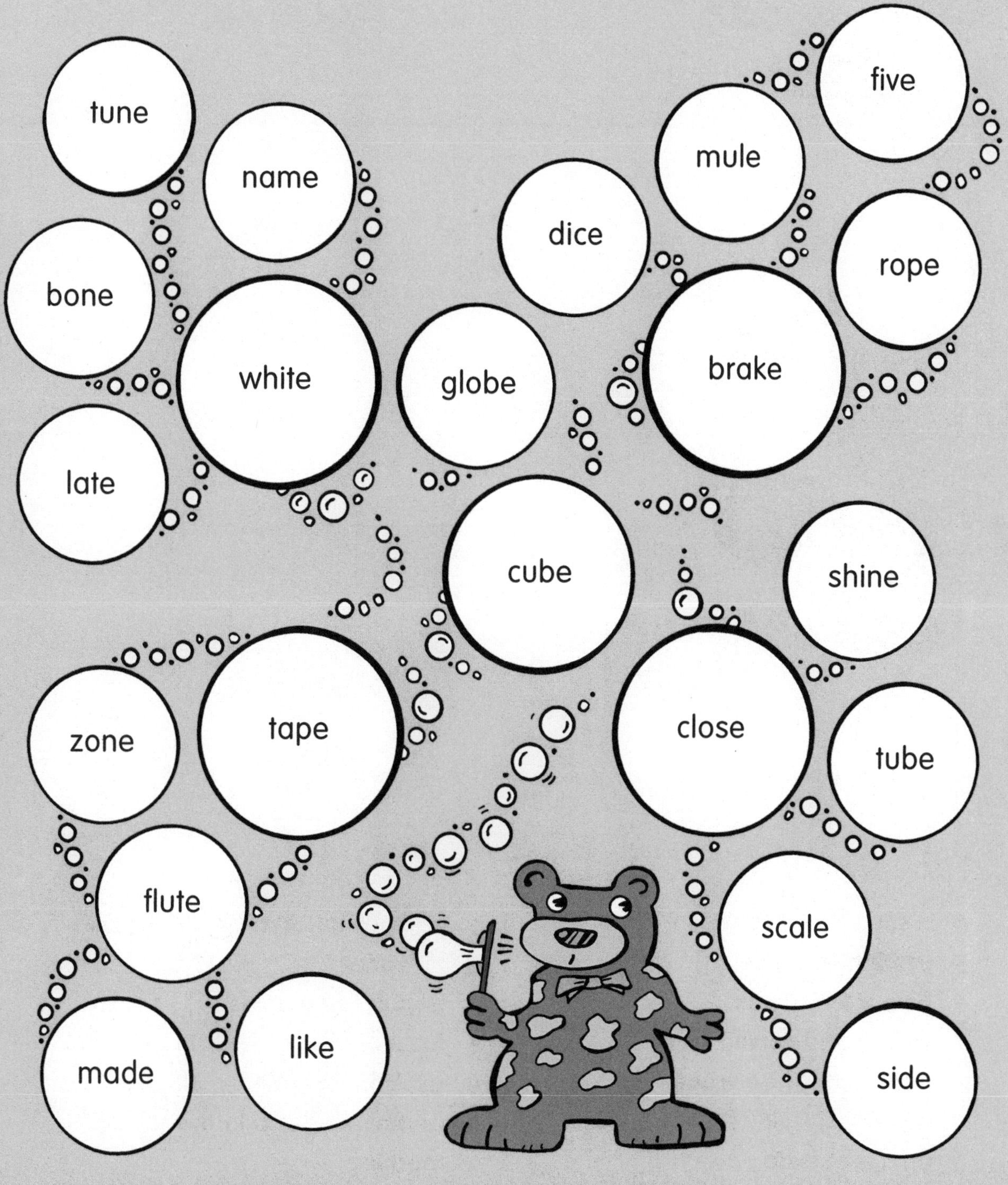

tune
name
five
mule
dice
rope
bone
white
globe
brake
late
cube
shine
zone
tape
close
tube
flute
scale
made
like
side

Fruity Delights

Solve the crossword.

Across

4. a summer treat
5. used to make jelly
6. homonym of pair
7. yellow and curved
10. on top of an ice cream sundae
11. a soft red fruit with tiny seeds on the outside

Down

1. a Hawaiian fruit
2. ___ ade
3. popular in muffins
6. fuzzy fruit used in cobbler
8. as American as ___ pie
9. perfect for juice in the morning

Circle the two sunglasses that are the same.

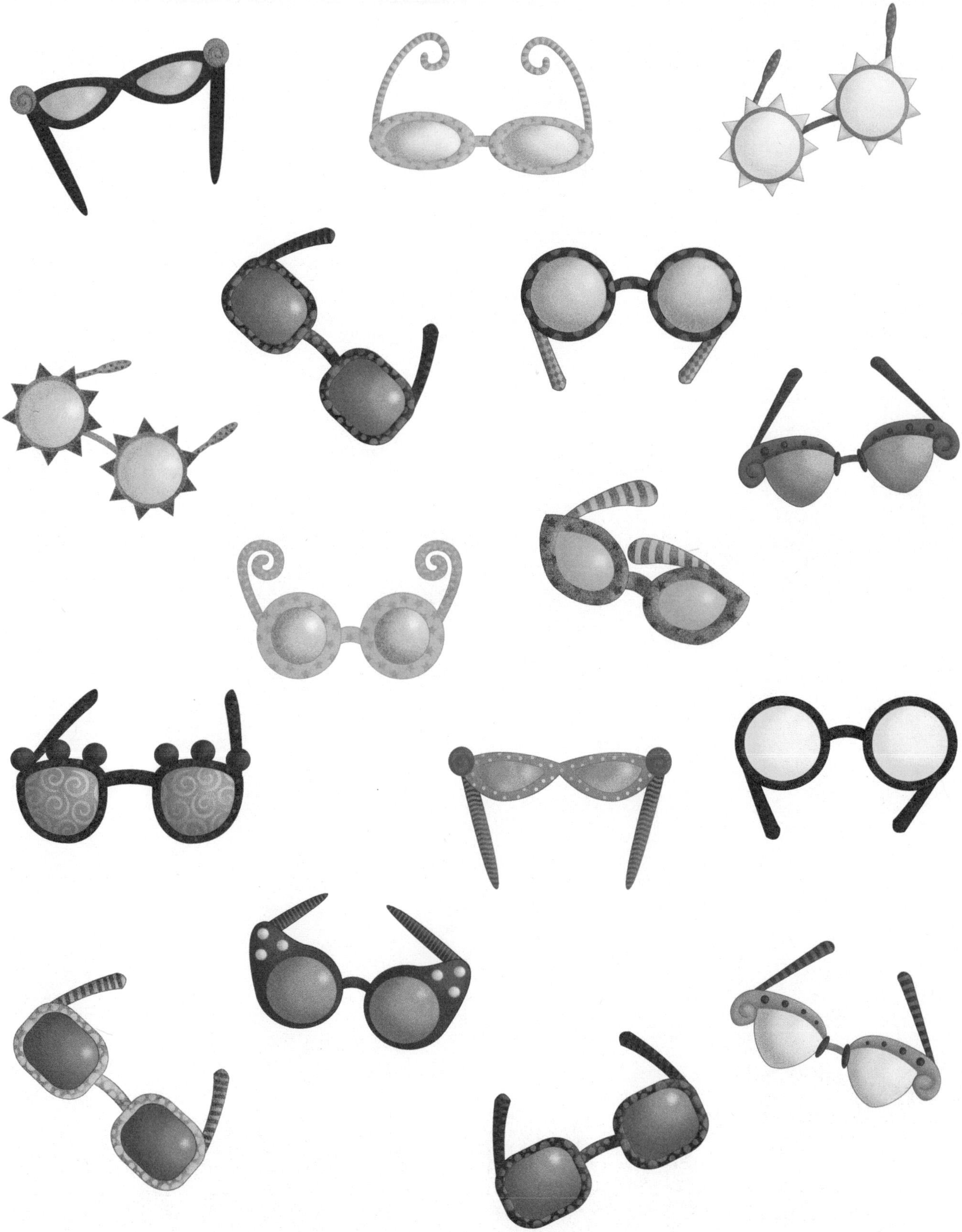

How many smaller words can you make using the letters in

elephant?

1 ______________________________

2 ______________________________

3 ______________________________

4 ______________________________

5 ______________________________

6 ______________________________

7 ______________________________

8 ______________________________

9 ______________________________

10 ______________________________

11 ______________________________

12 ______________________________

13 ______________________________

14 ______________________________

15 ______________________________

16 ______________________________

17 ______________________________

18 ______________________________

19 ______________________________

20 ______________________________

21 ______________________________

22 ______________________________

23 ______________________________

24 ______________________________

25 ______________________________

26 ______________________________

27 ______________________________

28 ______________________________

29 ______________________________

30 ______________________________

elephant (EL-uh-fuhnt) n. – a large mammal that has two ivory tusks and a long, flexible nose called a trunk

Help the ship get to the island.

Read the riddle. The answer is written in code.
Use the decoder to solve the riddle.

DECODER			
A	8	N	20
B	9	O	26
C	10	P	23
D	14	Q	1
E	2	R	3
F	25	S	18
G	5	T	24
H	6	U	4
I	13	V	21
J	15	W	12
K	17	X	16
L	7	Y	22
M	19	Z	11

Why do bats always live in gigantic groups?

9 2 10 8 4 18 2   24 6 2 22   7 26 21 2   24 26

6 8 20 5   26 4 24   12 13 24 6   24 6 2 13 3

25 3 13 2 20 14 18 !

Let's Make Music

Find the words below in the puzzle.
Words are hidden → and ↓.

BASS	CYMBALS	DRUM	FLUTE
GUITAR	HARP	KAZOO	MARACAS
OBOE	PIANO	TRIANGLE	VIOLIN

J	O	H	A	R	P	B	R	N	X
L	P	T	R	I	A	N	G	L	E
Y	M	A	R	A	C	A	S	B	K
U	P	I	A	N	O	C	C	E	A
B	O	W	V	G	Q	T	Y	Z	Z
O	G	B	I	D	R	U	M	L	O
B	U	K	O	C	F	N	B	D	O
O	I	I	L	B	A	X	A	L	R
E	T	K	I	A	P	T	L	S	O
L	A	C	N	S	T	C	S	M	K
H	R	U	P	S	F	L	U	T	E

What picture is missing?
Find the sticker on page 321. Add it to the pattern.

Draw your own pattern below.

Find each space with any, from, give, know, and put.
Color those spaces green. Then color the rest of the picture.

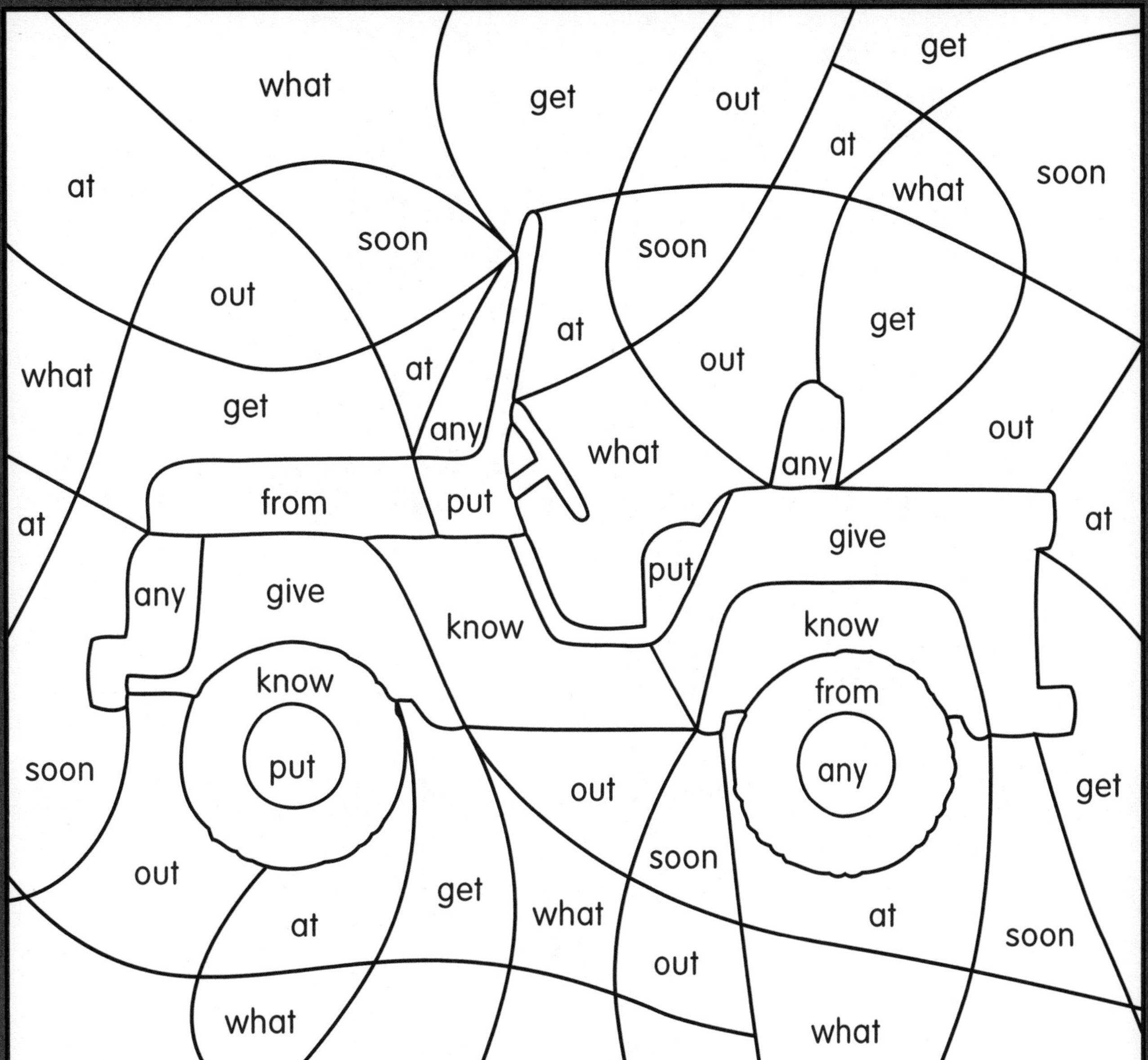
get
what
get
out
at
soon
at
what
soon
soon
out
get
at
out
at
what
get
out
any
what
any
from
put
at
at
give
put
any
give
know
know
know
from
soon
put
any
get
out
soon
out
get
what
at
at
soon
out
what
what
get
soon
out
get
at
out

Connect the dots from 11 to 38. Then color the picture.

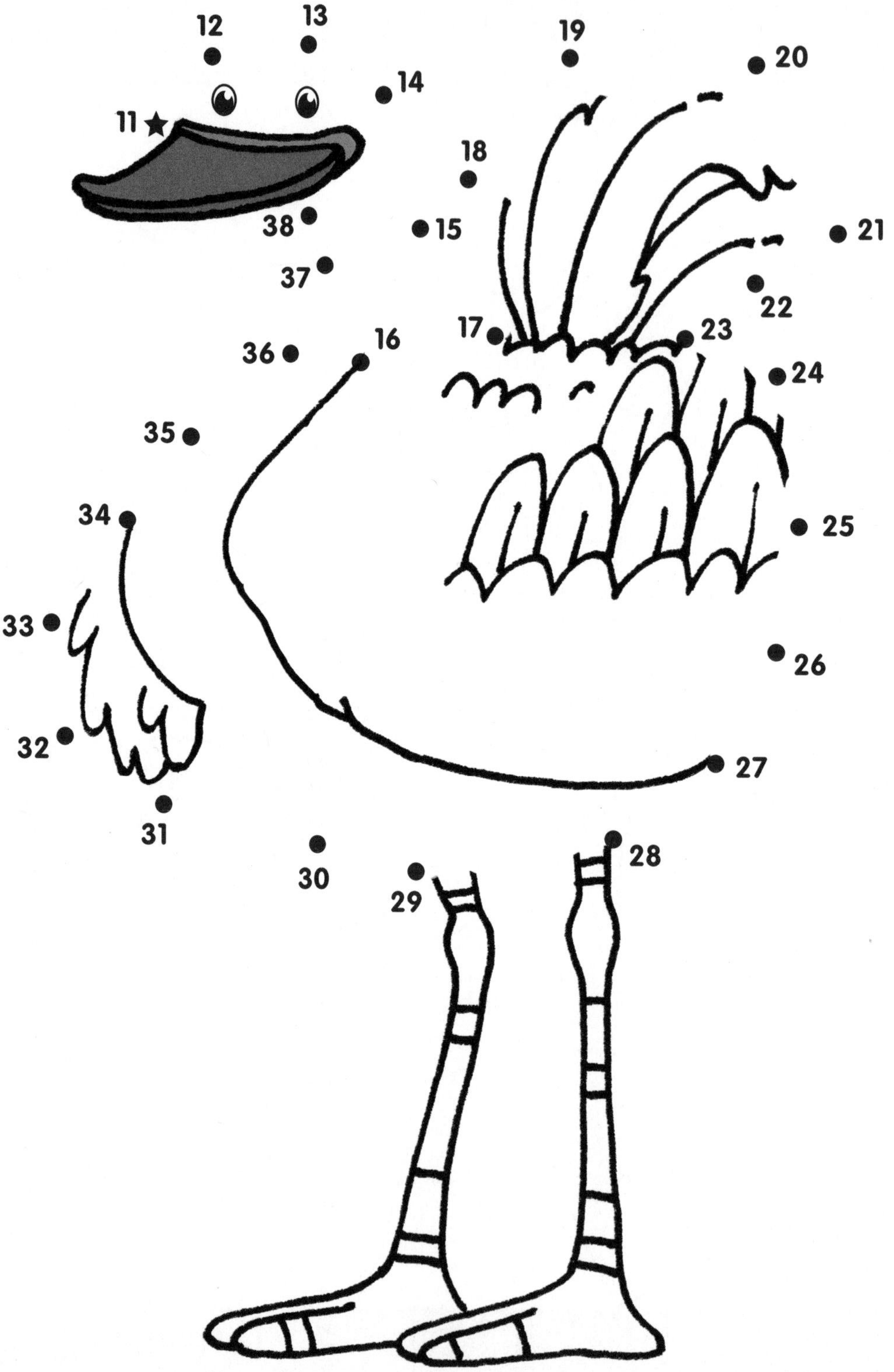
11
12
13
14
15
16
17
18
19
20
21
22
23
24
25
26
27
28
29
30
31
32
33
34
35
36
37
38

Add. Then use the code to answer the riddle below.

6 + 2 = ___ I	4 + 3 = ___ D	2 + 1 = ___ H	4 + 1 = ___ A
11 + 3 = ___ A	8 + 2 = ___ B	7 + 5 = ___ N	9 + 2 = ___ S
6 + 3 = ___ O	11 + 4 = ___ U	5 + 13 = ___ R	9 + 4 = ___ P

What has 88 keys but can't open a single door?

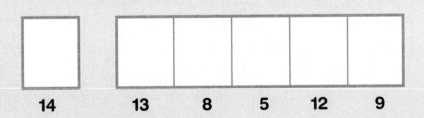

___	___	___	___	___	___
14	13	8	5	12	9

Read the riddle. The answer is written in code.
Use the decoder to solve the riddle.

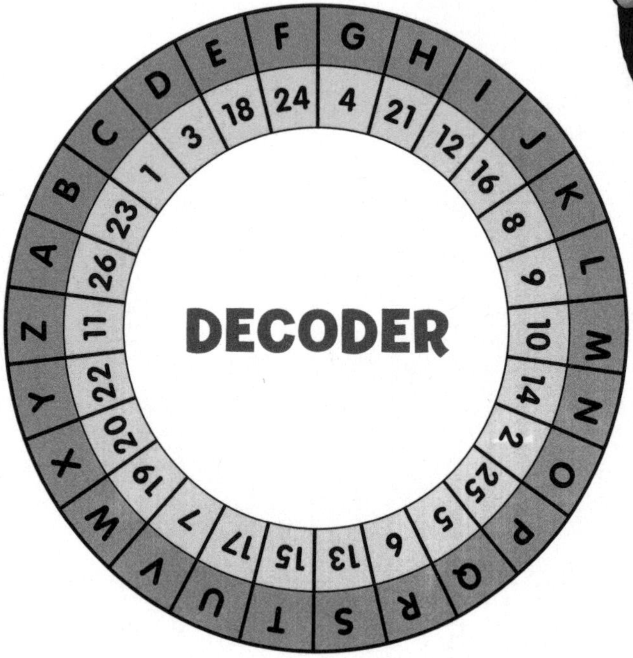
DECODER
A 26
B 23
C 1
D 3
E 18
F 24
G 4
H 21
I 12
J 16
K 8
L 9
M 10
N 14
O 2
P 25
Q 5
R 6
S 13
T 15
U 17
V 7
W 19
X 20
Y 22
Z 11

Why did King Kong climb to the top of the Empire State Building?

___ ___ ___ ___ ___ ___ ___   ___ ___   ___ ___ ___ ___ ___

23 18 1 26 17 13 18   21 18   1 2 17 9 3

14 2 15   24 12 15   12 14 13 12 3 18   15 21 18

18 9 18 7 26 15 2 6 !

Circle the lights that should be turned off.
Circle the leaky faucets.

SPOT

How many things did you circle? ______

LIN
FIN
MIN

Circle six differences.

LIN
FIN
MIN

Draw stars to complete the grid.
Each row, column, and minigrid should have one of each color.

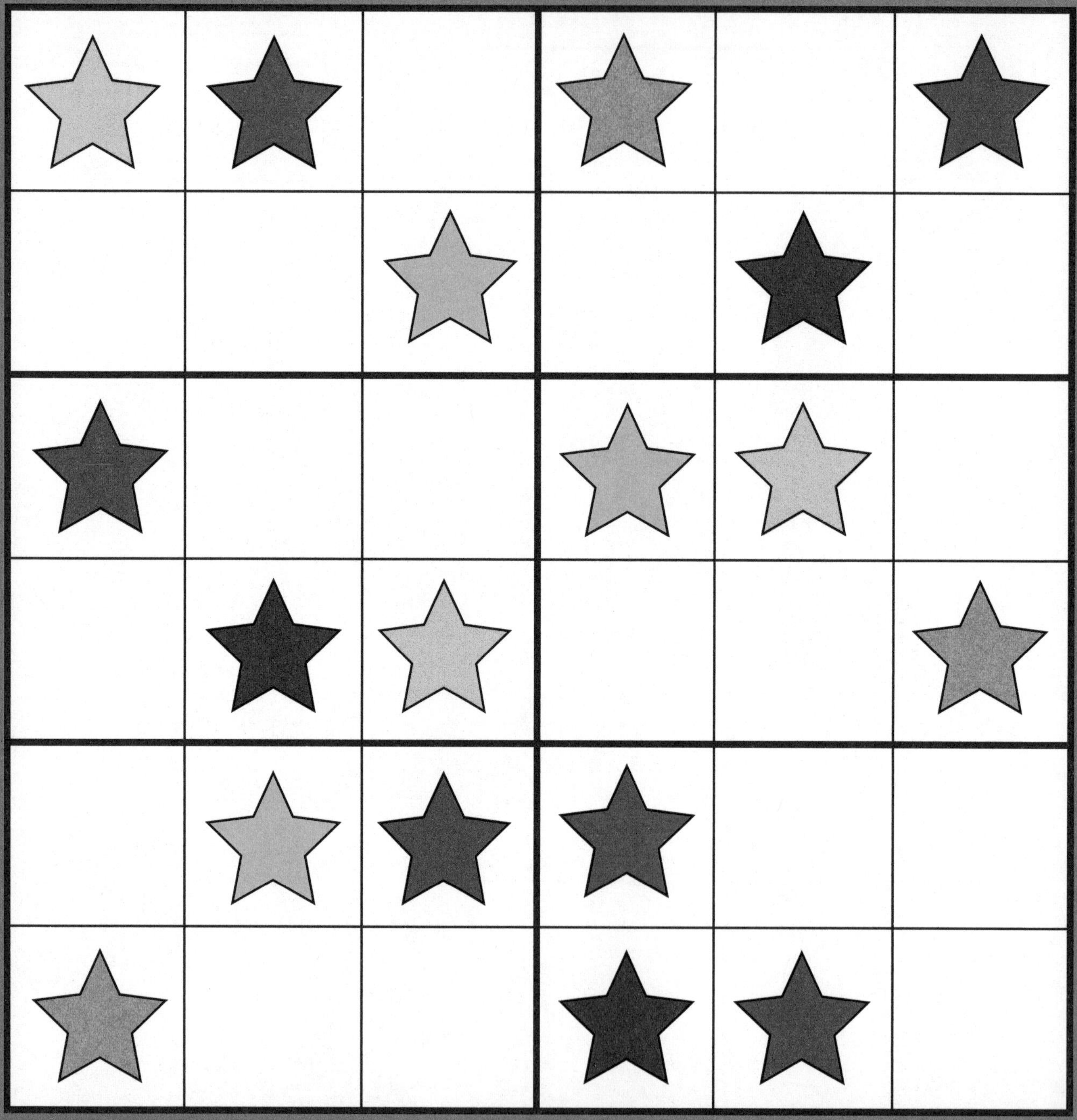

Change fin into train. Use the picture clues and letter tiles. Start at the bottom and climb to the top.

i n r f t a

Who would you give a medal to? What would it look like?

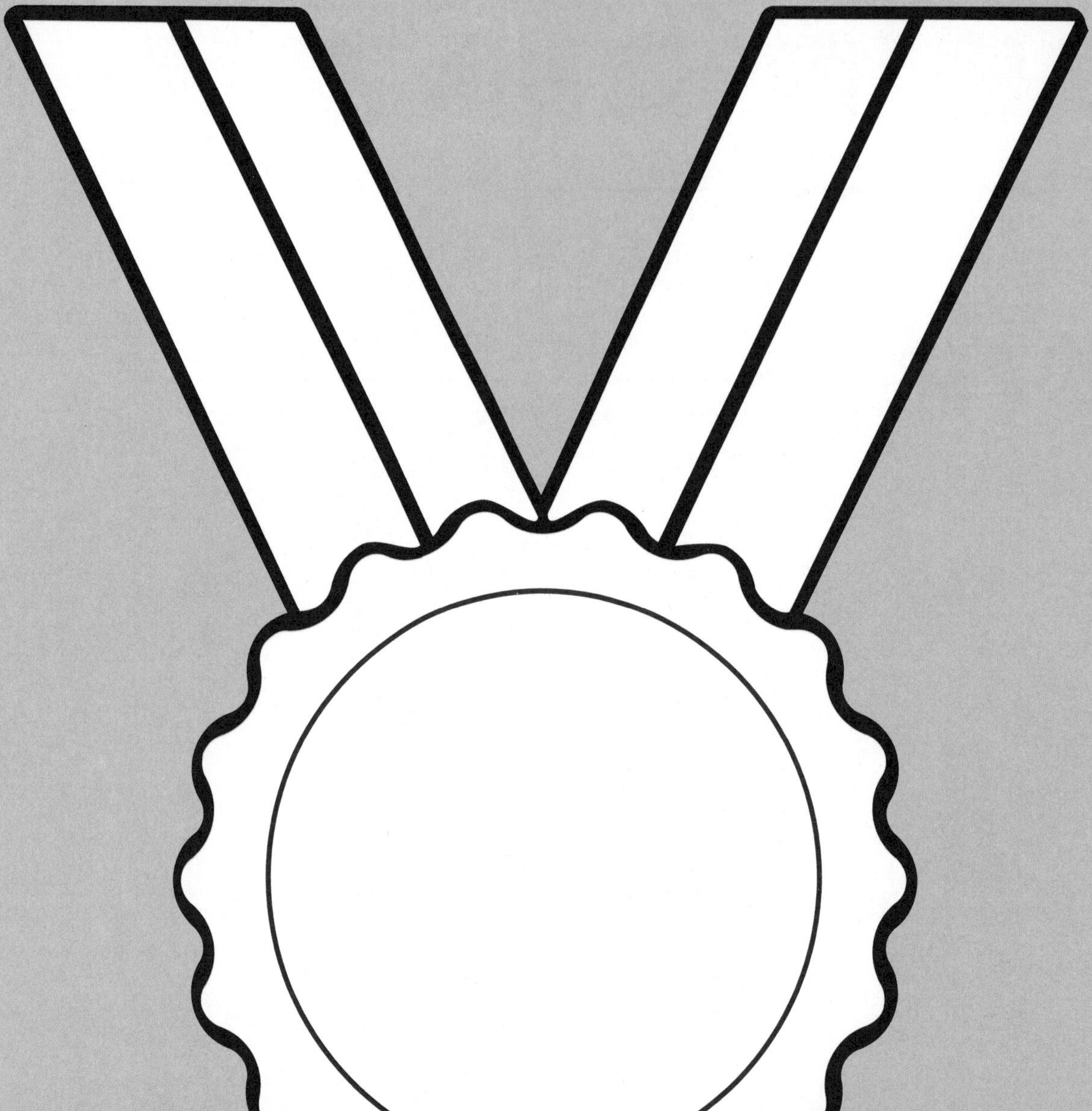

This medal is presented to ______________________

for ____________________________________.

Swimming Lessons

Read the story. Number the pictures in the order that they happened.

Last summer I learned how to swim. First, the teacher told me to hold my breath. Then I learned to put my head under water. I practiced kicking my feet. While I held on to a float, I paddled around the pool. Next, I floated to my teacher with my arms straight out. Finally, I swam using both my arms and my legs. I did it! Swimming is fun! This summer, I want to learn to dive off the diving board.

Add. Color the picture. Use the color key below.

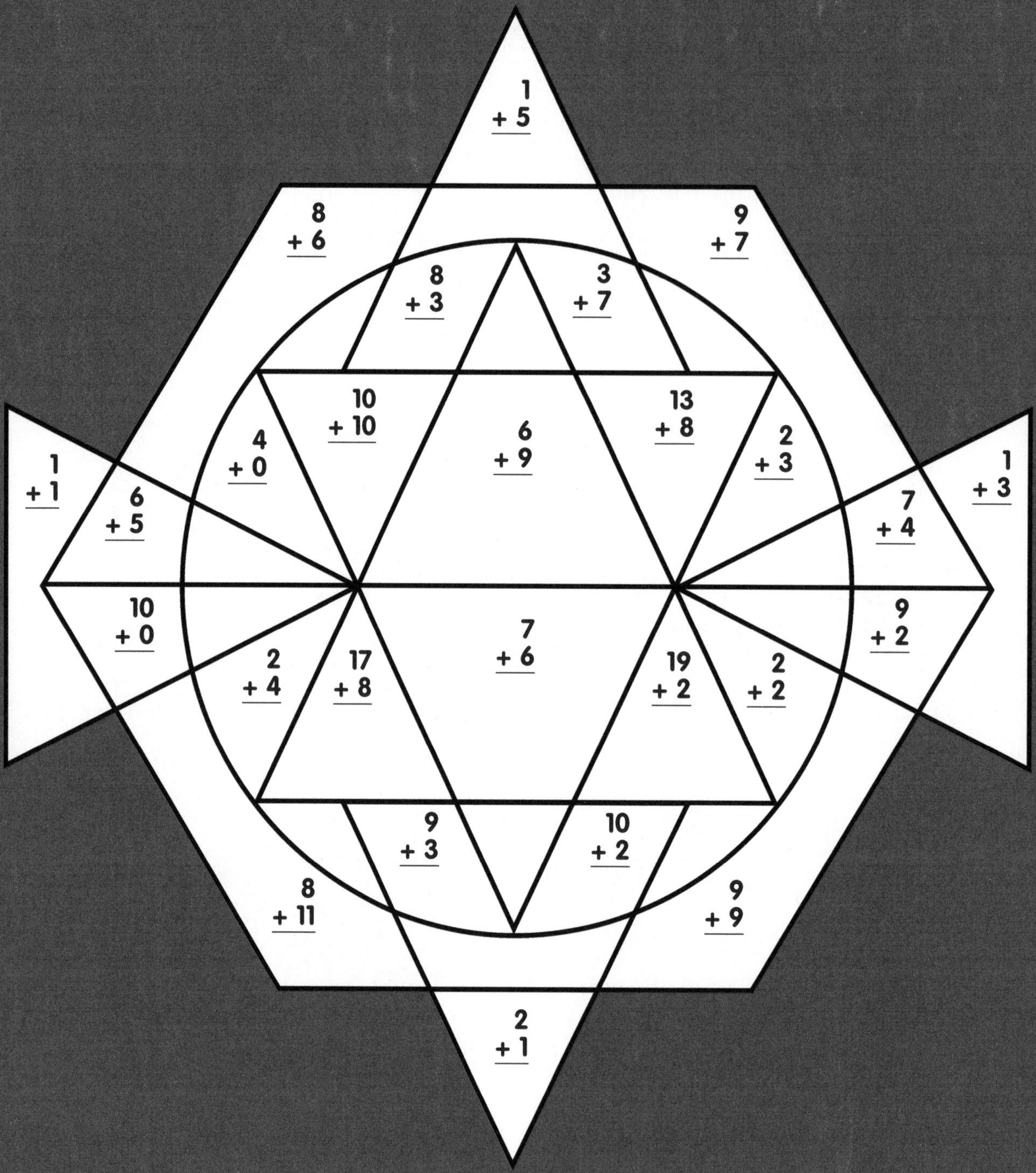
1 + 5
8 + 6
9 + 7
8 + 3
3 + 7
10 + 10
13 + 8
4 + 0
6 + 9
2 + 3
1 + 1
6 + 5
7 + 4
1 + 3
10 + 0
7 + 6
9 + 2
2 + 4
17 + 8
19 + 2
2 + 2
9 + 3
10 + 2
8 + 11
9 + 9
2 + 1

If the sum is between	Color the space
1 and 6	green
7 and 12	red
13 and 19	yellow
20 and 25	black

Fill in the other spaces with colors of your choice.

At the Marina

Read the clues. Write the words.
Start at the bottom and climb to the top.

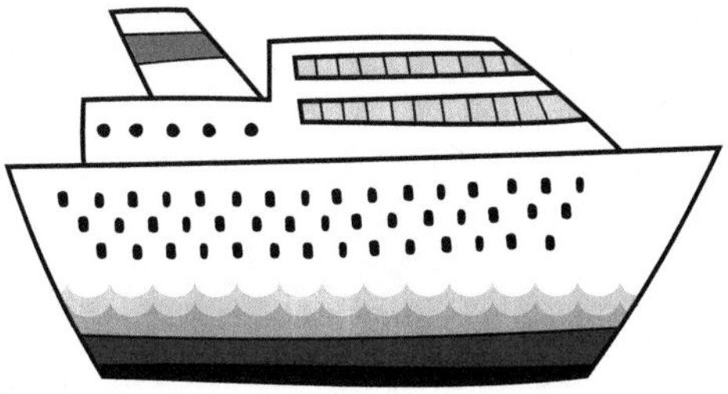

a large boat
add a letter to the beginning

___ ___ ___ ___

side of the body below the waist
change the first letter

___ ___ ___

synonym of *tear*
change the first letter

___ ___ ___

a hint
change the last letter

___ ___ ___

t i e

Connect the dots from 20 to 46. Then color the picture.

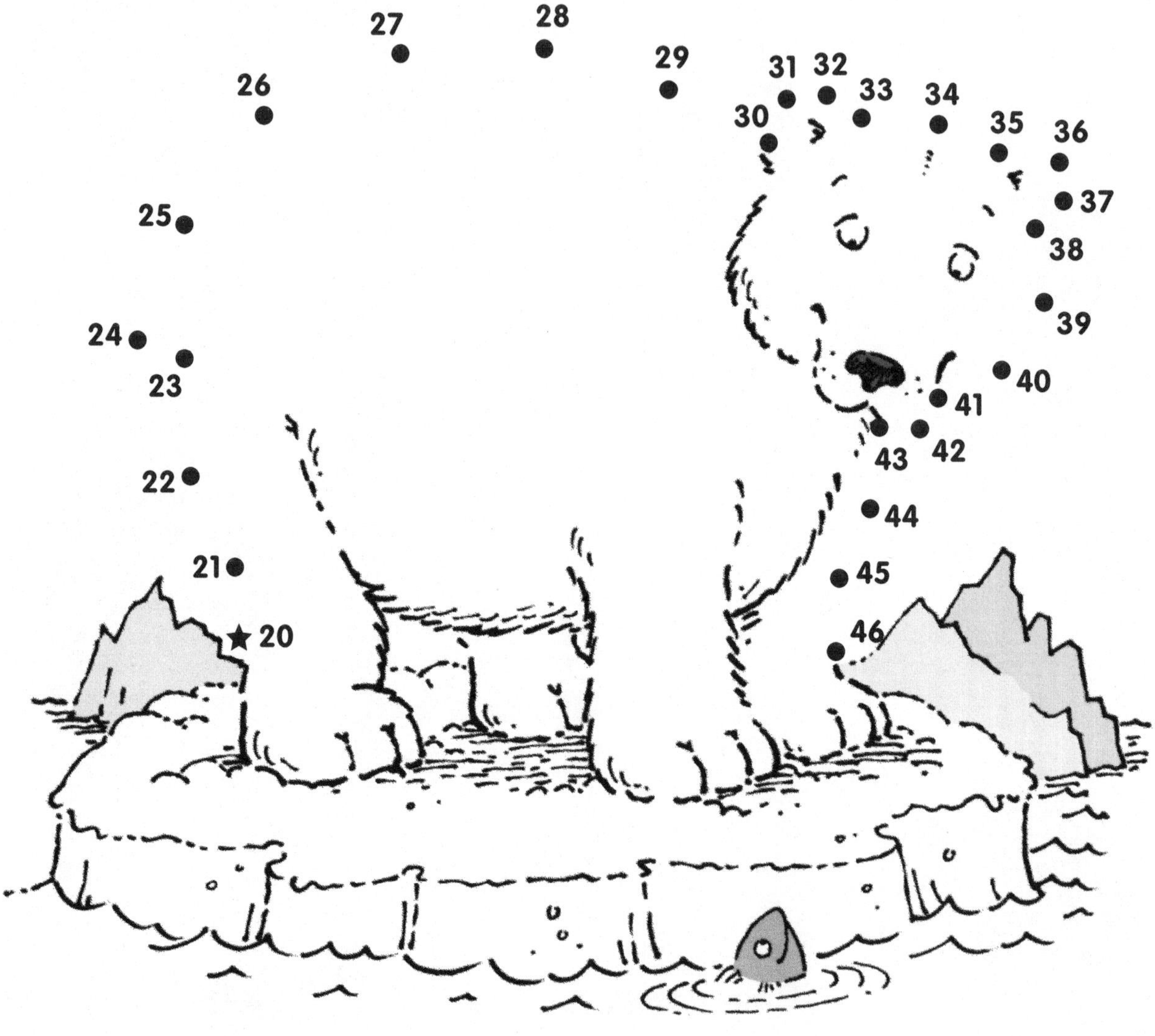

20
21
22
23
24
25
26
27
28
29
30
31
32
33
34
35
36
37
38
39
40
41
42
43
44
45
46

Favorite Pets

Solve the crossword. Use the Word Box and picture clues.

Across

2

3

6

7

8

9

Down

3

1

4

5

Word Box

CAT	DOG
FISH	FROG
GUINEA PIG	HAMSTER
LIZARD	PARROT
RABBIT	TURTLE

Math Tic-Tac-Toe

Subtract. Draw a line through the three problems in a row with the same answer. The row can go →, ↓, ↘ or ↗.

23 − 11	33 − 12	25 − 9
19 − 7	44 − 6	32 − 26
18 − 6	29 − 8	22 − 9

52 − 18	63 − 29	43 − 9
38 − 5	19 − 16	48 − 36
29 − 12	11 − 8	52 − 9

59 − 7	67 − 25	42 − 15
37 − 12	53 − 25	38 − 23
76 − 19	68 − 11	88 − 31

35 − 11	77 − 53	25 − 13
66 − 42	44 − 32	38 − 26
18 − 6	20 − 7	52 − 26

Draw the items shown to complete the grid.
Each row, column, and minigrid should have one of each item.

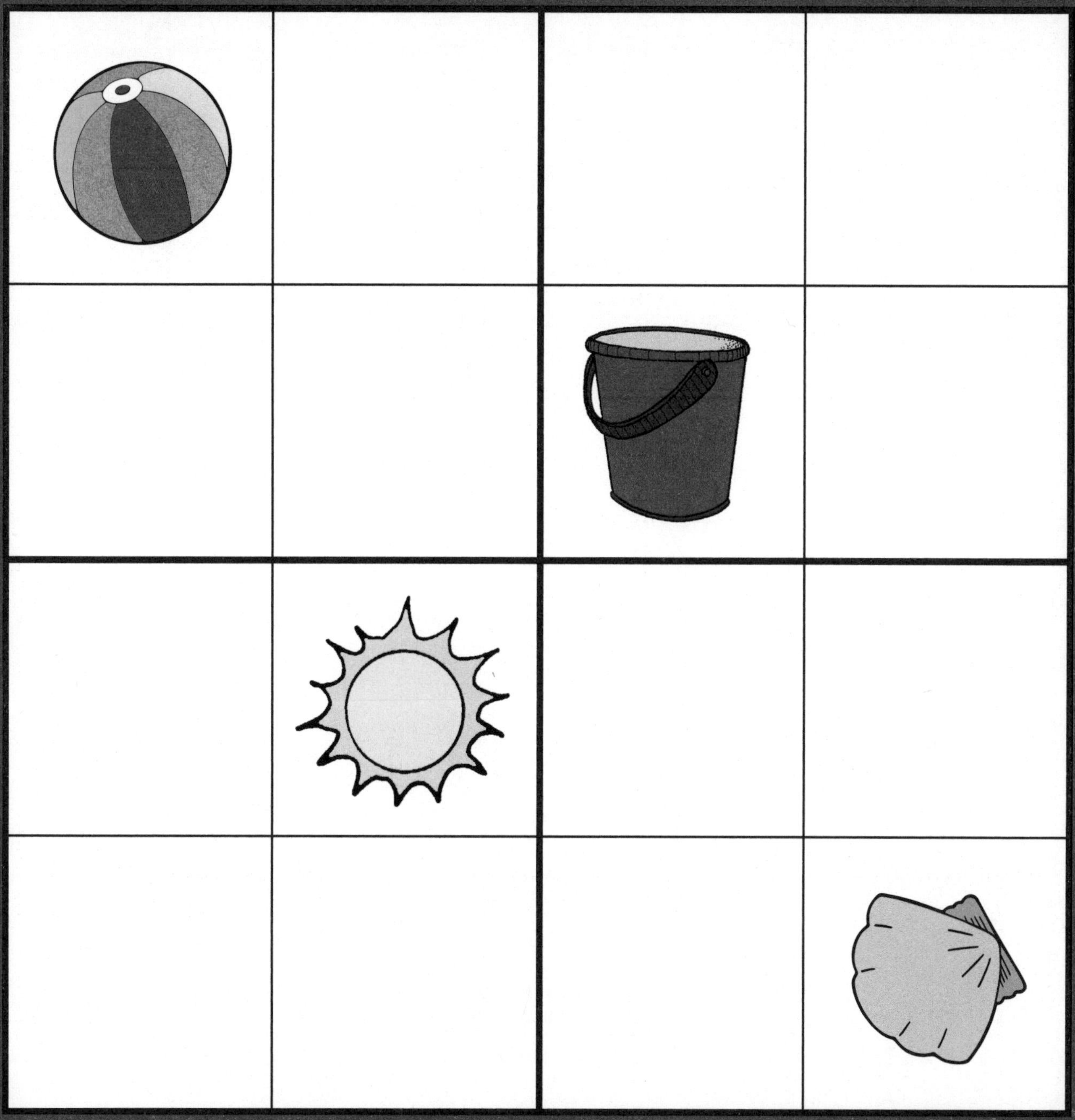

Find the two drawings that are the same.

The New England Scramble

Unscramble the name of each state.

CONTUICECTN

MAENI

SMSATSAHESTUC

WEN IHAMPESHR

RDEHO SAILDN

VROENMT

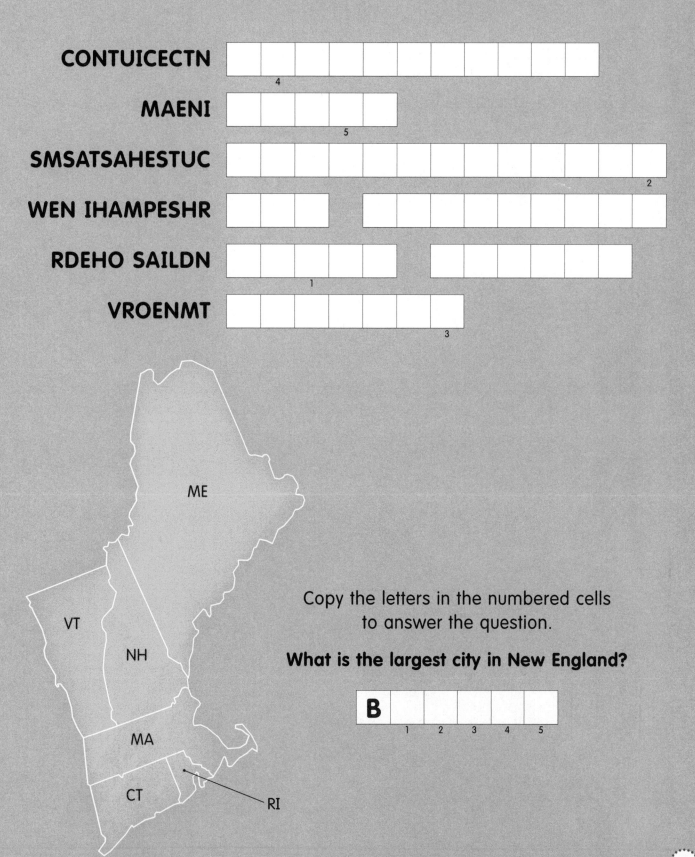

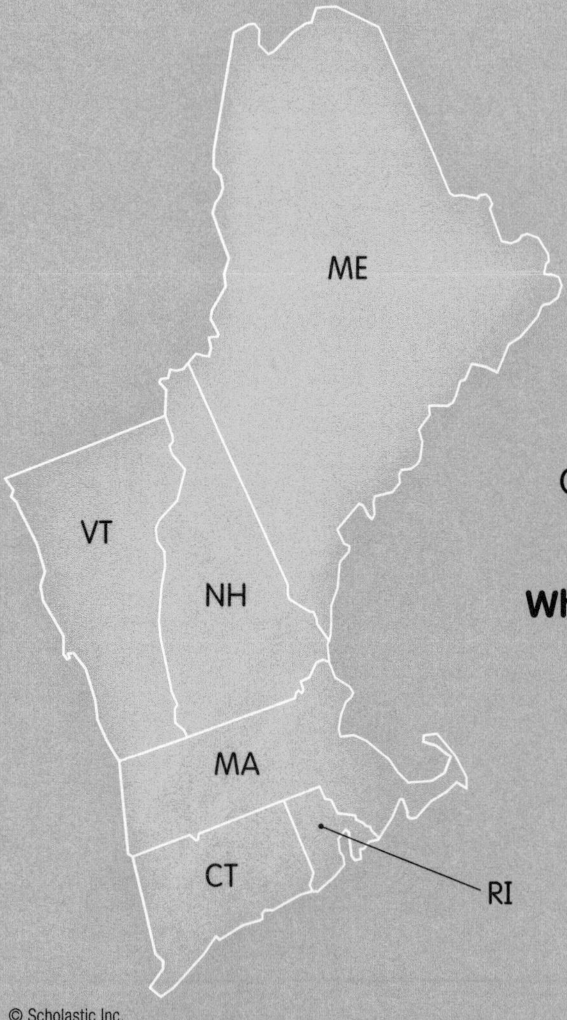
ME
VT
NH
MA
CT
RI

Copy the letters in the numbered cells to answer the question.

What is the largest city in New England?

B	1	2	3	4	5

How will people get around in the future? Draw a picture.

How Do You Feel?

Find the words below in the puzzle.
Words are hidden →, ↓, ↘ and ↗.

BORED	EXCITED	GLAD	GREAT
HAPPY	LUCKY	NERVOUS	SAD
SICK	THANKFUL	THRILLED	TIRED

N	I	T	Y	E	X	C	I	T	E	D	S	I
T	K	H	Q	P	N	V	M	B	B	I	R	N
H	L	R	Y	K	L	J	R	U	O	Z	N	C
A	T	I	C	Q	I	X	D	X	A	R	B	Z
N	A	L	C	S	F	S	X	V	Q	L	E	S
K	E	L	A	B	I	J	G	L	A	D	K	D
F	J	E	G	O	A	C	R	N	I	P	A	G
U	M	D	U	I	O	D	K	M	Y	B	I	X
L	S	M	K	X	B	Z	O	Z	O	L	C	R
N	E	R	V	O	U	S	M	S	W	D	M	X
S	H	U	X	R	F	J	E	O	A	U	L	H
L	U	C	K	Y	A	Z	W	S	S	E	T	A
W	M	B	P	A	G	D	Z	X	J	Y	U	P
T	I	R	E	D	C	G	F	D	W	G	U	P
K	N	F	G	D	G	G	R	E	A	T	V	Y

Help Mama rabbit find her baby rabbits.

Change king into pin. Use the picture clues and letter tiles. Start at the bottom and climb to the top.

w n i p g k

___ ___ ___

___ ___ ___

___ ___ ___

___ ___ ___ ___

___ ___ ___ ___

Color the picture. Use the color key.

If the word has the same vowel sound as			
Color the space	yellow	red	green

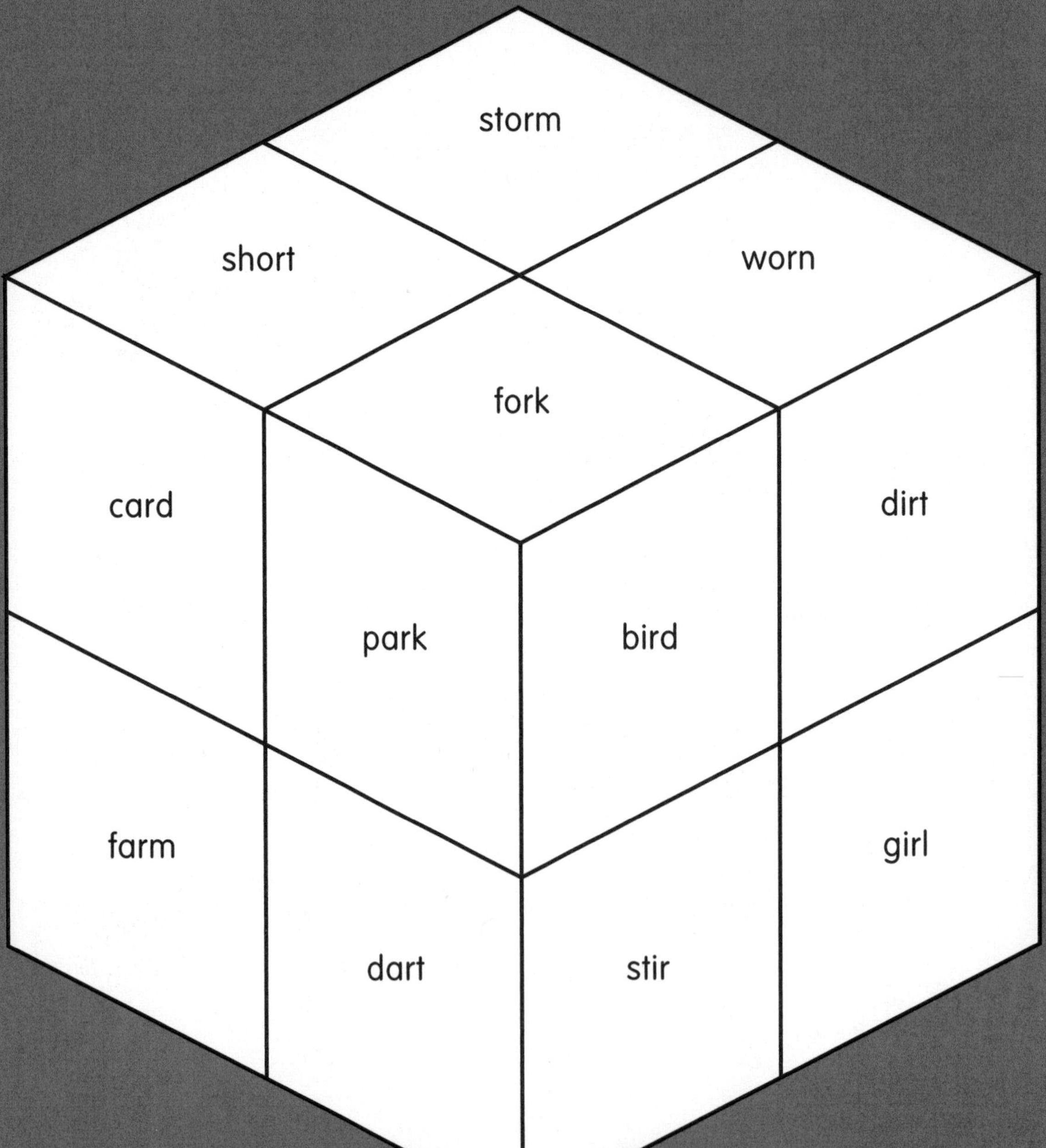
storm
short
worn
fork
card
dirt
park
bird
farm
girl
dart
stir

Label each picture. Use the Word Box.
Match the pictures with words that sound the same.

Word Box							
BLEW	BLUE	CHILI	CHILLY	HAIR	HARE	ROSE	ROWS

____

____

____

____

____

____

____

____

Find and circle each item in the big picture.

Magic Triangles

In these magic triangles, fill in the numbers from the oval next each, so that each side of the triangle adds up to the same sum.

Example

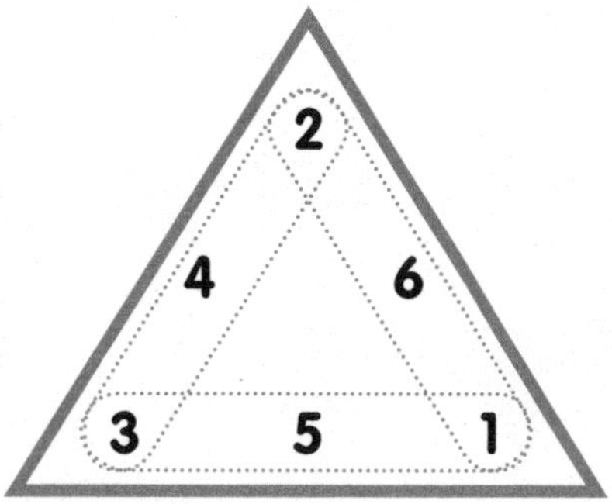
2
4
6
3
5
1

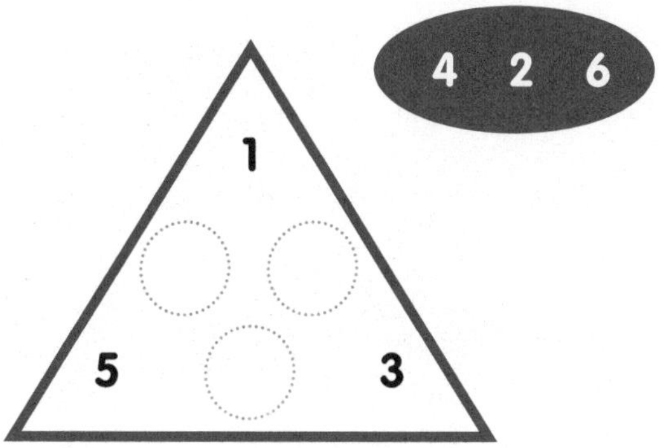
4 2 6
1
5
3

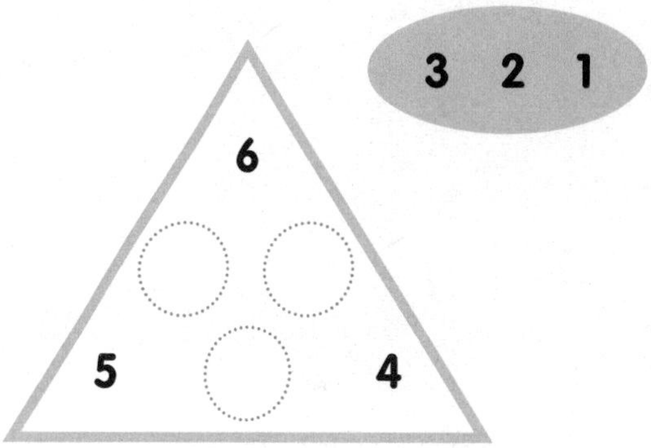
3 2 1
6
5
4

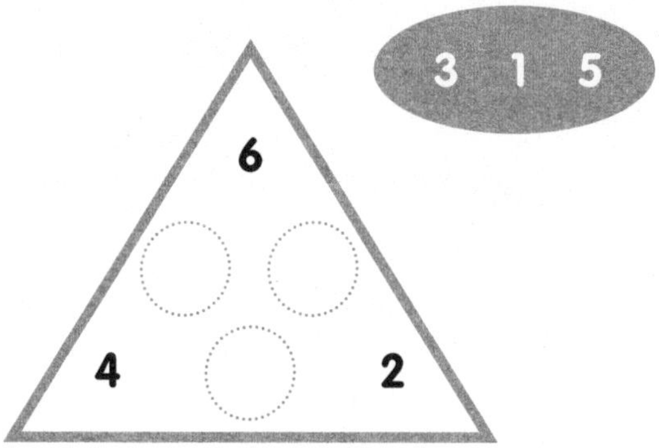
3 1 5
6
4
2

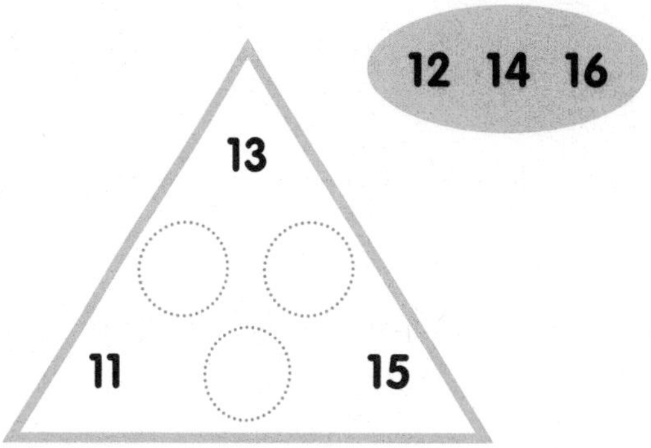
12 14 16
13
11
15

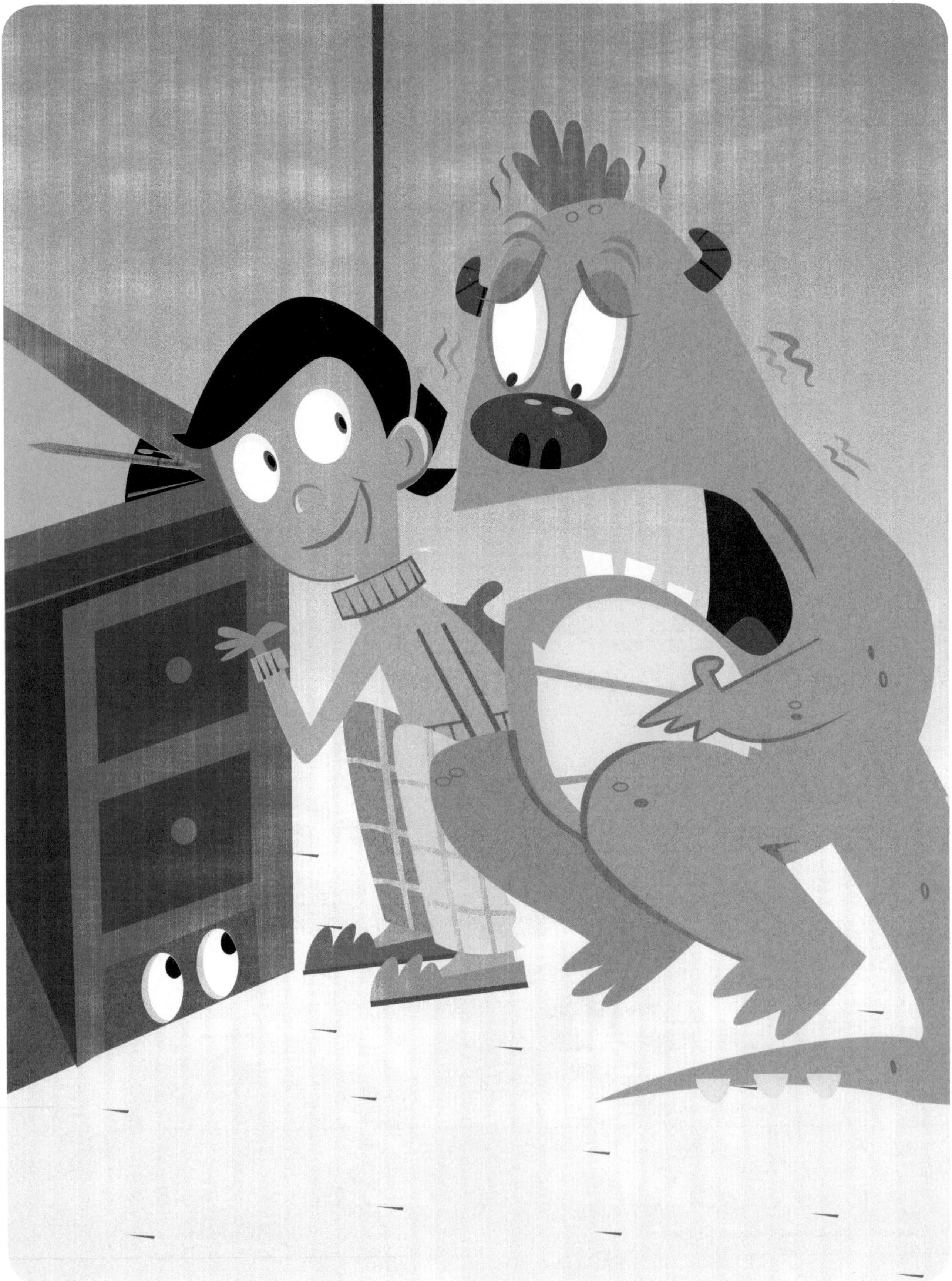

Circle six differences.

© Scholastic Inc.

How many smaller words can you make using the letters in

international?

1 ____________________ 16 ____________________
2 ____________________ 17 ____________________
3 ____________________ 18 ____________________
4 ____________________ 19 ____________________
5 ____________________ 20 ____________________
6 ____________________ 21 ____________________
7 ____________________ 22 ____________________
8 ____________________ 23 ____________________
9 ____________________ 24 ____________________
10 ____________________ 25 ____________________
11 ____________________ 26 ____________________
12 ____________________ 27 ____________________
13 ____________________ 28 ____________________
14 ____________________ 29 ____________________
15 ____________________ 30 ____________________

international (in-ter-NASH-uh-nuhl) adj. – involving two or more countries

Help the mouse find the strawberry basket.

Striped Critters

Read the story. Then solve the crossword.

Skunks are small animals that live in the woods. They have black fur with one or two white stripes down their backs. Bugs are their favorite food. They also eat mice. If a skunk raises its tail, run away! Skunks can spray a very smelly liquid at anyone who bothers them.

Across

2 What color are the stripes on a skunk's fur?

5 What is a skunk's favorite food?

Down

1 What is another thing that skunks like to eat?

2 Where do skunks live?

3 What does a skunk raise when it is getting ready to spray?

4 What should you do if a skunk raises its tail?

1
2
3
4
5

My best friends are . . .

Skip count by 2 to connect the dots. Then color the picture.

2
4
6
8
10
12
14
16
18
20
22
24
26
28
30
32
34
36
38
40
42
44
46
48
50
52

Add. Color the picture. Use the color key below.

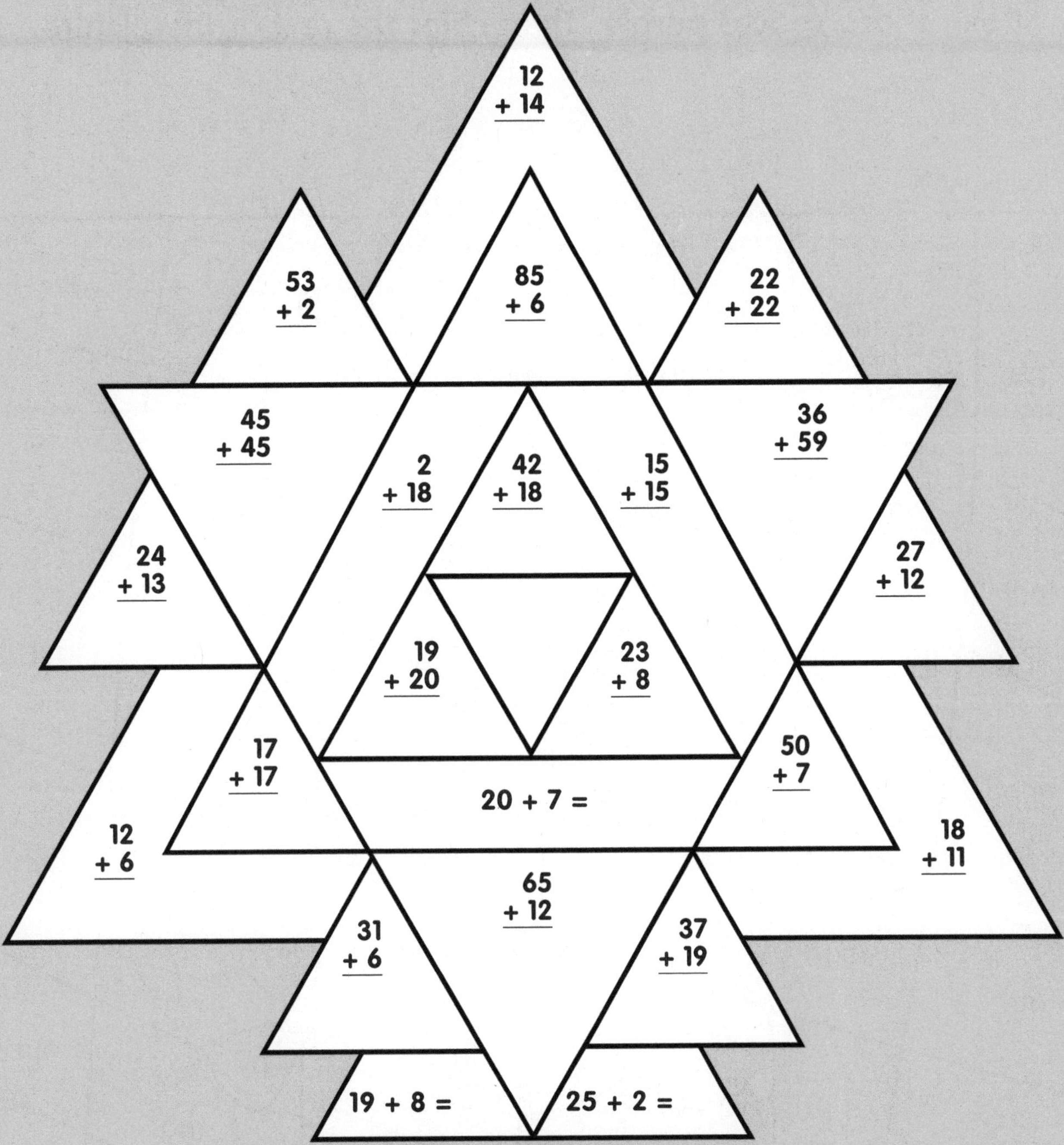
12 + 14
53 + 2
85 + 6
22 + 22
45 + 45
36 + 59
2 + 18
42 + 18
15 + 15
24 + 13
27 + 12
19 + 20
23 + 8
17 + 17
50 + 7
20 + 7 =
12 + 6
18 + 11
65 + 12
31 + 6
37 + 19
19 + 8 =
25 + 2 =

If the sum is between	Color the space
1 and 30	purple
31 and 60	orange
61 and 99	yellow

Fill in the other spaces with colors of your choice.

Find each space with by, going, let, round, and walk. Color those spaces purple. Then color the rest of the picture.

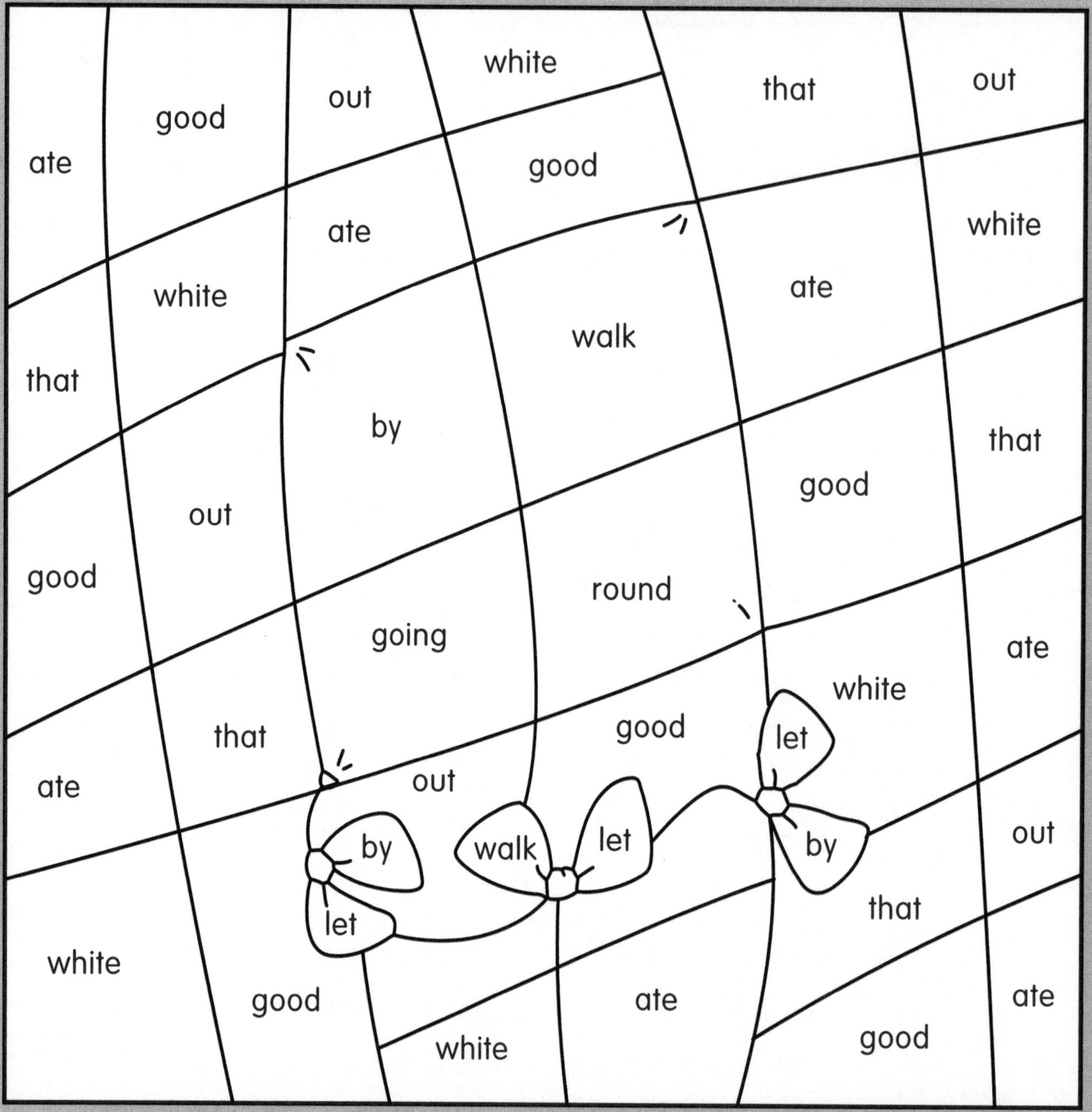
ate
good
out
white
that
out
good
ate
white
white
ate
walk
that
by
that
out
good
good
round
going
ate
white
that
good
let
ate
out
by
walk
let
by
out
let
that
white
good
ate
ate
white
good

Read the riddle. The answer is written in code.
Use the decoder to solve the riddle.

DECODER

A	☺	N	❐
B	🕓	O	💧
C	➦	P	❄
D	☆	Q	◆
E	★	R	📫
F	⌛	S	⍰
G	✿	T	😐
H	✋	U	✈
I	✖	V	❖
J	✓	W	☹
K	◯	X	⚑
L	☸	Y	☼
M	⚐	Z	🖱

Why did the chicken cross the playground?

__ __   __ __ __ __ __ __   __ __   __ __ __

✋ ★   ☹ ☺ ❐ 😐 ★ ☆   😐 💧   ✿ ★ 😐

__ __   __ __ __   __ __ __ __ __   __ __ __ __ __ !

😐 💧   😐 ✋ ★   💧 😐 ✋ ★ 📫   ⍰ ☸ ✖ ☆ ★

What picture is missing?
Find the sticker on page 321. Add it to the pattern.

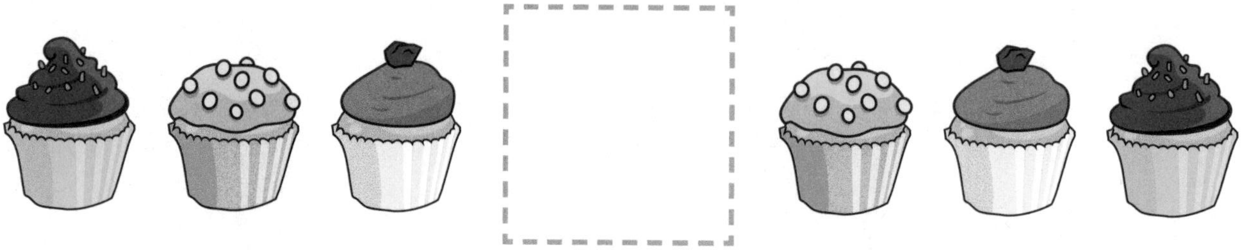

Draw your own pattern below.

Do Your Chores

Solve the crossword.

Across

4 water these every few days
5 make something to eat
7 set this before a meal
10 mow it in the summer
11 do yours after school
12 tidy yours before going out to play
13 make yours in the morning

Down

1 wash these after dinner
2 a chore involving snow
3 clean up the fallen leaves
6 help do this for dirty clothes
8 feed it, take it for a walk, or change its litter box
9 take this out at the end of the day
11 put dirty clothes here

Let's Go Sailing!

Read the clues. Write the words.
Start at the bottom and climb to the top.

___ ___ ___ ___

this is used to go sailing **change the third letter**

a flash of lightning **change the vowel**

___ ___ ___ ___

___ ___ ___ ___

worn around the waist **change the last letter**

ring this when visiting someone **change the vowel**

___ ___ ___ ___

used to play with **change the first letter**

___ ___ ___ ___

synonym of *drop* **change the second vowel**

___ ___ ___ ___

opposite of *succeed* **change the first letter**

___ ___ ___ ___

s a i l

We Love Sports!

Find the words below in the puzzle.
Words are hidden → and ↓.

BASEBALL	BASKETBALL	BOWLING	FOOTBALL
GYMNASTICS	HOCKEY	ROWING	RUNNING
SKATING	SOCCER	SWIMMING	TENNIS

B	A	S	K	E	T	B	A	L	L
O	R	T	B	E	H	A	F	B	S
W	O	N	P	G	O	S	M	R	K
L	W	S	O	C	C	E	R	U	A
I	I	X	B	L	K	B	W	N	T
N	N	J	C	A	E	A	D	N	I
G	G	O	V	P	Y	L	T	I	N
F	O	O	T	B	A	L	L	N	G
Q	S	W	I	M	M	I	N	G	R
G	P	T	E	N	N	I	S	I	N
G	Y	M	N	A	S	T	I	C	S

Subtract. Color the picture. Use the color key below.

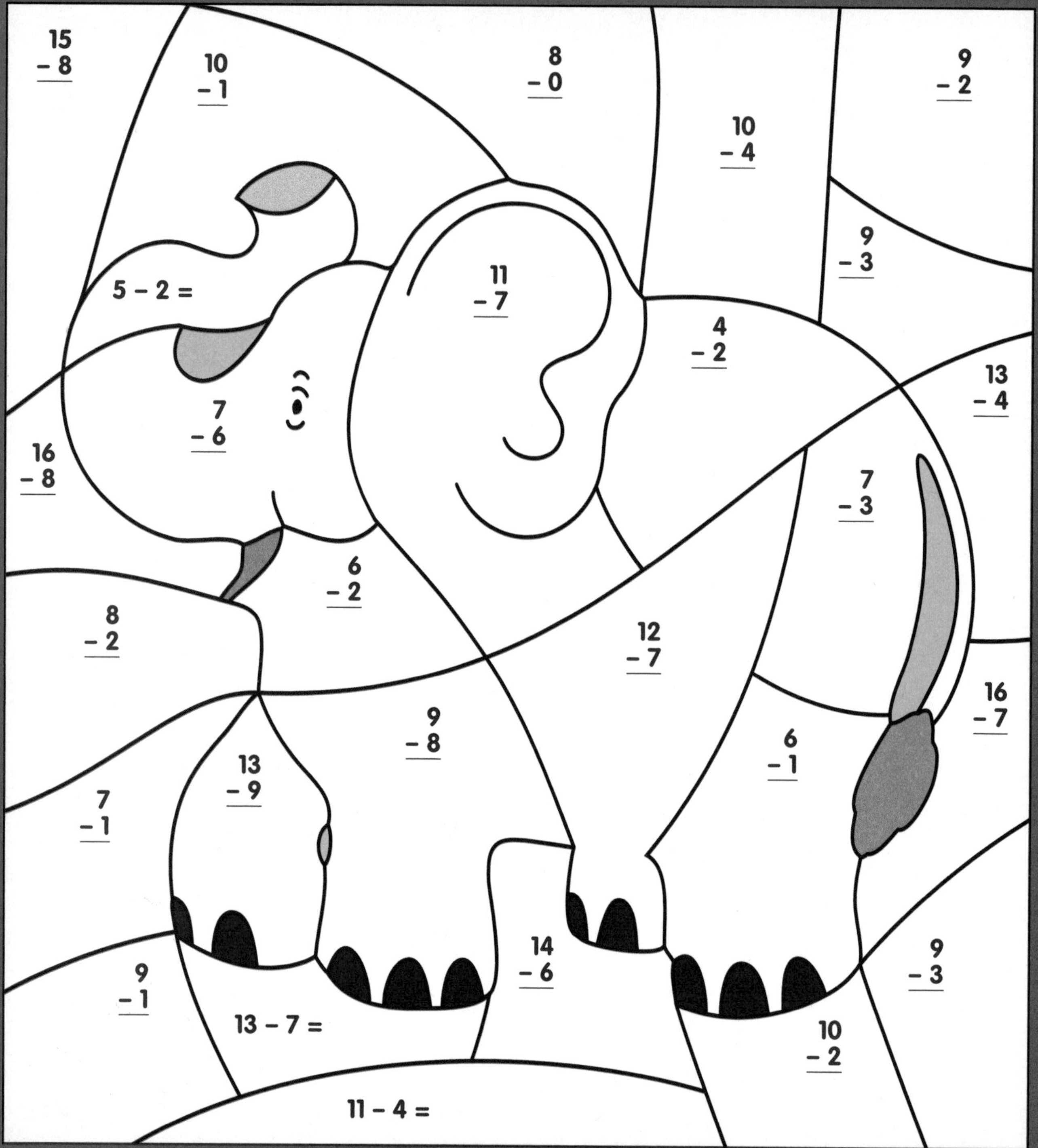

15 – 8
10 – 1
8 – 0
9 – 2
10 – 4
9 – 3
5 – 2 =
11 – 7
4 – 2
13 – 4
7 – 6
16 – 8
7 – 3
6 – 2
8 – 2
12 – 7
16 – 7
9 – 8
13 – 9
6 – 1
7 – 1
14 – 6
9 – 3
9 – 1
13 – 7 =
10 – 2
11 – 4 =

If the difference is between	Color the space
1 and 5	grey
6 and 9	green

Change clay into pan. Use the picture clues and letter tiles. Start at the bottom and climb to the top.

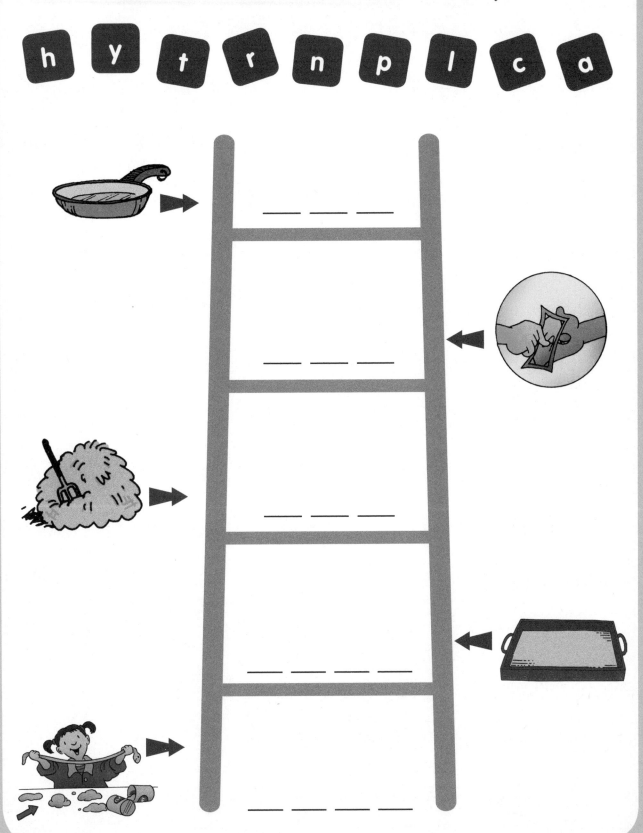

h y t r n p l c a

___ ___ ___

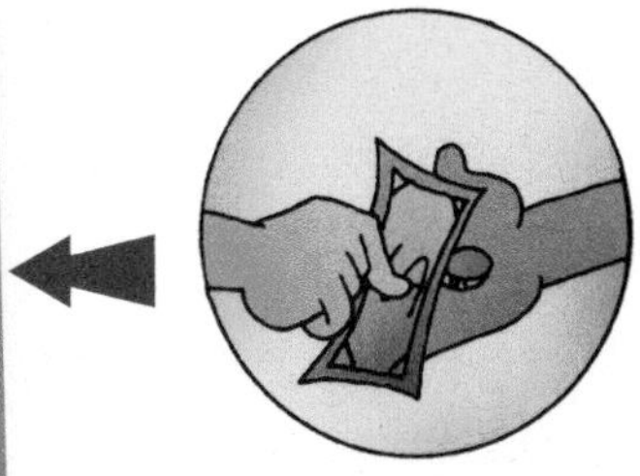

___ ___ ___

___ ___ ___

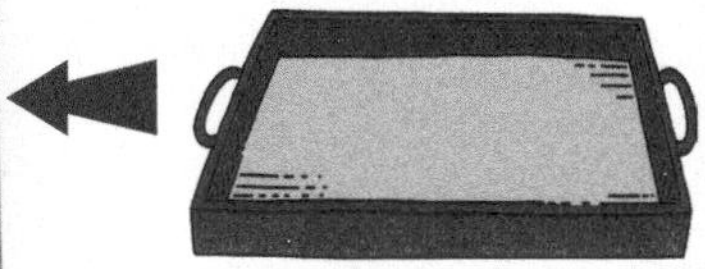

___ ___ ___ ___

___ ___ ___ ___

This is what I look like when I wake up in the morning.

Circle the two totem poles that are the same.

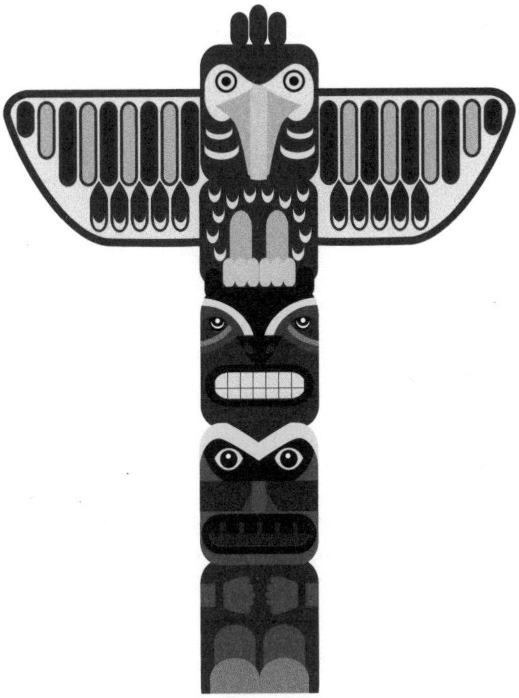

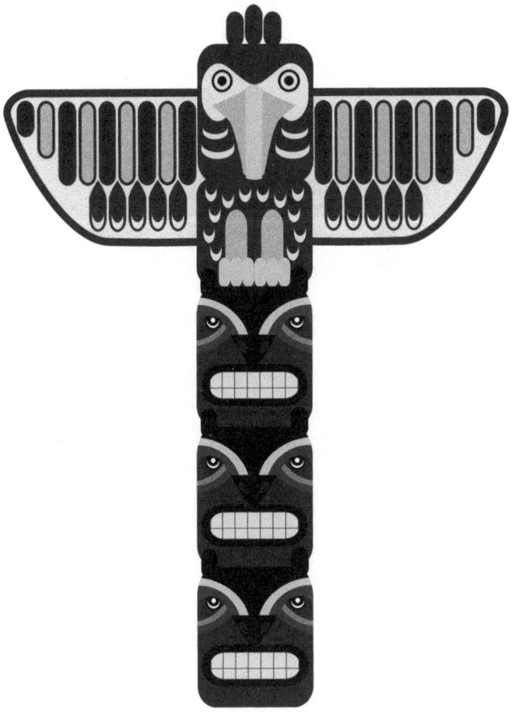

Connect the dots from A to Z. Then color the picture.

A
B
C
D
E
F
G
H
I
J
K
L
M
N
O
P
Q
R
S
T
U
V
W
X
Y
Z

**Color the word path each dog follows to its bone.
Use the color key.**

If the word has the same vowel sound as			
Color the space	blue	red	green

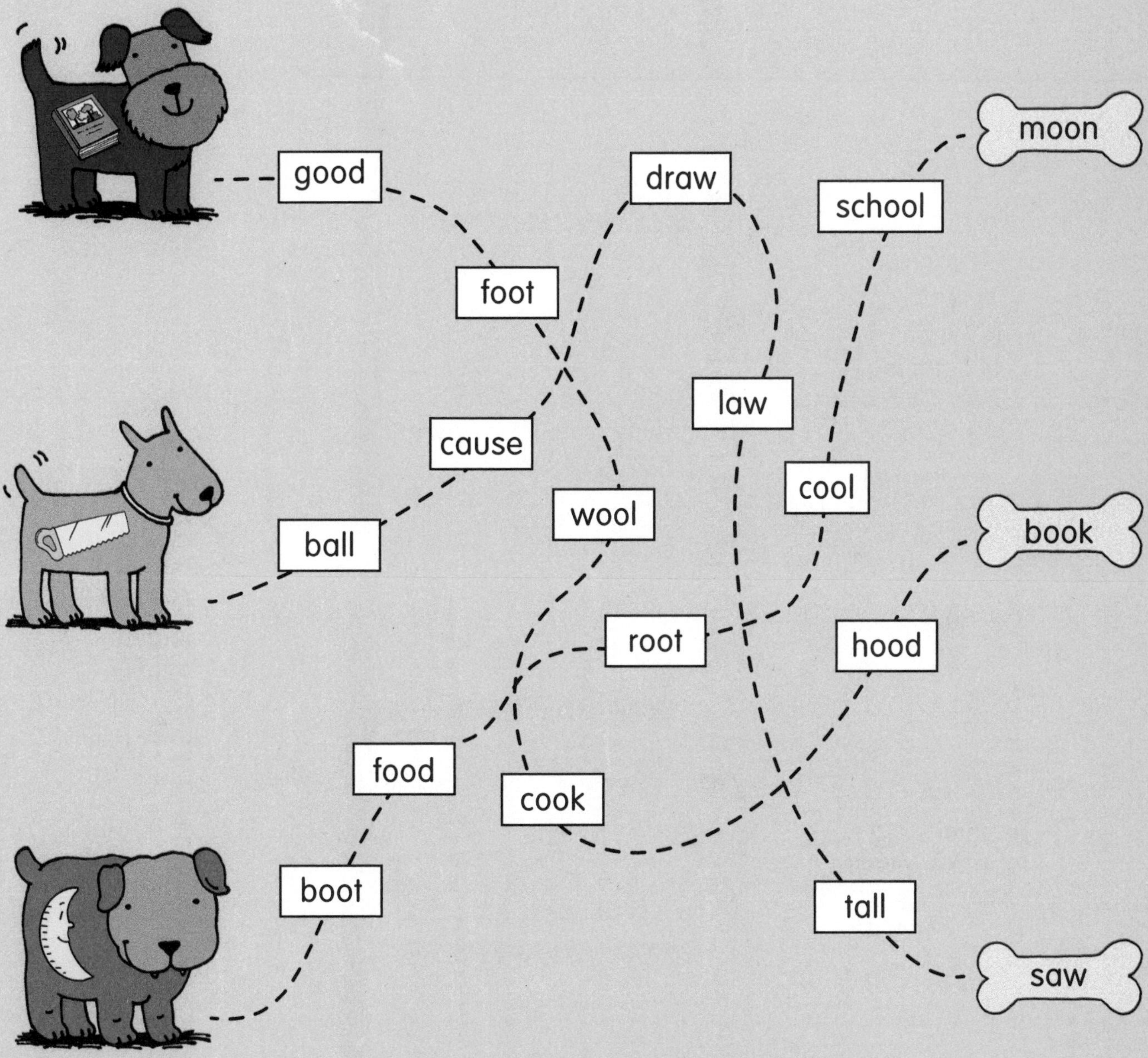

good
draw
school
moon
foot
law
cause
cool
wool
ball
book
root
hood
food
cook
boot
tall
saw

It Only Gets Better!

Read the clues. Write the words.
Start at the bottom and climb to the top.

better than the rest
change the third letter

worn around the waist
change the vowel

a flash of lightning
change the last letter

synonym of *brave*
change the first letter

a metal used to make jewelry
change the second vowel

___ ___ ___ ___
___ ___ ___ ___
___ ___ ___ ___
___ ___ ___ ___
___ ___ ___ ___
g o o d

Help the frog find the fly.

Add. Color the picture. Use the color key below.

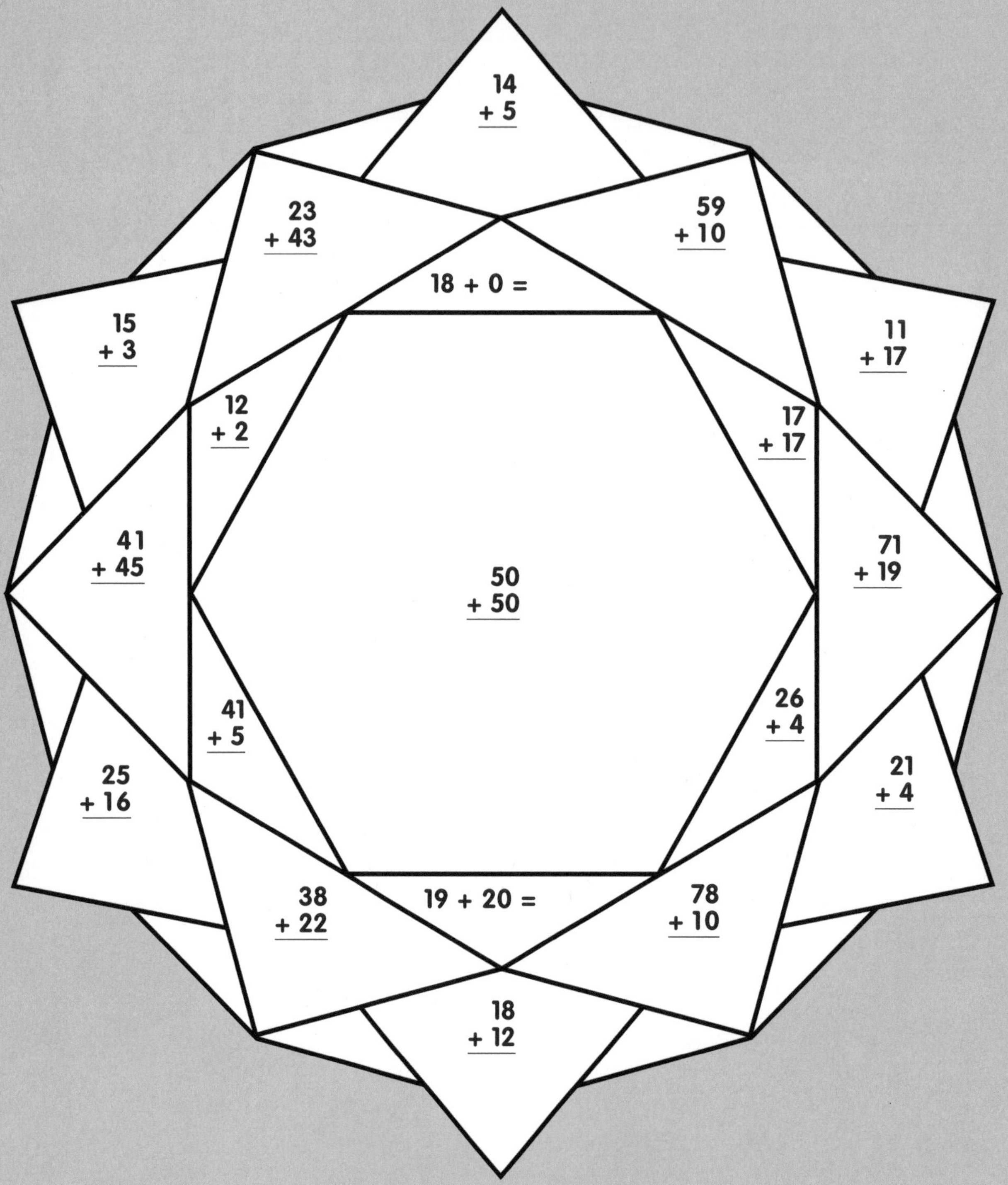
14 + 5
23 + 43
59 + 10
18 + 0 =
15 + 3
11 + 17
12 + 2
17 + 17
41 + 45
50 + 50
71 + 19
41 + 5
26 + 4
25 + 16
21 + 4
38 + 22
19 + 20 =
78 + 10
18 + 12

If the sum is between	Color the space
1 and 50	blue
51 and 100	yellow

Fill in the other spaces with colors of your choice.

Change coat into snow. Use the picture clues and letter tiles. Start at the bottom and climb to the top.

n l c o s w b t a

What picture is missing?
Find the sticker on page 321. Add it to the pattern.

Draw your own pattern below.

Find each word that has the same vowel sound as *shirt* and *purse*. Color that space green.

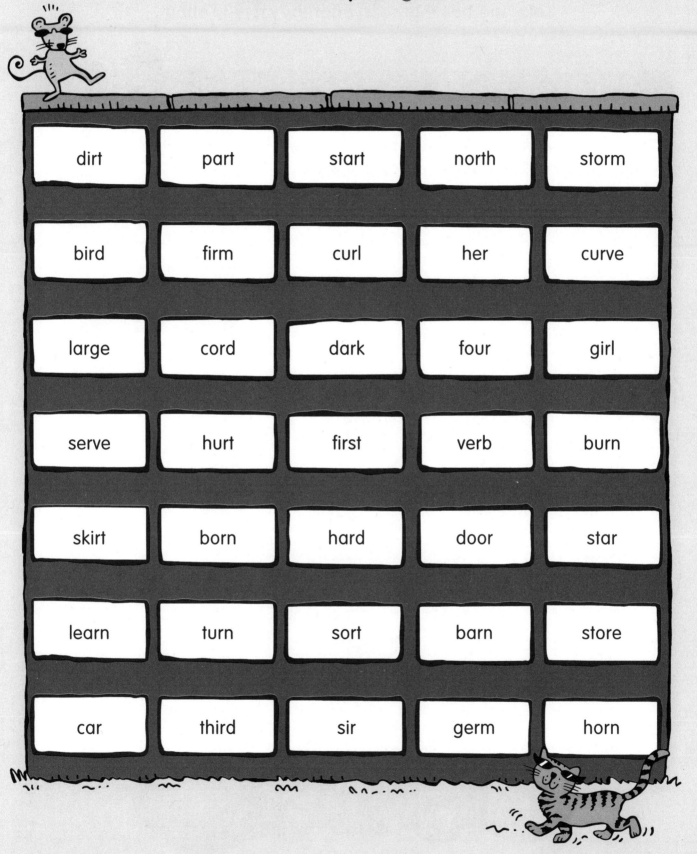

dirt	part	start	north	storm
bird	firm	curl	her	curve
large	cord	dark	four	girl
serve	hurt	first	verb	burn
skirt	born	hard	door	star
learn	turn	sort	barn	store
car	third	sir	germ	horn

Party Clowns

Color the ball that tells what the story is about.

Today I went to Chrissa's birthday party. There were two clowns at the party! Clowns can do funny tricks. The clown named Fancy Pants juggled balls while he was singing a funny song. Happy Hal made balloons into animal shapes. At the end of the party, the clowns squeezed into a very tiny car and rode away. This was one of the best parties ever!

Clowns drive tiny cars.

Balloons can be shaped like animals.

Clowns sing while juggling.

Clowns can do funny tricks.

Fancy Pants sang a song.

Find each space with had, live, of, some, and stop.
Color those spaces red. Then color the rest of the picture.

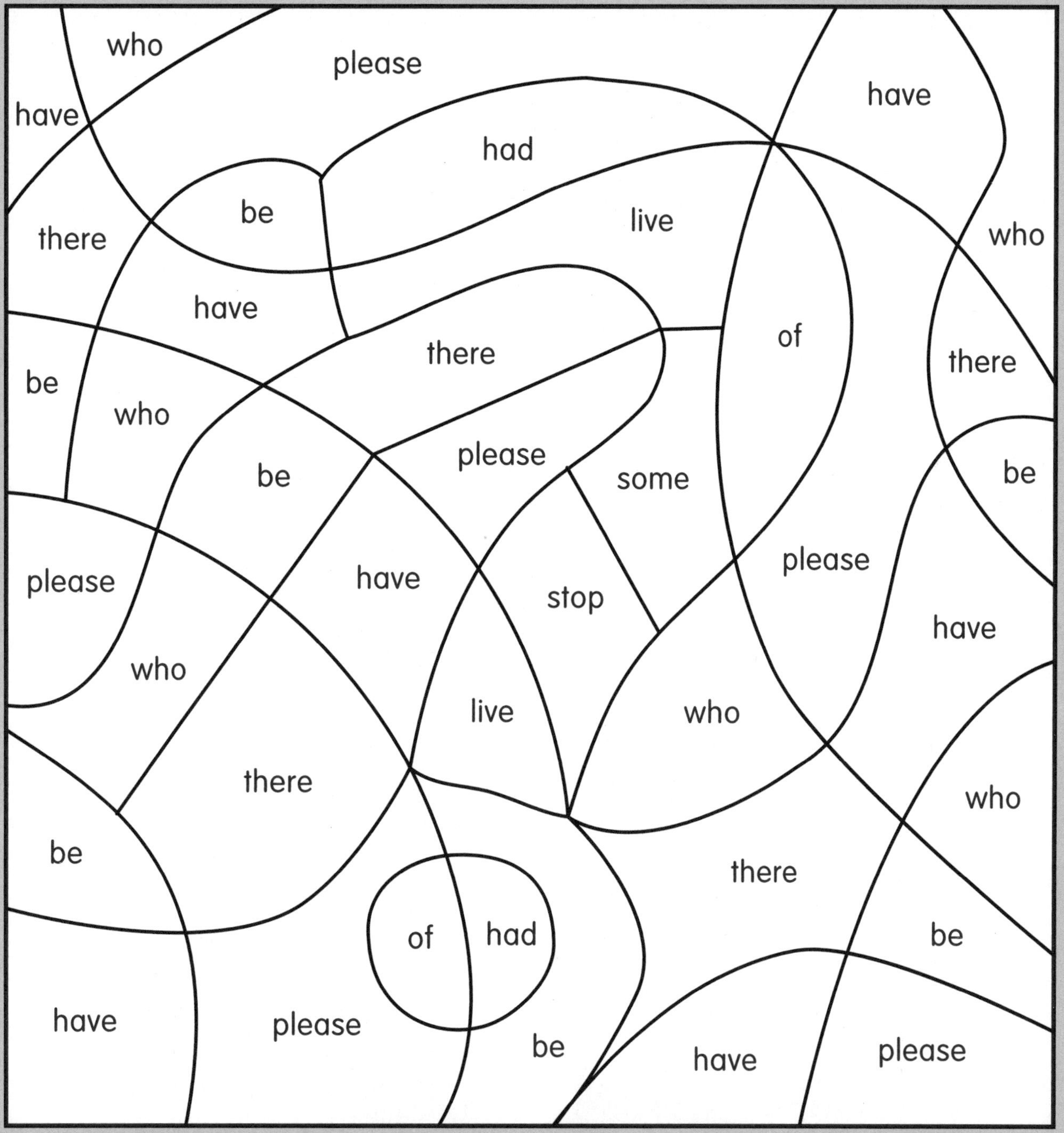
who
please
have
have
had
be
live
there
who
have
of
there
there
be
who
please
be
some
be
please
have
please
stop
have
who
live
who
there
who
be
there
of
had
be
have
please
be
have
please

Connect the dots from 30 to 56. Then color the picture.

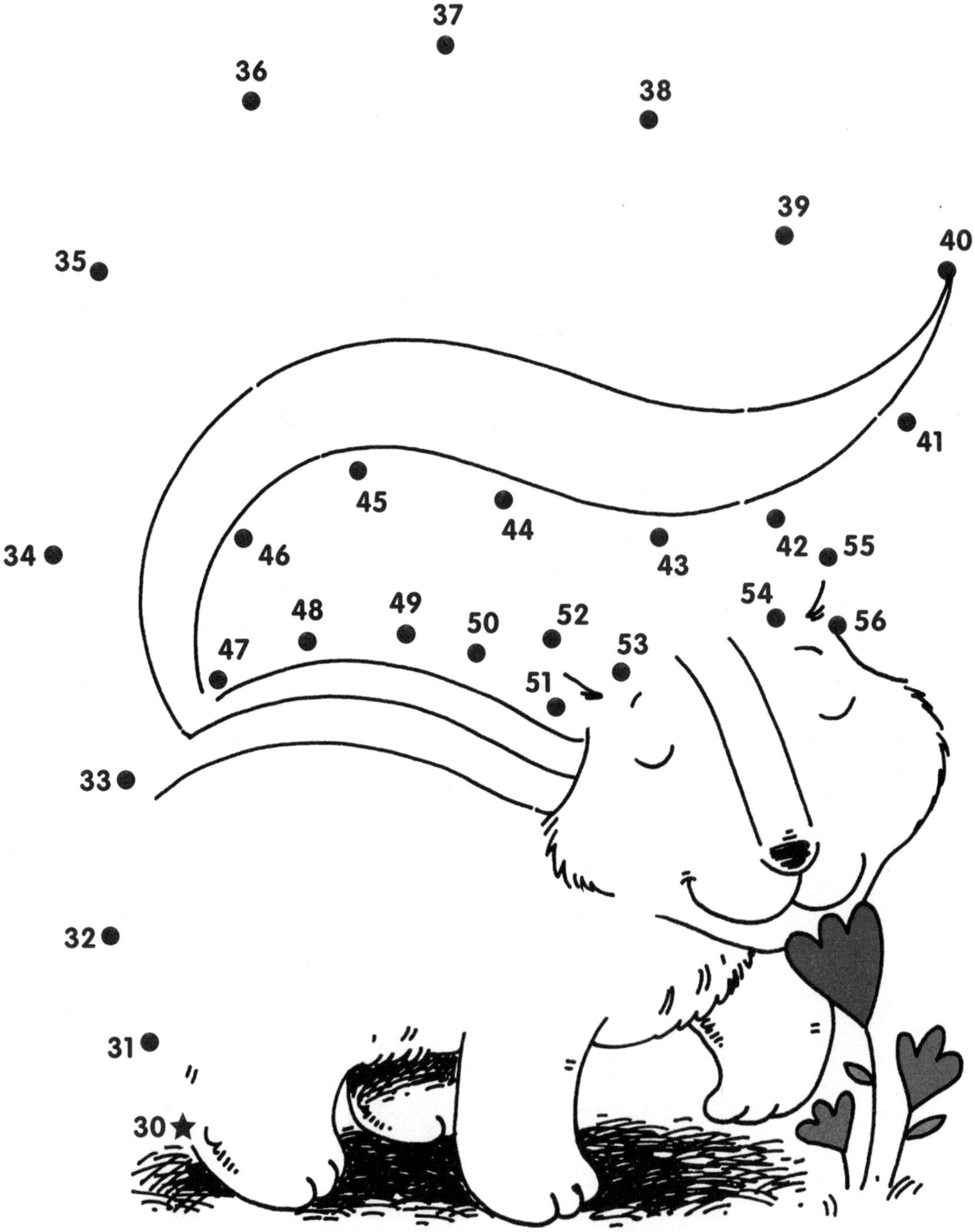

37
36
38
39
40
35
41
45
44
34
46
43
42
55
54
56
48
49
52
50
47
53
51
33
32
31
30

Do You Speak the Language?

Find the words below in the puzzle.
Words are hidden →, ↓, ↘ and ↗.

BIT	BYTE	DATA	DELETE
EMAIL	INTERNET	KEYBOARD	MEMORY
MONITOR	MOUSE	PRINTER	WEBSITE

M	O	N	I	T	O	R	D	L	N	N	B	P
F	T	Y	Q	V	D	I	V	B	I	S	I	L
H	P	E	P	C	M	N	J	M	N	I	I	K
V	R	X	M	R	I	T	Y	O	M	D	K	I
Z	I	K	X	A	U	K	D	U	O	Z	H	N
M	N	Q	O	D	I	X	X	S	Q	Y	D	T
X	T	S	F	M	K	L	M	E	F	J	N	E
B	E	F	R	R	E	B	S	D	S	U	R	R
Y	R	W	B	G	Y	S	G	W	O	P	M	N
R	R	P	A	H	B	A	B	E	C	U	E	E
B	F	D	H	Y	O	G	Y	B	J	Q	M	T
I	X	G	A	P	A	F	T	S	Z	T	O	O
T	M	T	N	Q	R	V	E	I	Y	O	R	G
C	A	G	P	J	D	N	N	T	W	G	Y	H
D	E	L	E	T	E	V	Y	E	P	E	B	W

HIGHLAND PARK
Hank's Hotdogs
Visit
Washington
D.C.

Circle six differences.

HIGHLAND PARK
Hank's Hotdogs
Visit Washington D.C.

Design your dream bedroom.

Brilliant Blends

Solve the crossword. Use the Word Box and picture clues.

Across

2
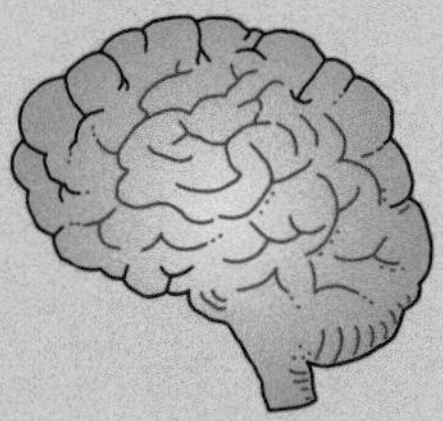

4

6

8
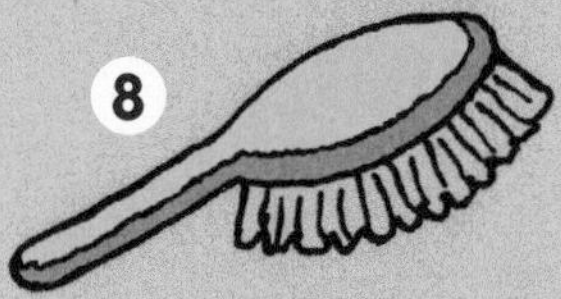

Word Box

BRACELET
BRAIN
BREAD
BRICKS
BRIDE
BRIDGE
BROOM
BRUSH

Down

1
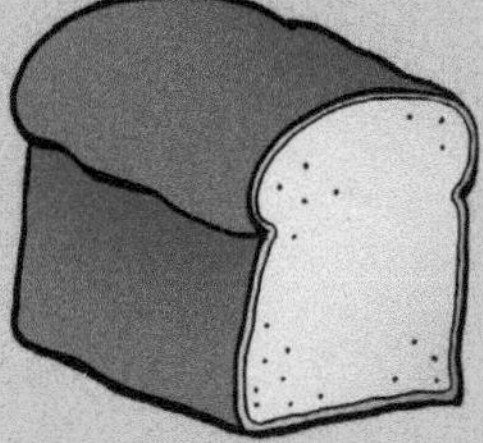

3

7

5

Find the missing number.
Match each answer on the left with one on the right.

1. 1, 4, 7, ________
2. 10, 20, ________ , 40
3. 6, ________ , 18, 24
4. ________ , 10, 15, 20
5. 36, 38, ________ , 42
6. 100, 200, 300, ________

A. 3, 6, 9, ________
B. 200, ________ , 600, 800
C. 2, 6, ________ , 14
D. 2, 3, 4, ________
E. 20, ________ , 60, 80
F. 15, 20, 25, ________

Color the picture. Use the color key.

If the word has the same ending sound as			
Color the space	yellow	orange	green

mouth
lunch
watch
dish
bush
with
cloth
inch
wash
path
fresh
hatch

My Favorites

This page is all about you!
Read the categories and write your own answers.

My Favorite TV Shows

My Favorite Foods

My Favorite Sports

Draw two of your favorite people here and write their names.

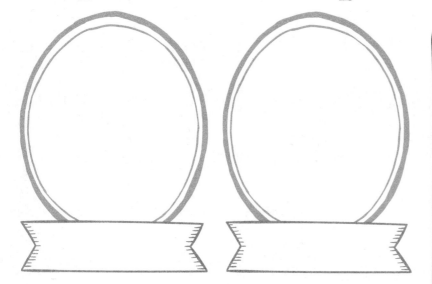

Favorite Color

Favorite Holiday

Favorite Song

Favorite Movie

Favorite School Subject

Favorite Thing to Do After School

Favorite Thing to Do With My Family

Help the alien reach the blue planet.

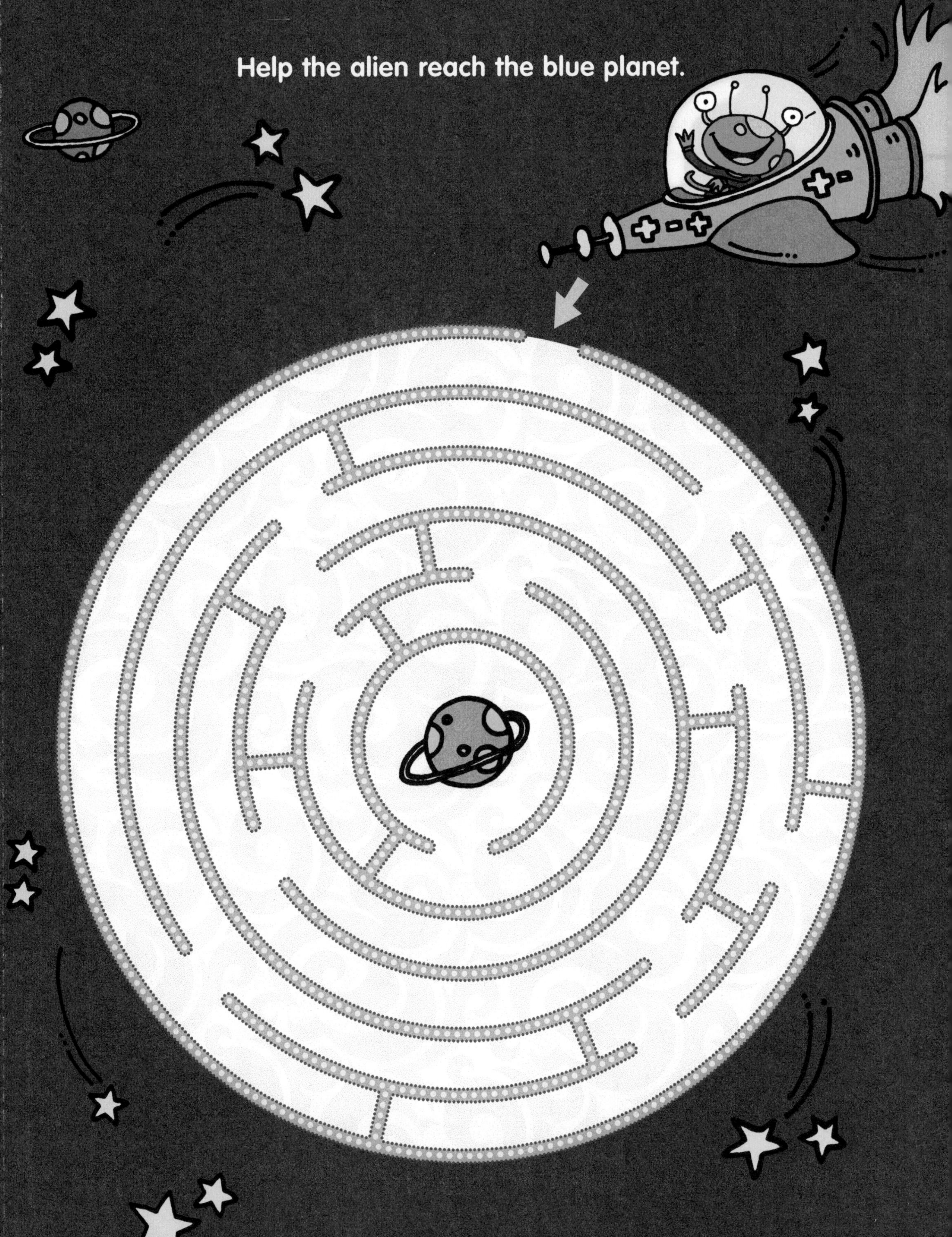

Skip count by 2 to connect the dots. Then color the picture.

52
2
50
4
48
6
8
10
46
12
14
44
16
42
40
18
38
20
36
22
34
24
32
30
28
26

The Midwest Scramble

Unscramble the name of each state.

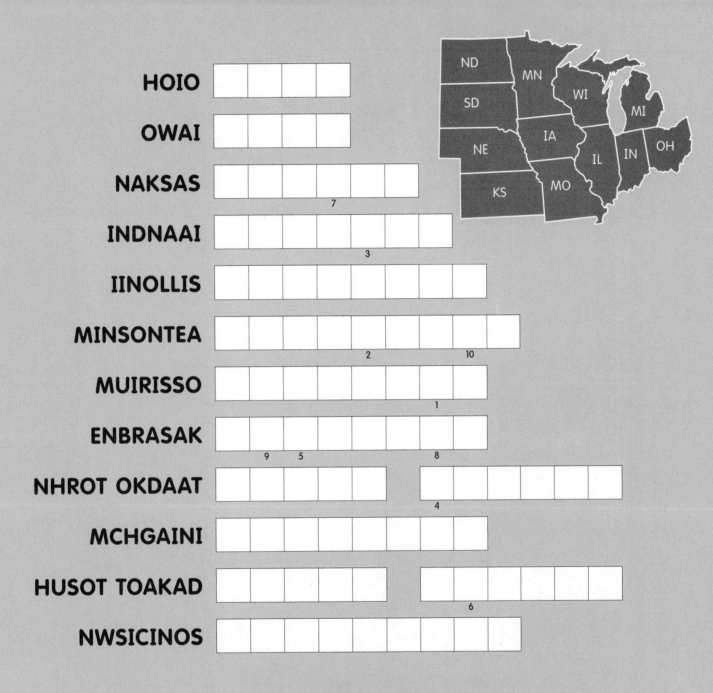

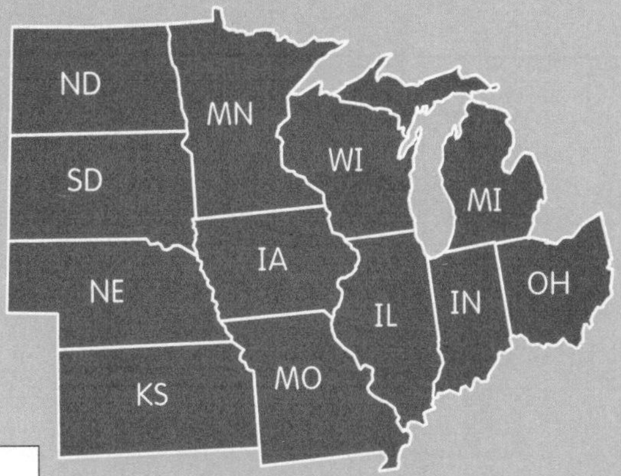

ND
MN
WI
SD
MI
IA
NE
OH
IN
IL
KS
MO

HOIO

OWAI

NAKSAS 7

INDNAAI 3

IINOLLIS

MINSONTEA 2 10

MUIRISSO 1

ENBRASAK 9 5 8

NHROT OKDAAT 4

MCHGAINI

HUSOT TOAKAD 6

NWSICINOS

Copy the letters in the numbered cells to answer the question.

What is the Midwest sometimes called?

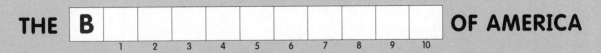

THE B _ _ _ _ _ _ _ _ _ _ **OF AMERICA**

1 2 3 4 5 6 7 8 9 10

Design your family's flag.

Read the riddle. The answer is written in code.
Use the decoder to solve the riddle.

DECODER			
A	8	N	20
B	9	O	26
C	10	P	23
D	14	Q	1
E	2	R	3
F	25	S	18
G	5	T	24
H	6	U	4
I	13	V	21
J	15	W	12
K	17	X	16
L	7	Y	22
M	19	Z	11

Why are bees always humming?

9 2 10 8 4 18 2   24 6 2 22   10 8 20

20 2 21 2 3   3 2 19 2 19 9 2 3

8 7 7   26 25   24 6 2   12 26 3 14 18 !

Summer Scramble

Unscramble each word. To help you get started, the first and last letter and some vowels are filled in.

CBHAE	B	E			H					
FYLREIF	F	I					Y			
FERIRKSWO	F			E		O			S	
CEI CAMER	I		E		C		E		M	
AKLE	L			E						
NICPIC	P				I	C				
SNASDLA	S	A					S			
WMSI	S			M						
WALMOTREEN	W						E			N

How many smaller words can you make using the letters in

Washington?

1 ______

2 ______

3 ______

4 ______

5 ______

6 ______

7 ______

8 ______

9 ______

10 ______

11 ______

12 ______

13 ______

14 ______

15 ______

16 ______

17 ______

18 ______

19 ______

20 ______

21 ______

22 ______

23 ______

24 ______

25 ______

26 ______

27 ______

28 ______

29 ______

30 ______

Washington, George (WASH-ing-ton) n. – the first president of the United States (1789–97)

Let's Have Breakfast

Read the clues. Write the words.
Start at the bottom and climb to the top.

this is used to eat cereal **add a letter to the end**

___ ___ ___ ___

a type of tie **change the first letter**

___ ___ ___

what is done to the lawn **change the last letter**

___ ___ ___

tool for washing floors **change the first letter**

___ ___ ___

synonym of *police officer* **change the vowel**

___ ___ ___

c u p

Find and circle all the animals and insects in the big picture.

How many of each animal did you find?

_____ _____ _____ _____ _____

Find the pattern that is unique.

Friendship

Find the words below in the puzzle.
Words are hidden → and ↓.

CARE	COOPERATE	HELP	KINDNESS
LAUGHTER	LISTEN	MEMORIES	PLAY
RESPECT	SHARE	TOGETHER	TRUST

M	E	M	O	R	I	E	S	A	B
F	K	I	N	D	N	E	S	S	T
L	L	S	O	L	P	L	R	P	O
I	M	H	T	A	C	X	E	M	G
S	Q	A	R	U	A	I	S	P	E
T	J	R	U	G	R	D	P	L	T
E	T	E	S	H	E	M	E	A	H
N	F	O	T	T	J	M	C	Y	E
C	O	O	P	E	R	A	T	E	R
T	L	P	N	R	Z	M	O	J	A
U	N	Z	Y	R	H	E	L	P	L

Label each picture. Use the Word Box.
Match the pictures that use the same word.

Word Box			
CRANE	MOUSE	NAIL	PITCHER

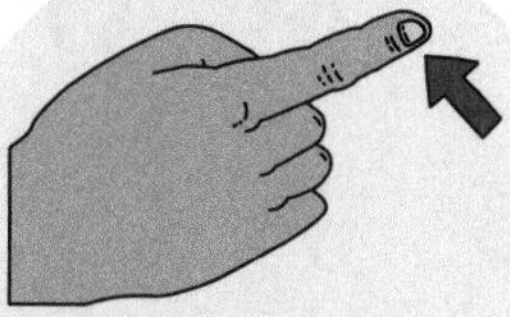

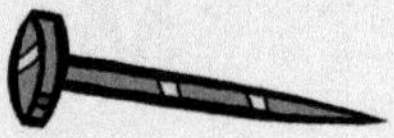

Color the squares to complete the grid. Each row, column, and minigrid should have one square of each color.

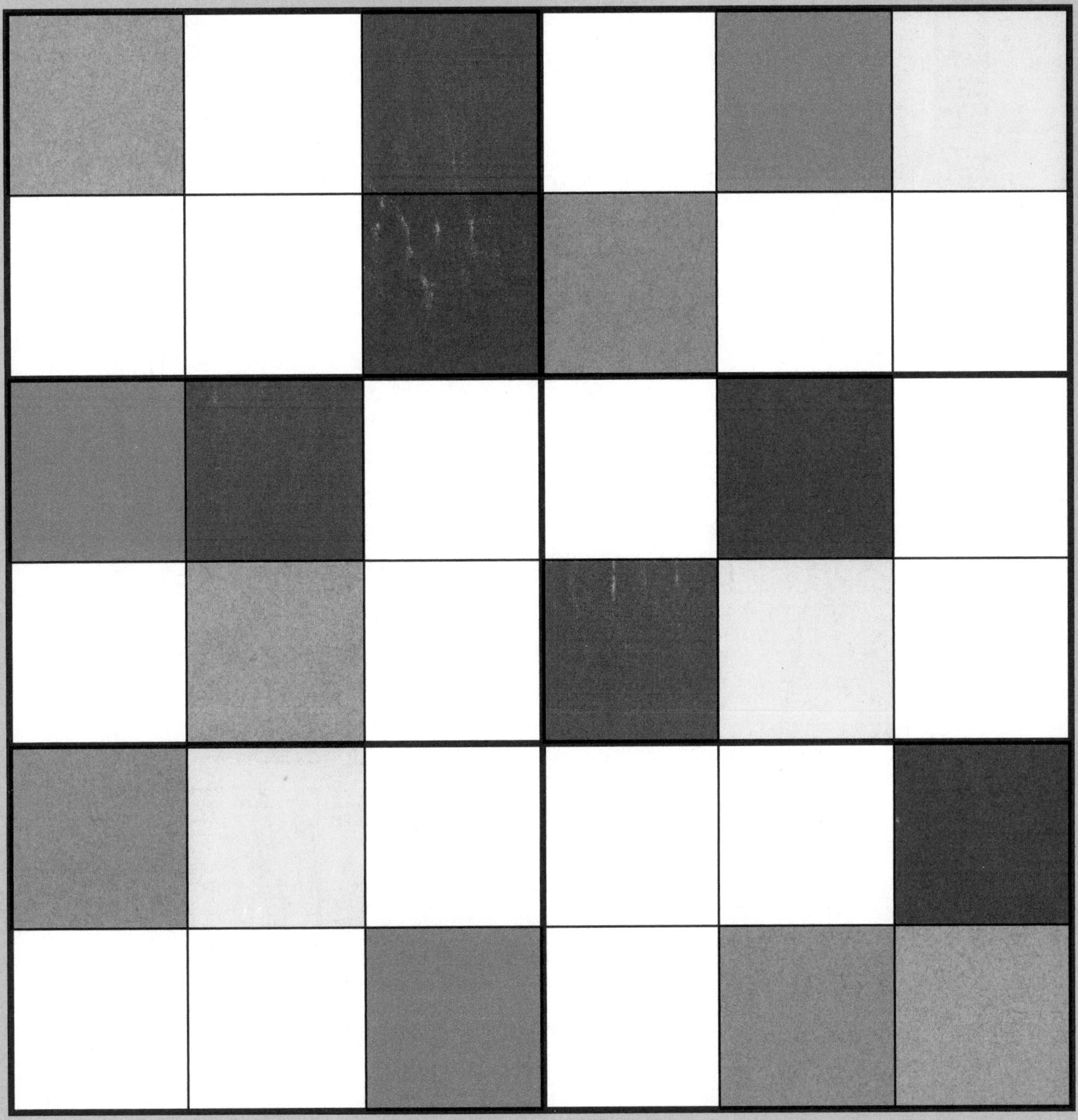

P
ZZZZZ

Circle six differences.

P
ZZZZZZ

Magic Circles

For each puzzle, use the numbers from the box on the right to fill in the magic circles.

The sum of the three circles in each vertical and diagonal line must be 12.

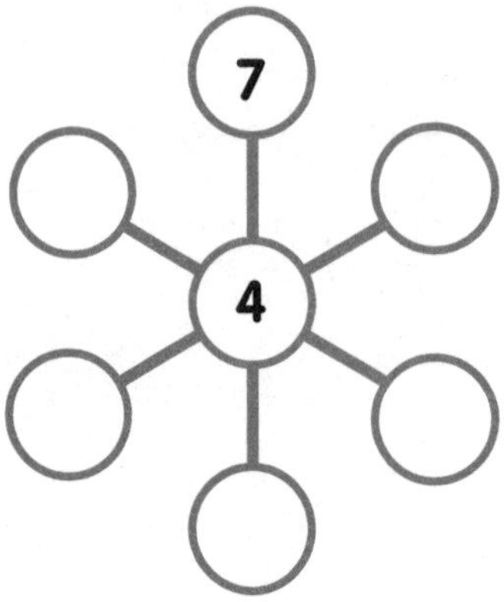
7
4

1 3 5 6 2

The sum of the three circles in each vertical and diagonal line must be 18.

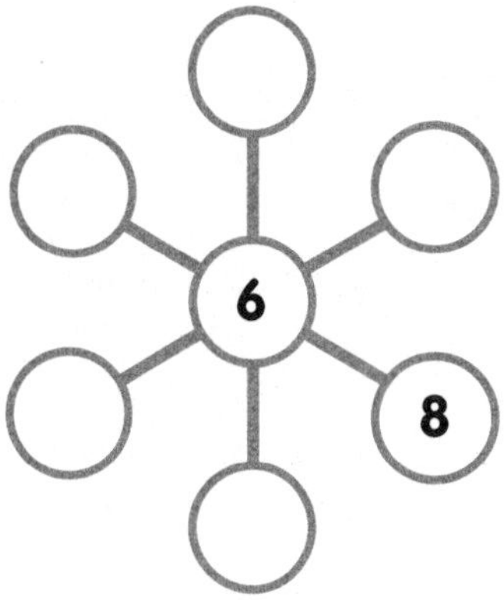
6
8

5 3 4 7 9

The sum of the three circles in each vertical and diagonal line must be 24.

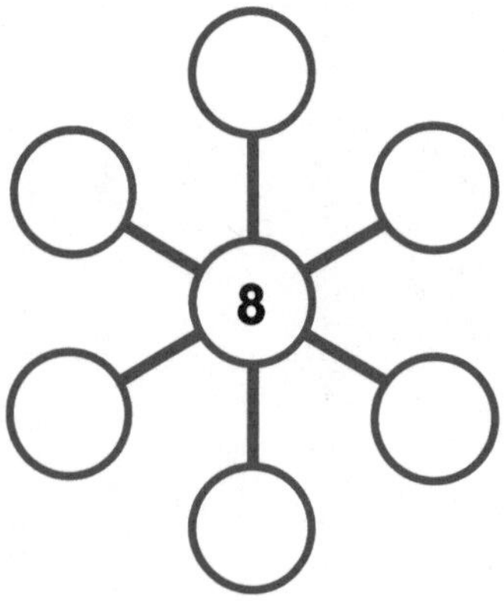
8

12 4 6 14 10 2

Help the bees get to the hive.

Change bell into mail. Use the picture clues and letter tiles. Start at the bottom and climb to the top.

e b l m i t a

Find each space with **every**, **has**, **old**, **once**, and **take**.
Color those spaces brown. Then color the rest of the picture.

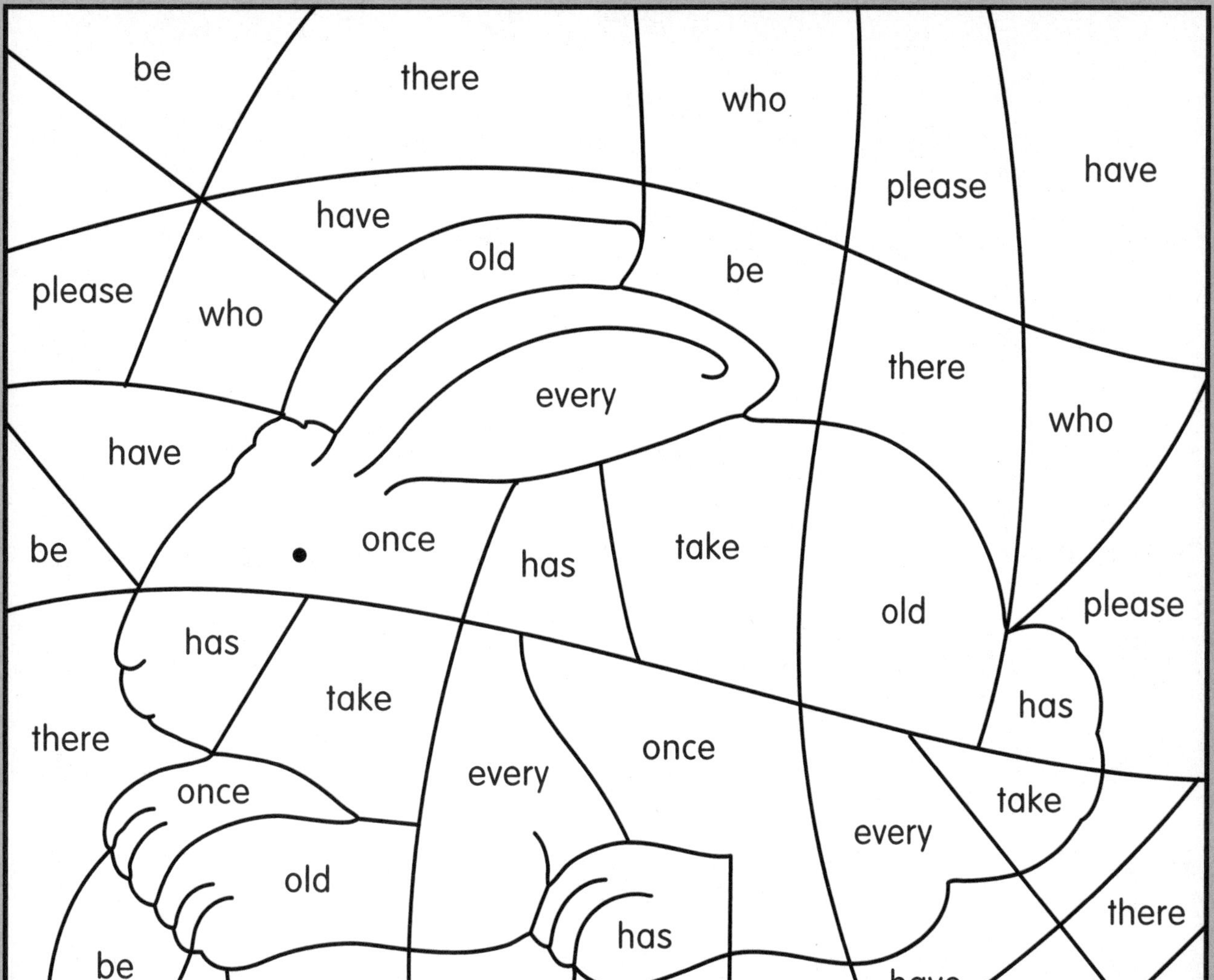
be
there
who
please
have
have
old
please
who
be
there
every
who
have
be
once
has
take
old
please
has
take
has
there
once
every
once
take
every
old
there
has
be
have
be
please
be
who
have
who
please
have
there
who
there
have
there

Think of an idea for a book. Design a cover for it.
Write the title on the cover.

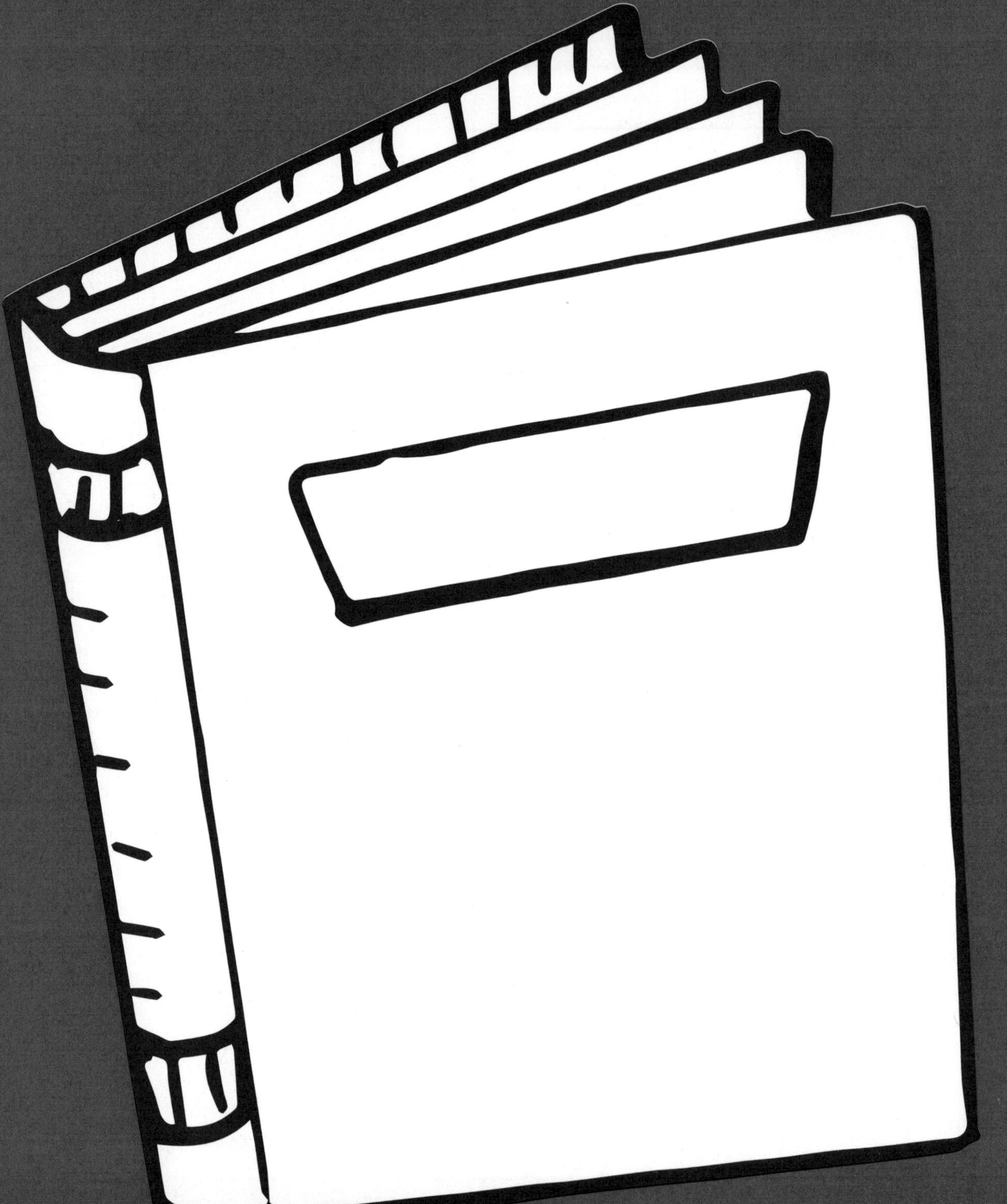

Read the riddle. The answer is written in code.
Use the decoder to solve the riddle.

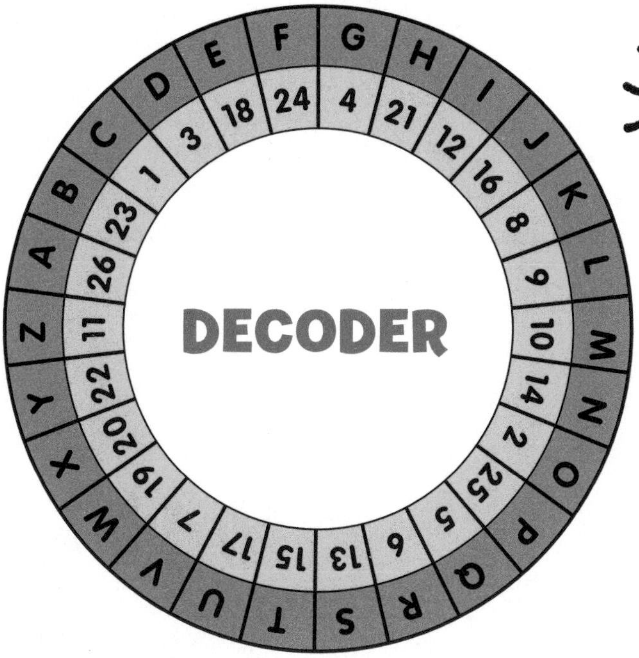
DECODER
A B C D E F G H I J K L M N O P Q R S T U V W X Y Z
26 23 1 3 18 24 4 21 12 16 8 9 10 14 2 25 5 6 13 15 17 7 19 20 22 11

What did the pony say when he had a sore throat?

"___ ___ ___ ___ ___ ___   ___ ___,   ___   ___ ___   ___

18 20 1 17 13 18   10 18   12   26 10   26

___ ___ ___ ___ ___ ___   ___ ___ ___ ___ ___."

9 12 15 15 9 18   21 2 6 13 18

All Kinds of Animals

Solve the crossword. Use the words in the Word Bank.

Word Box

ALLIGATOR	BEAR	DOLPHIN	LION
OCTOPUS	PENGUIN	PIG	SNAKE

Across

2 This mammal hibernates in the winter.

5 This reptile has a long mouth and very sharp teeth.

6 This mammal makes an "oink" sound.

7 This mammal has a mane.

8 This reptile has no arms or legs.

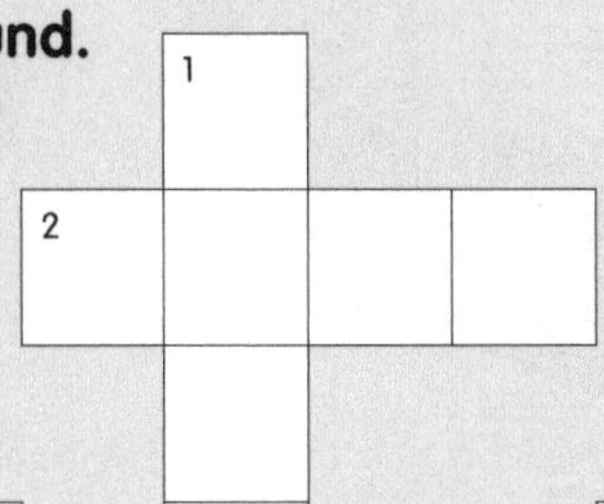

1
2

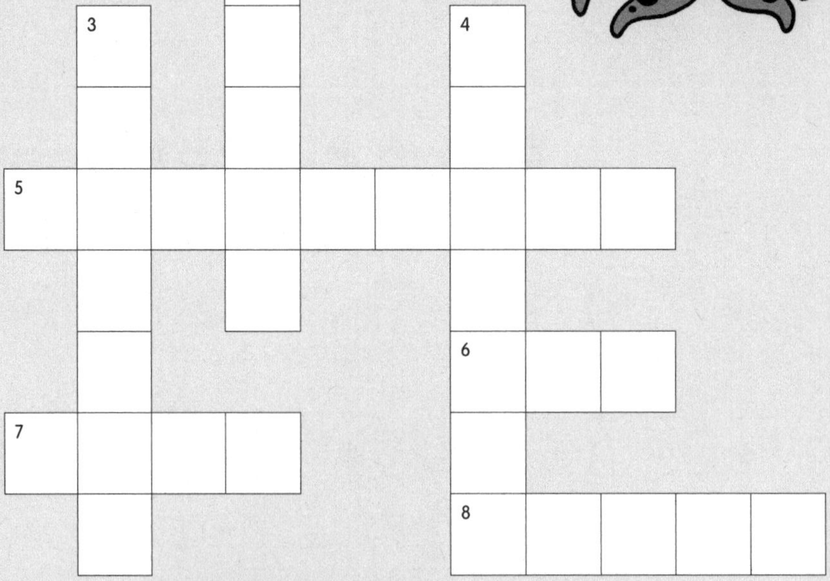

3
4
5
6
7
8

Down

1 This bird uses its wings to swim.

3 This mammal lives like a fish.

4 This sea creature has eight arms.

Skip count by 2 to connect the dots. Then color the picture.

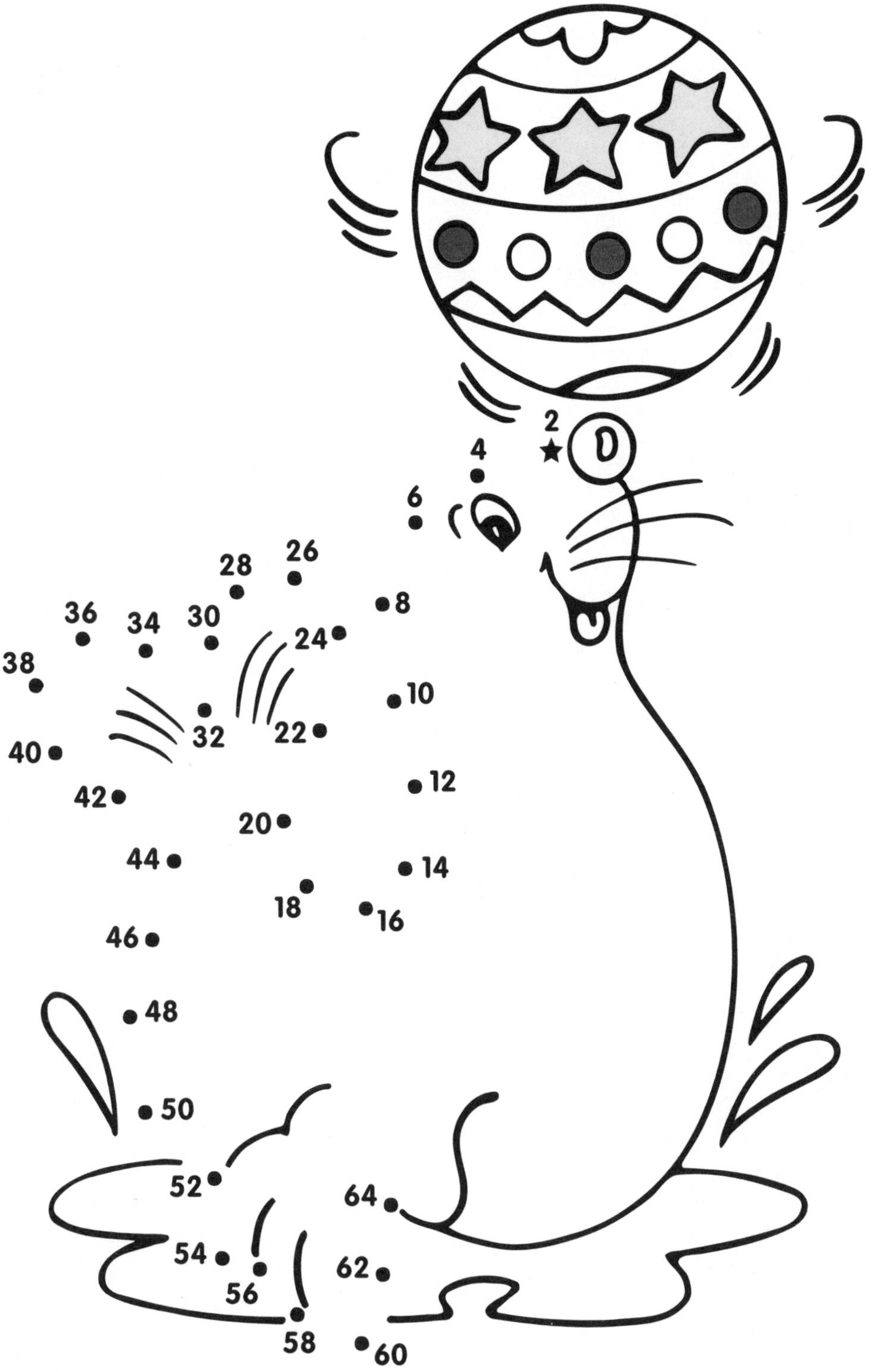
2
4
6
8
10
12
14
16
18
20
22
24
26
28
30
32
34
36
38
40
42
44
46
48
50
52
54
56
58
60
62
64

Circle six differences.

Add. Color the picture. Use the color key below.

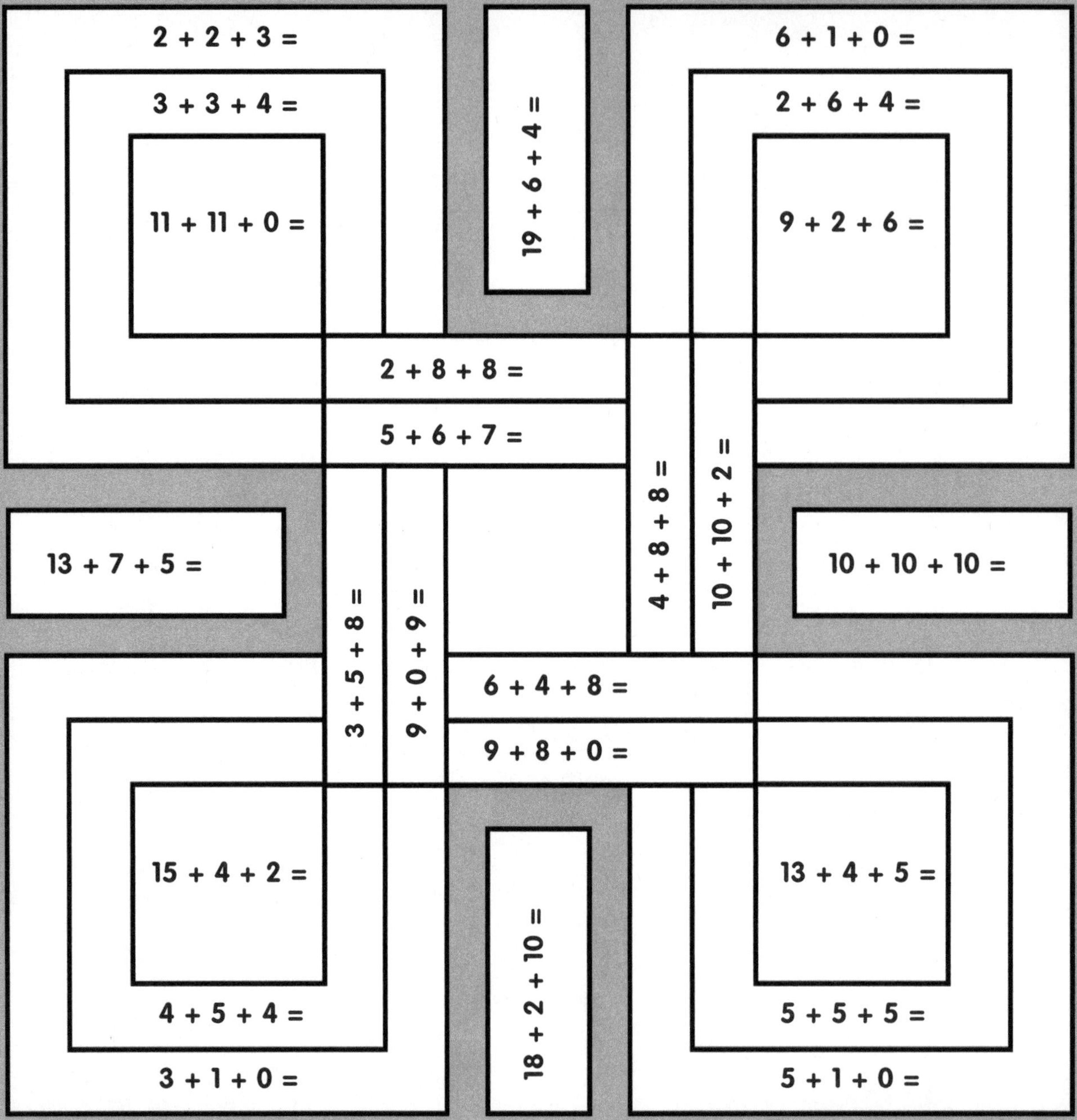
2 + 2 + 3 =
3 + 3 + 4 =
11 + 11 + 0 =
19 + 6 + 4 =
6 + 1 + 0 =
2 + 6 + 4 =
9 + 2 + 6 =
2 + 8 + 8 =
5 + 6 + 7 =
4 + 8 + 8 =
10 + 10 + 2 =
13 + 7 + 5 =
10 + 10 + 10 =
3 + 5 + 8 =
9 + 0 + 9 =
6 + 4 + 8 =
9 + 8 + 0 =
15 + 4 + 2 =
18 + 2 + 10 =
13 + 4 + 5 =
4 + 5 + 4 =
5 + 5 + 5 =
3 + 1 + 0 =
5 + 1 + 0 =

If the sum is between	Color the space
1 and 7	red
8 and 15	gray
16 and 22	blue
23 and 30	purple

Fill in the other spaces with colors of your choice.

My Body

Read the clues. Write the words.
Start at the bottom and climb to the top.

this is what you walk on **change the last letter**

___ ___ ___ ___

this is what you eat **change the third letter**

___ ___ ___ ___

have a liking or love **change the first letter**

___ ___ ___ ___

a link between people **change the vowel**

___ ___ ___ ___

a group that plays music **change the first letter**

___ ___ ___ ___

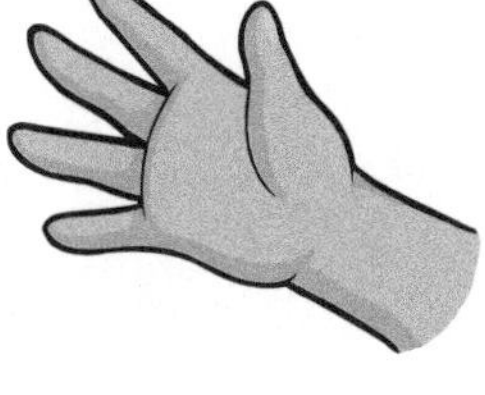

h a n d

What picture is missing?
Find the sticker on page 321. Add it to the pattern.

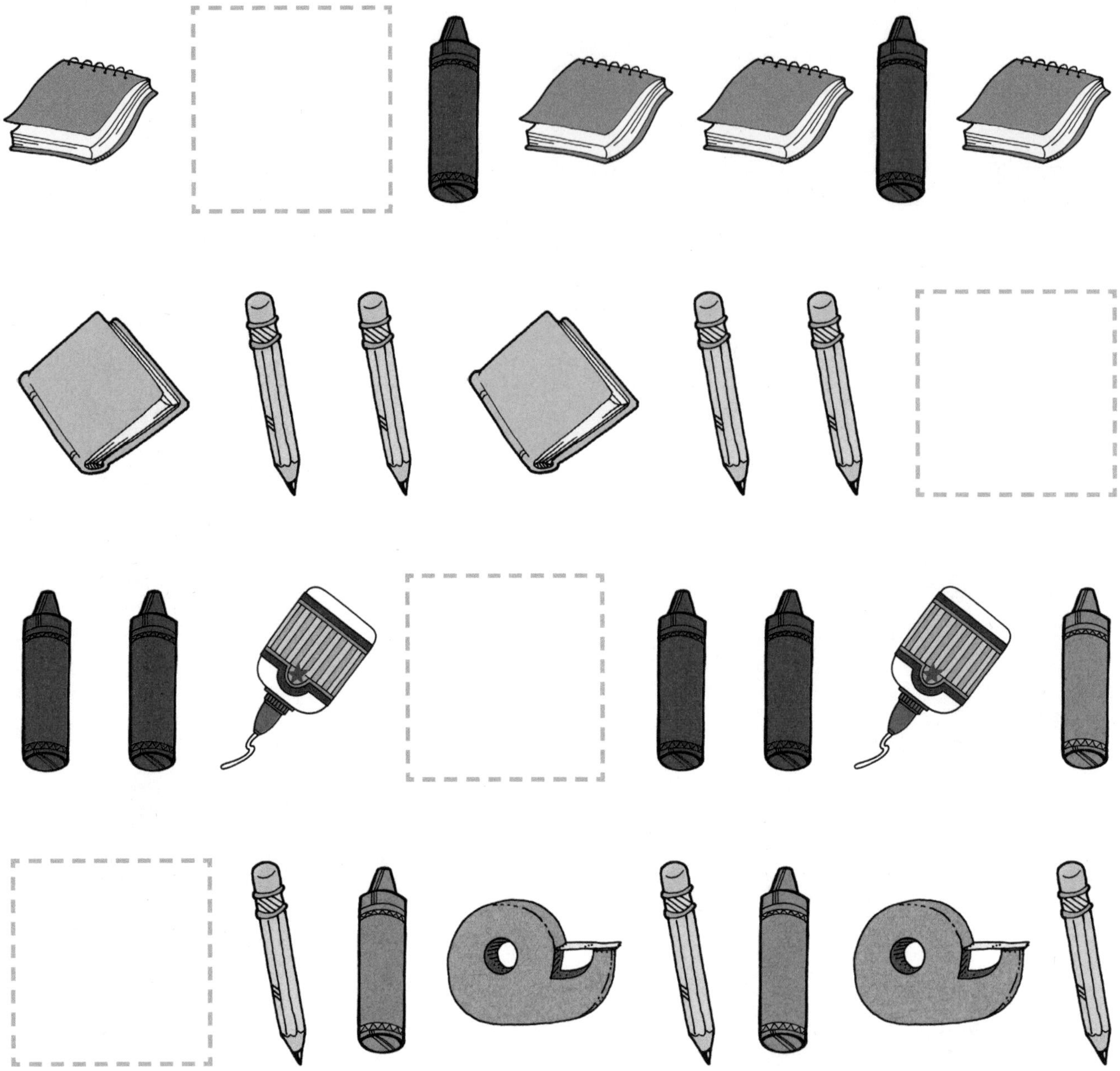

Draw your own pattern below.

Color the picture. Use the color key.

If a letter matches the beginning sound of		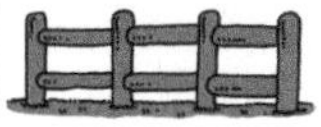	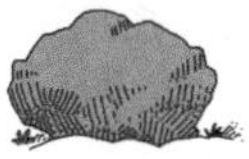
Color the space	yellow	blue	orange

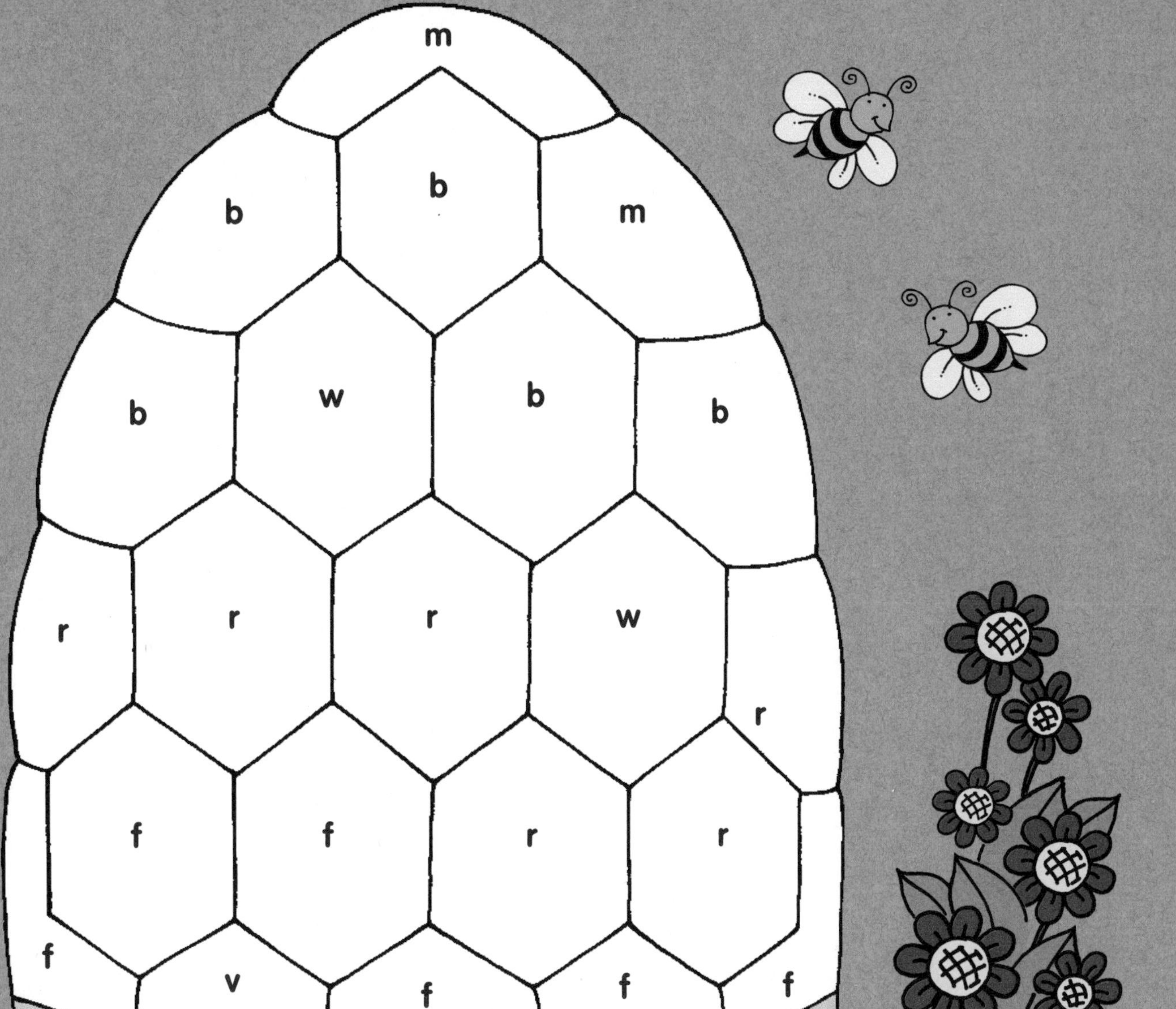
m
b
b
m
b
w
b
b
r
r
r
w
r
f
f
r
r
f
v
f
f
f

Summer Fun!

Find the words below in the puzzle.
Words are hidden →, ↓, ↘ and ↗.

BEACH	CAMP	FIREWORKS	ICE CREAM
LAKE	PICNIC	POOL	SLUMBER PARTY
SWIM	VACATION	WATER PARK	WATERMELON

F	I	R	E	W	O	R	K	S	I	W	V	R
J	T	P	N	L	C	L	R	E	M	W	A	C
C	S	O	J	L	C	D	K	Q	C	A	C	Y
C	X	O	N	P	U	A	J	V	N	T	A	I
C	E	L	P	M	L	T	W	Z	S	E	T	D
A	A	P	V	I	X	K	L	Y	J	R	I	X
V	Z	M	Z	K	C	T	U	V	L	M	O	L
L	E	D	P	Z	M	N	G	C	B	E	N	B
G	G	P	T	S	S	W	I	M	M	L	U	Z
Y	W	C	E	V	R	K	L	C	X	O	T	T
R	I	L	W	U	B	E	A	C	H	N	E	J
U	A	E	W	C	K	G	N	Y	X	P	V	I
W	A	T	E	R	P	A	R	K	W	F	J	C
G	E	E	V	I	C	E	C	R	E	A	M	F
S	L	U	M	B	E	R	P	A	R	T	Y	F

Circle the two patterns that do not have a match.

Help the mouse find the cheese.

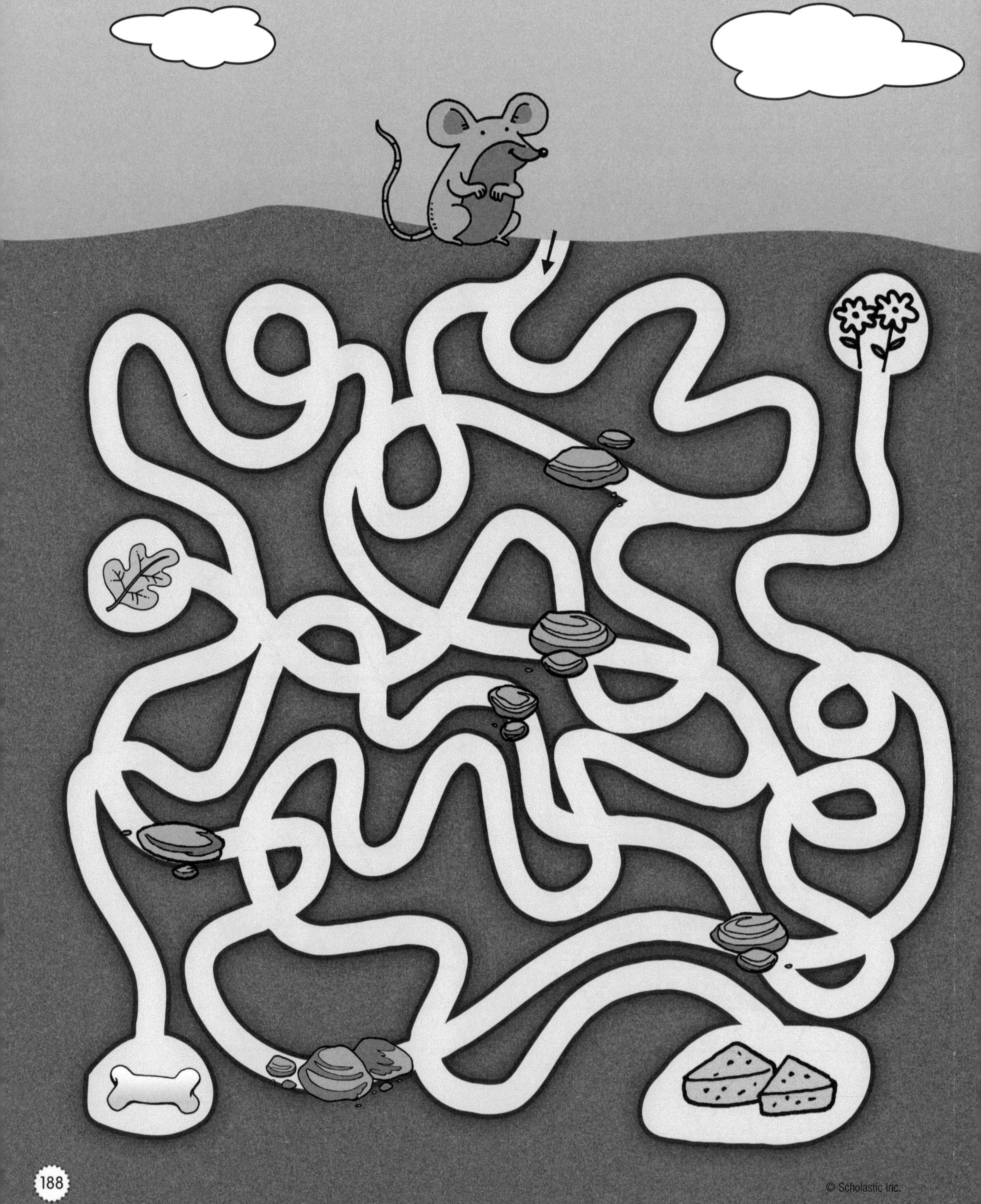

Math Tic-Tac-Toe

Add or subtract. Draw a line through the three problems in a row with the same answer. The row can go →, ↓, ↘ or ↗.

22 + 15	18 + 19	33 + 14
25 + 18	24 + 13	42 + 15
32 + 15	19 + 18	23 + 17

45 − 18	33 − 25	42 − 15
62 − 21	52 − 11	67 − 26
36 − 12	82 − 70	44 − 13

48 − 5	67 − 25	32 − 29
35 − 2	88 − 85	38 − 14
15 − 12	43 − 24	19 − 12

28 + 15	34 + 19	62 + 58
33 + 62	18 + 25	28 + 13
52 + 14	48 + 16	19 + 24

Add. Color the boxes with odd answers orange.
Color the boxes with even answers blue.

22 + 2 = _____	12 + 7 = _____	20 + 8 = _____
5 + 10 = _____	12 + 4 = _____	10 + 13 = _____
17 + 1 = _____	4 + 15 = _____	11 + 11 = _____
22 + 3 = _____	12 + 16 = _____	21 + 4 = _____
16 + 2 = _____	3 + 24 = _____	7 + 11 = _____
14 + 5 = _____	12 + 4 = _____	23 + 6 = _____
6 + 12 = _____	11 + 4 = _____	20 + 8 = _____

Change food into goat. Use the picture clues and letter tiles. Start at the bottom and climb to the top.

f o d t b a g

Circle six differences.

Color the picture. Use the color key.

If the letter makes the sound at the end of	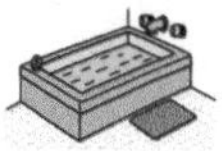			10	
Color the space	green	blue	yellow	orange	red

p
p
m
n
m
n
n
n
n
n
p
d
b
p
d
m
p
n
p

Ouch!

Read the story. Then answer the question below.

Mia and Rosa were playing hospital. Mia was the patient, and Rosa was the doctor. Rosa pretended to take Mia's temperature. "You have a fever," she said. "You will have to lie down." Mia climbed onto the top bunk bed. "You need to sleep," Dr. Rosa said. Mia rolled over too far and fell off the top bunk. "O-o-o-h, my arm!" yelled Mia. Her mother came to look. It was broken!

What do you think happened next?

____

Find out if your answer is correct.
Color each space with a dot to finish the sentence below.

Mia had to go to

Skip count by 5 to connect the dots. Then color the picture.

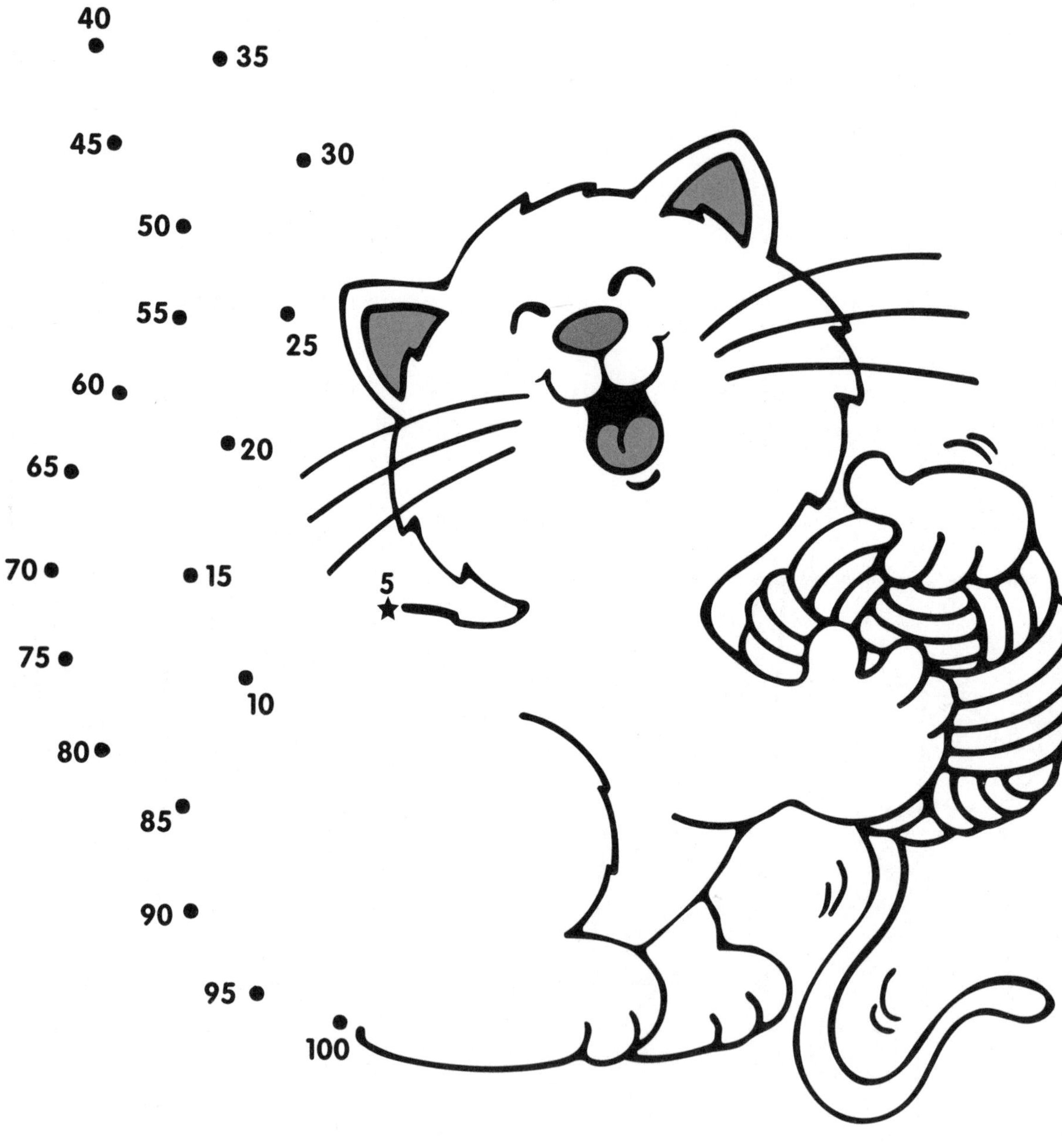

40
35
45
30
50
55
25
60
20
65
70
15
5
75
10
80
85
90
95
100

Subtract. Color the picture. Use the color key below.

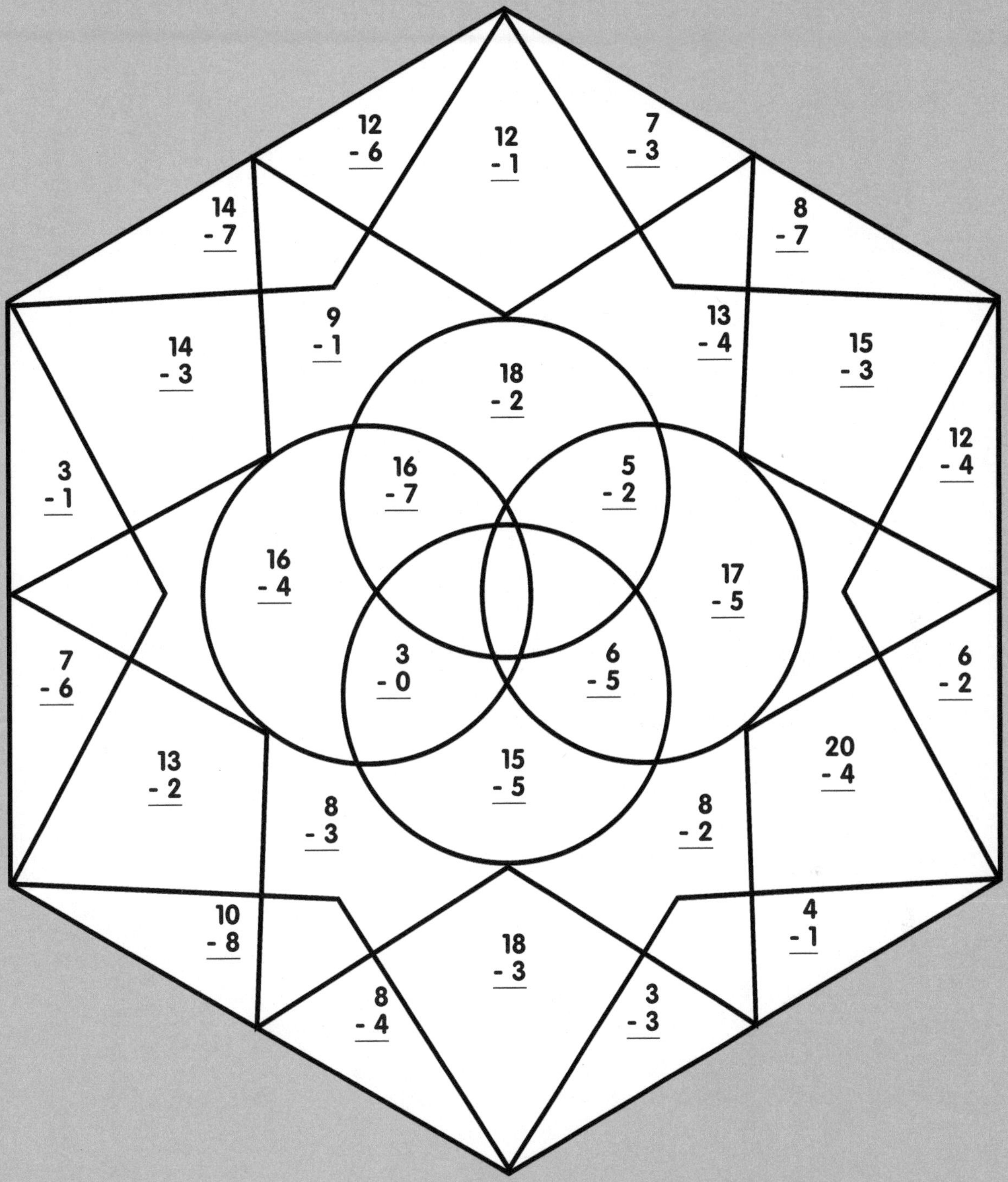
12 - 6
12 - 1
7 - 3
14 - 7
8 - 7
9 - 1
13 - 4
14 - 3
15 - 3
18 - 2
12 - 4
3 - 1
16 - 7
5 - 2
16 - 4
17 - 5
7 - 6
3 - 0
6 - 5
6 - 2
13 - 2
15 - 5
20 - 4
8 - 3
8 - 2
10 - 8
4 - 1
18 - 3
8 - 4
3 - 3

If the difference is between	Color the space
0 and 9	gray
10 and 18	red

Fill in the other spaces with colors of your choice.

Help the girl find her way home.

Read the riddle. The answer is written in code.
Use the decoder to solve the riddle.

DECODER

A	☺	N	❒
B	🕓	O	💧
C	➦	P	❄
D	☆	Q	◆
E	★	R	📫
F	⌛	S	◇?
G	❀	T	😐
H	✋	U	✈
I	✖	V	❖
J	✓	W	☹
K	◑	X	⚑
L	☸	Y	☼
M	⚐	Z	🖱

What happened when the owl lost his voice?

__ __ __ __ __ __ __ , __ __ __ __ __ __ __ __ __
❒ 💧 😐 ✋ ✖ ❒ ❀ 🕓 ★ ➦ ☺ ✈ ◇? ★ ✋ ★

__ __ __ __ __ __ __ __ __ __ __ __ __ __ __ !
☆ ✖ ☆ ❒ 💧 😐 ❀ ✖ ❖ ★ ☺ ✋ 💧 💧 😐

0123 Keep Counting

Read the clues. Write the words.
Start at the bottom and climb to the top.

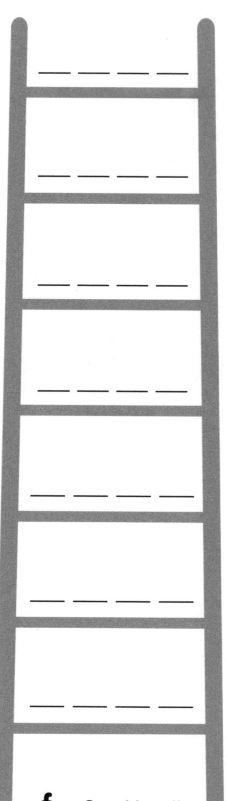

___ ___ ___ ___

one more than four
change the third letter

___ ___ ___ ___

synonym of *okay*
change the last letter

___ ___ ___ ___

present tense of *found*
change the vowel

___ ___ ___ ___

have a liking or love
change the second vowel

___ ___ ___ ___

what you eat
change the last letter

___ ___ ___ ___

to trick
change the second vowel

___ ___ ___ ___

reason for a penalty in soccer
change the last letter

4

f o u r

Find and circle 6 animals that live in the park.
Cross out 7 pieces of litter.

Awesome Short-a Words

Solve the crossword. Use the words in the Word Box.

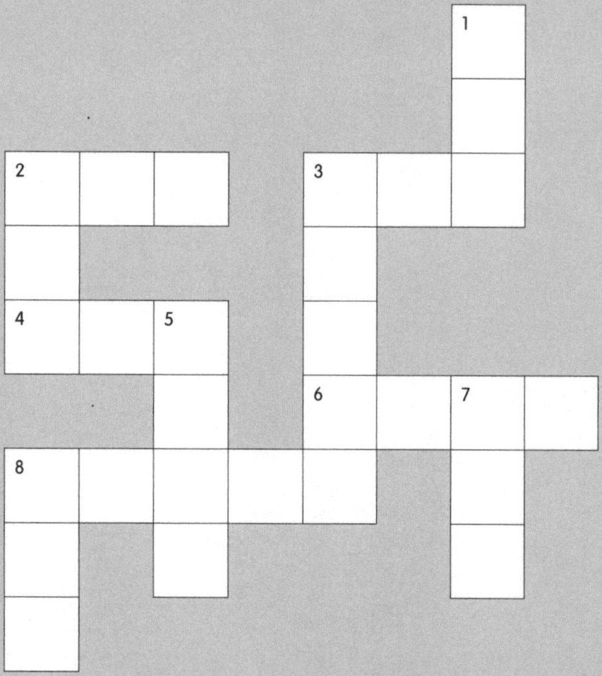
1
2
3
4
5
6
7
8

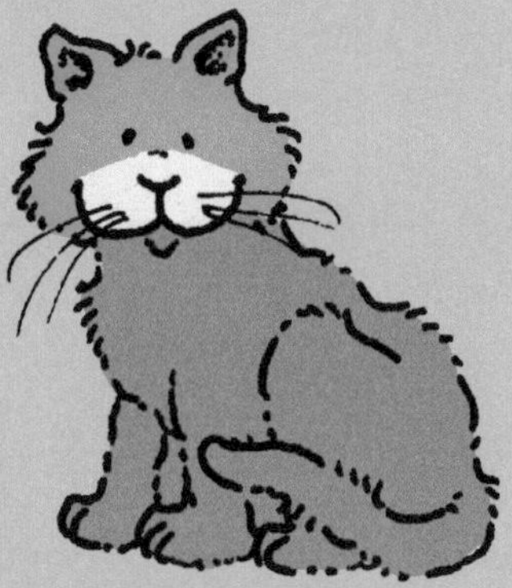

Across

2. a grown kitten
3. used in baseball
4. another name for sack
6. a baby cow
8. something to eat

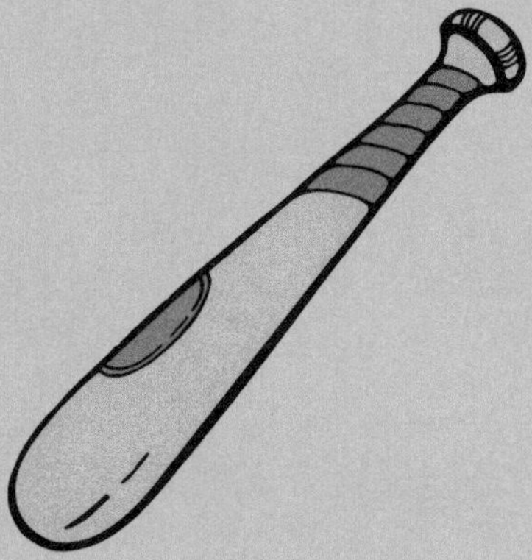

Word Box

BAG
BAT
BLACK
CAB
CALF
CAT
GLAD
HAT
LAD
SAD
SNACK

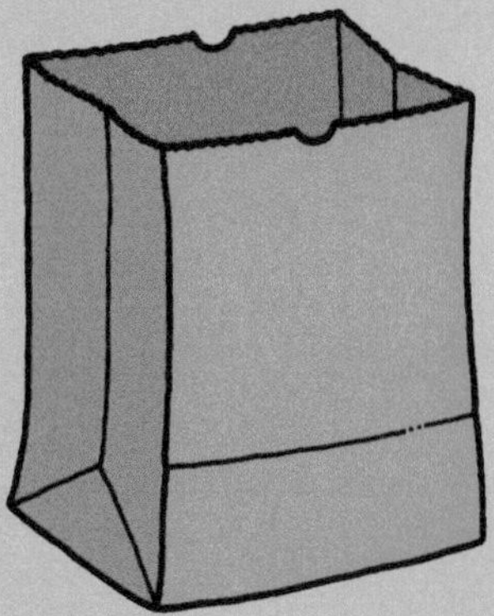

Down

1. something worn on your head
2. a taxi
3. opposite of white
5. opposite of sad
7. a boy
8. opposite of happy

Draw a sailboat. Give it a name.

How many smaller words can you make using the letters in

happiness?

1 _______________
2 _______________
3 _______________
4 _______________
5 _______________
6 _______________
7 _______________
8 _______________
9 _______________
10 _______________
11 _______________
12 _______________
13 _______________
14 _______________
15 _______________
16 _______________
17 _______________
18 _______________
19 _______________
20 _______________
21 _______________
22 _______________
23 _______________
24 _______________
25 _______________
26 _______________
27 _______________
28 _______________
29 _______________
30 _______________

happiness (HAP-ee-nuhs) n. – joy; the state of being happy

Super Science

Find the words below in the puzzle.
Words are hidden → and ↓.

ANIMAL	EARTH	ENERGY	FOSSIL
LIFE CYCLE	MAGNET	MINERAL	PLANT
ROCK	SEA	SPACE	WEATHER

A	P	B	D	F	O	S	S	I	L
W	L	E	A	R	T	H	E	G	I
D	A	N	I	M	A	L	A	C	F
M	N	A	L	I	K	L	N	U	E
A	T	P	D	N	C	V	M	K	C
G	D	M	C	E	N	E	R	G	Y
N	X	O	A	R	Z	A	R	H	C
E	H	W	E	A	T	H	E	R	L
T	W	D	X	L	S	P	A	C	E
Z	E	O	I	W	A	H	D	M	P
P	R	O	C	K	N	X	O	T	C

Subtract. Color the picture. Use the color key below.

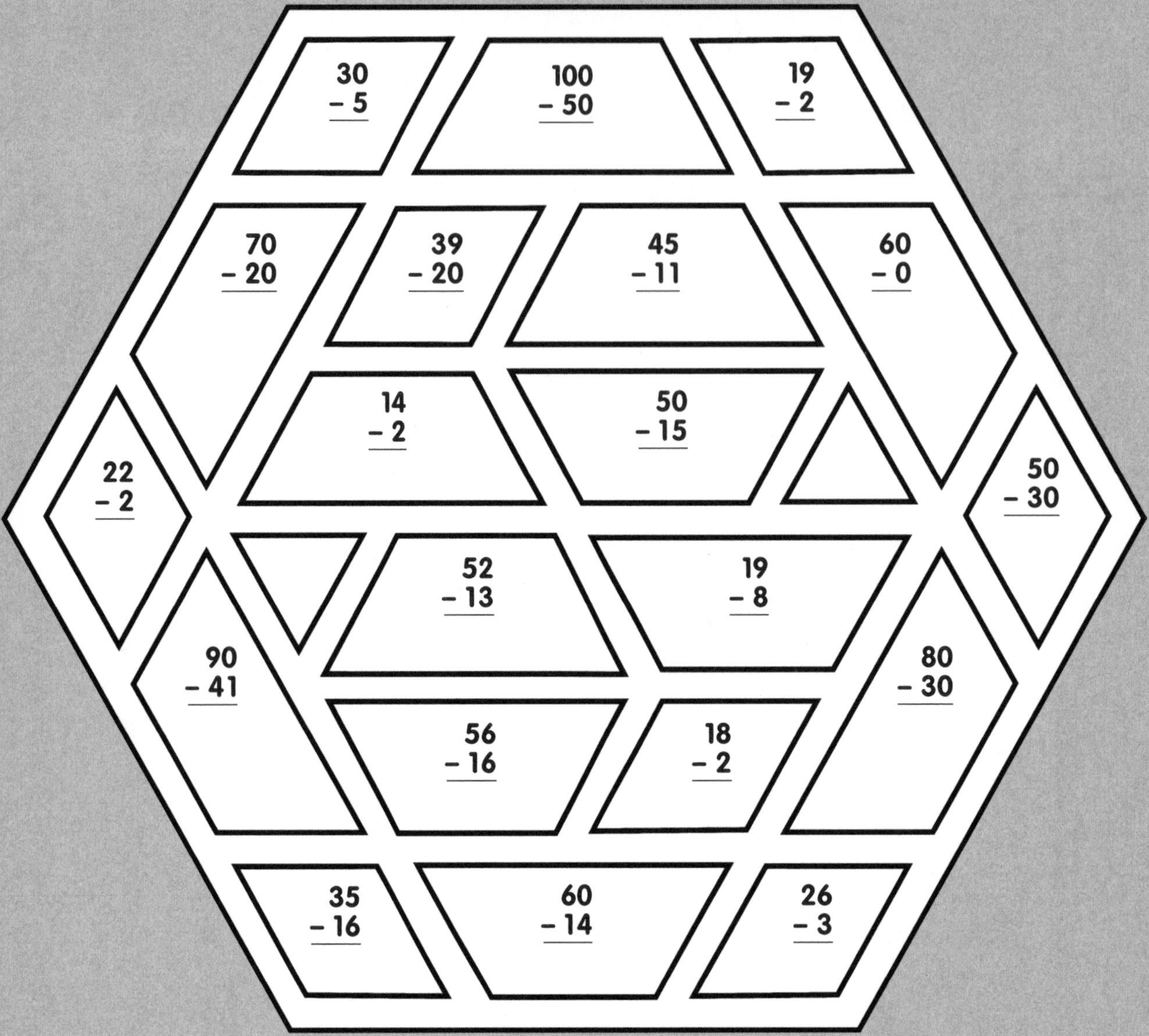

30
– 5
100
– 50
19
– 2
70
– 20
39
– 20
45
– 11
60
– 0
14
– 2
50
– 15
22
– 2
50
– 30
52
– 13
19
– 8
90
– 41
80
– 30
56
– 16
18
– 2
35
– 16
60
– 14
26
– 3

If the difference is between	Color the space
1 and 15	yellow
16 and 30	pink
31 and 45	purple
46 and 60	blue

Fill in the other spaces with colors of your choice.

Change duck into bump. Use the picture clues and letter tiles. Start at the bottom and climb to the top.

k m c p d u b j

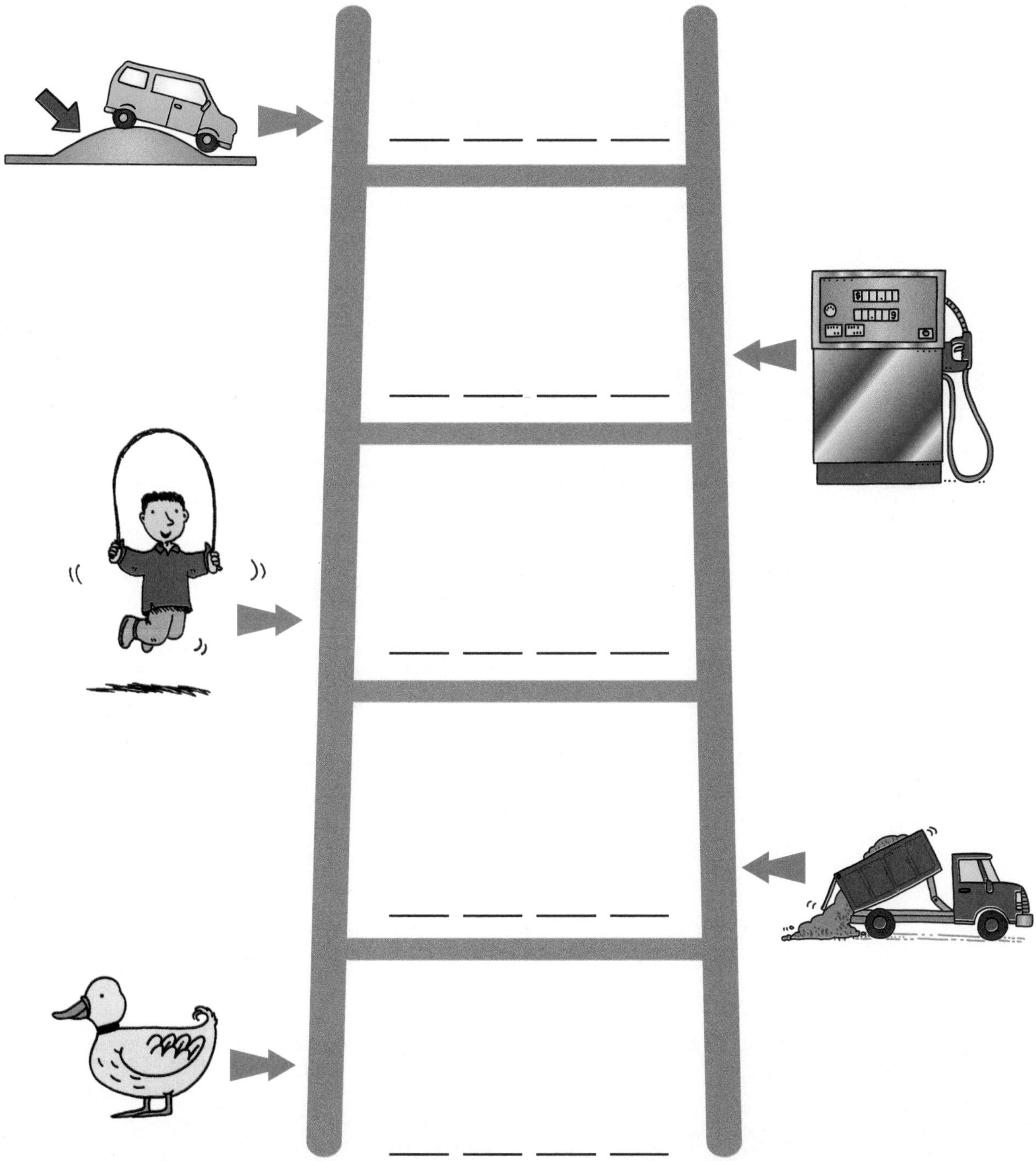

Draw shapes to complete the grid.
Each row, column, and minigrid should have one of each shape.

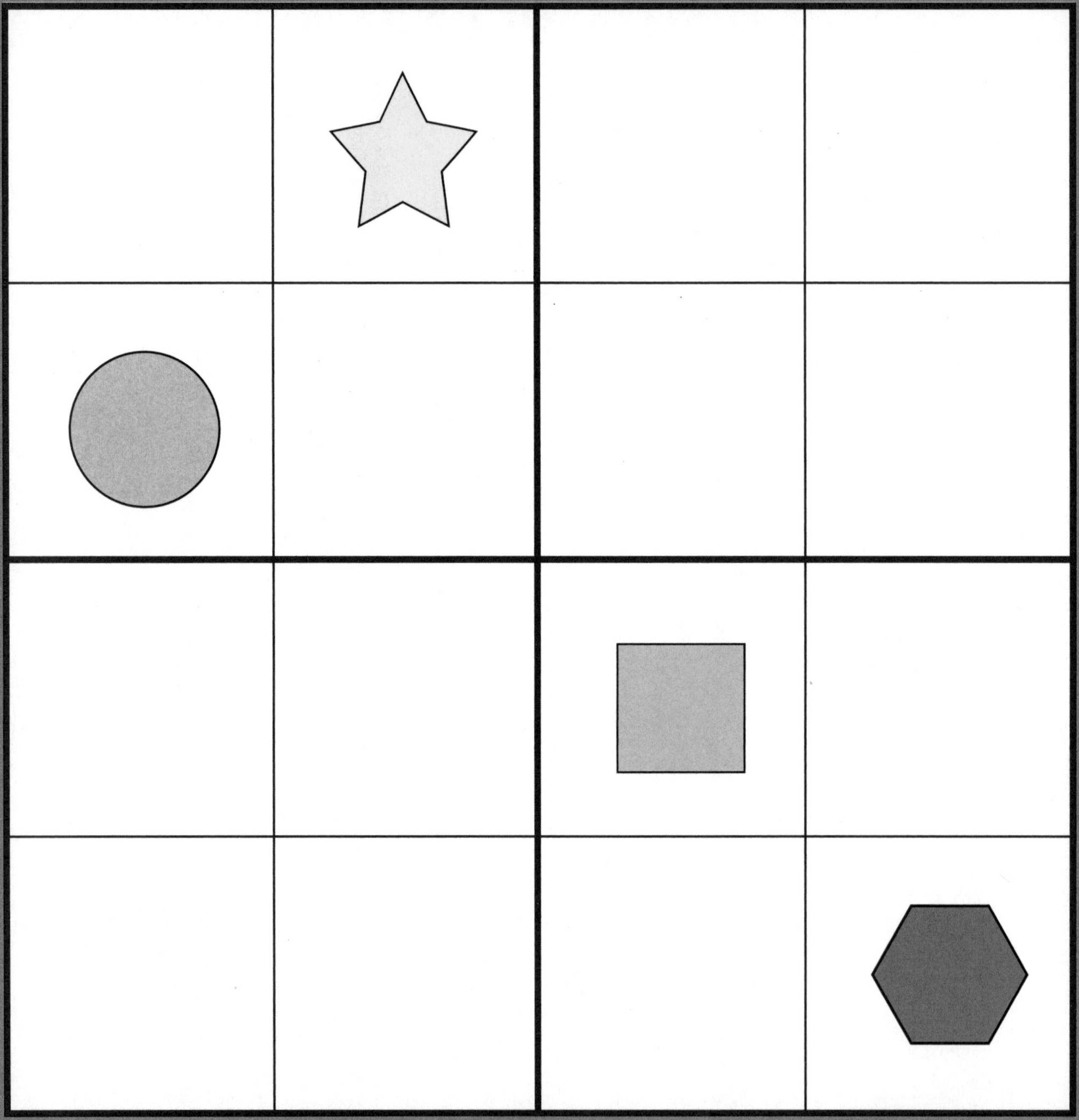

What Will Sam Do?

Read the story. Then answer the question below.

One day, Sam was riding his bike to the baseball game. He had to be on time. He was the pitcher. Just ahead, Sam saw a little boy who had fallen off his bike. His knee was bleeding, and he was crying. Sam asked him if he was okay, but the boy was crying too much to speak. Sam knew the boy needed help getting home. If he stopped to help, he might be late for the game. Sam thought about it. He knew he had to do the right thing.

What do you think Sam did next? There are two paths through the maze. Draw a line down the path that shows what you think Sam did next.

What sentence from the story gives a hint about what Sam decided to do? Write that sentence below.

Find each space with always, best, buy, could, and thank.
Color those spaces green. Then color the rest of the picture.

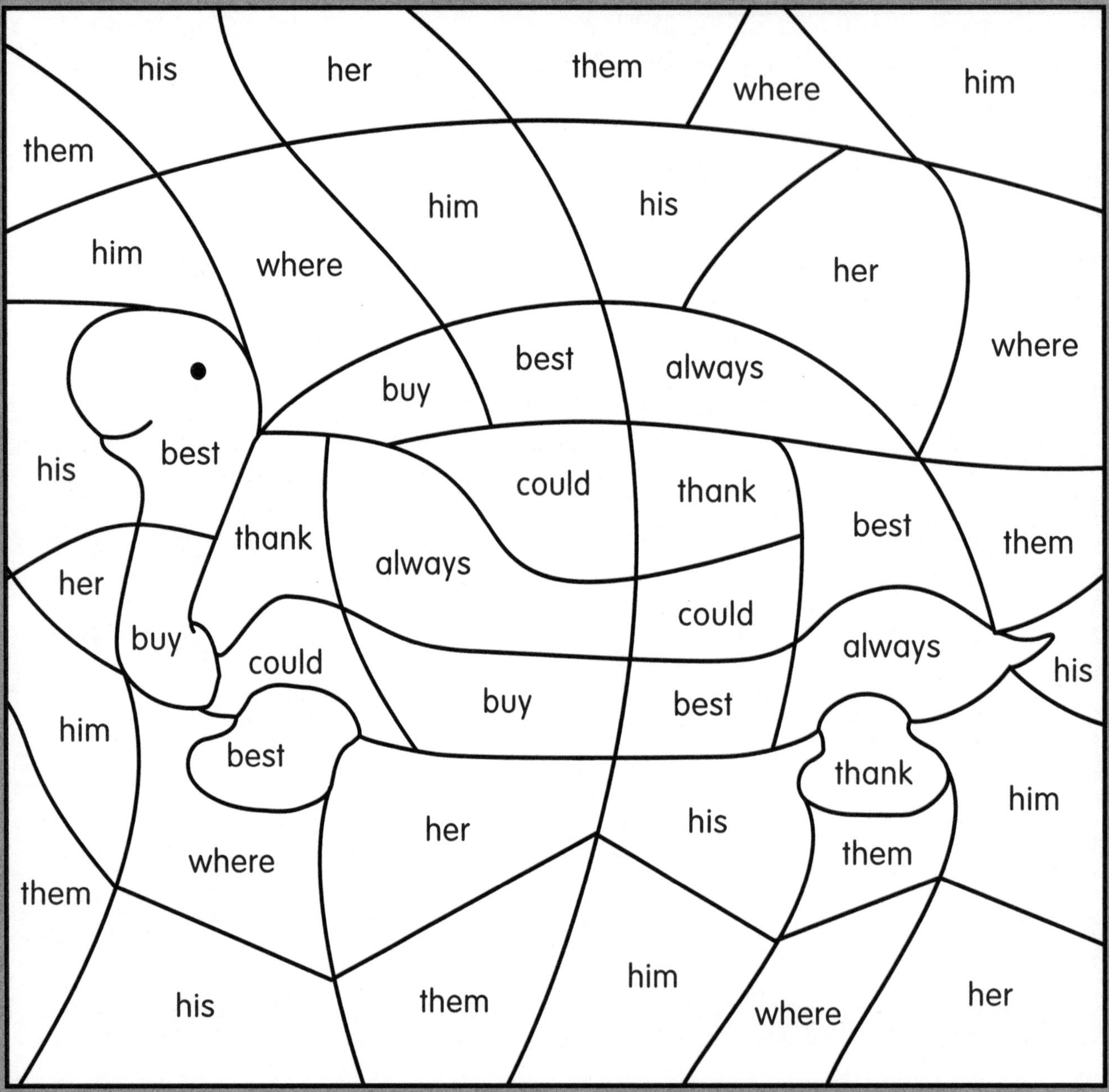
his
her
them
where
him
them
him
his
him
where
her
where
buy
best
always
his
best
could
thank
thank
best
them
always
her
could
buy
could
always
his
him
buy
best
best
thank
him
her
his
where
them
them
his
them
him
where
her

Connect the dots from 70 to 100. Then color the picture.

SOAP
70
71
72
73
74
75
76
77
78
79
80
81
82
83
84
85
86
87
88
89
90
91
92
93
94
95
96
97
98
99
100

Help the dog find the bone.

Add the missing numbers, letters, or symbols to each pattern.

1. ABC BCD _____ DEF _____ FGH GHI

2. 15 16 25 ____ 35 36 45 46 ____ 56 65 66

3. ▲ _____ ▲▲ ✖✖ ▲▲▲ ✖✖✖ _____ ✖✖✖✖

4. 99 88 77 ____ 55 ____ 33 22 11

5. a c e g i ____ m ____ q s u w

6. ↓ → ↑ ← ↓ ___ ↑ ← ↓ → ___ ←

7. z y ____ w v u ____ s r q ____ o

8. A Z ____ Y C X D ____ E V ____ U G

A Perfect Pizza

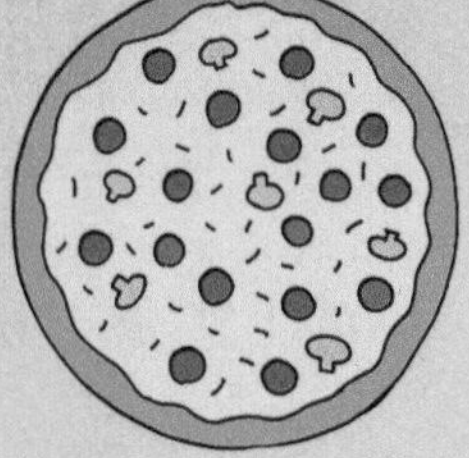

**Find the words below in the puzzle.
Words are hidden →, ↓, ↘ and ↗.**

ANCHOVIES	BROCCOLI	CHEESE	CHICKEN
HAM	MUSHROOMS	OLIVES	ONIONS
PEPPERONI	PEPPERS	SAUSAGES	TOMATOES

V	Q	G	I	S	R	B	L	Q	S	E	R	R
O	L	I	V	E	S	R	I	N	B	D	S	U
L	P	M	Q	S	I	N	O	S	I	E	N	Q
B	T	D	A	P	P	I	Y	P	G	B	H	O
R	L	H	O	D	N	G	X	A	U	G	A	Z
O	F	C	K	O	T	O	S	H	T	P	M	H
C	Q	L	H	S	N	U	C	O	A	E	I	A
C	A	K	E	E	A	R	A	S	S	P	E	N
O	H	P	K	S	E	I	Z	B	Q	P	Z	C
L	I	A	R	E	Q	S	V	D	C	E	K	H
I	A	C	H	I	C	K	E	N	C	R	S	O
T	O	M	A	T	O	E	S	G	C	S	X	V
I	U	P	E	P	P	E	R	O	N	I	A	I
G	I	D	E	N	Z	B	E	F	D	X	Y	E
F	F	G	C	M	U	S	H	R	O	O	M	S

Circle the two lamps that are the same.

Subtract. Color the picture. Use the color key below.

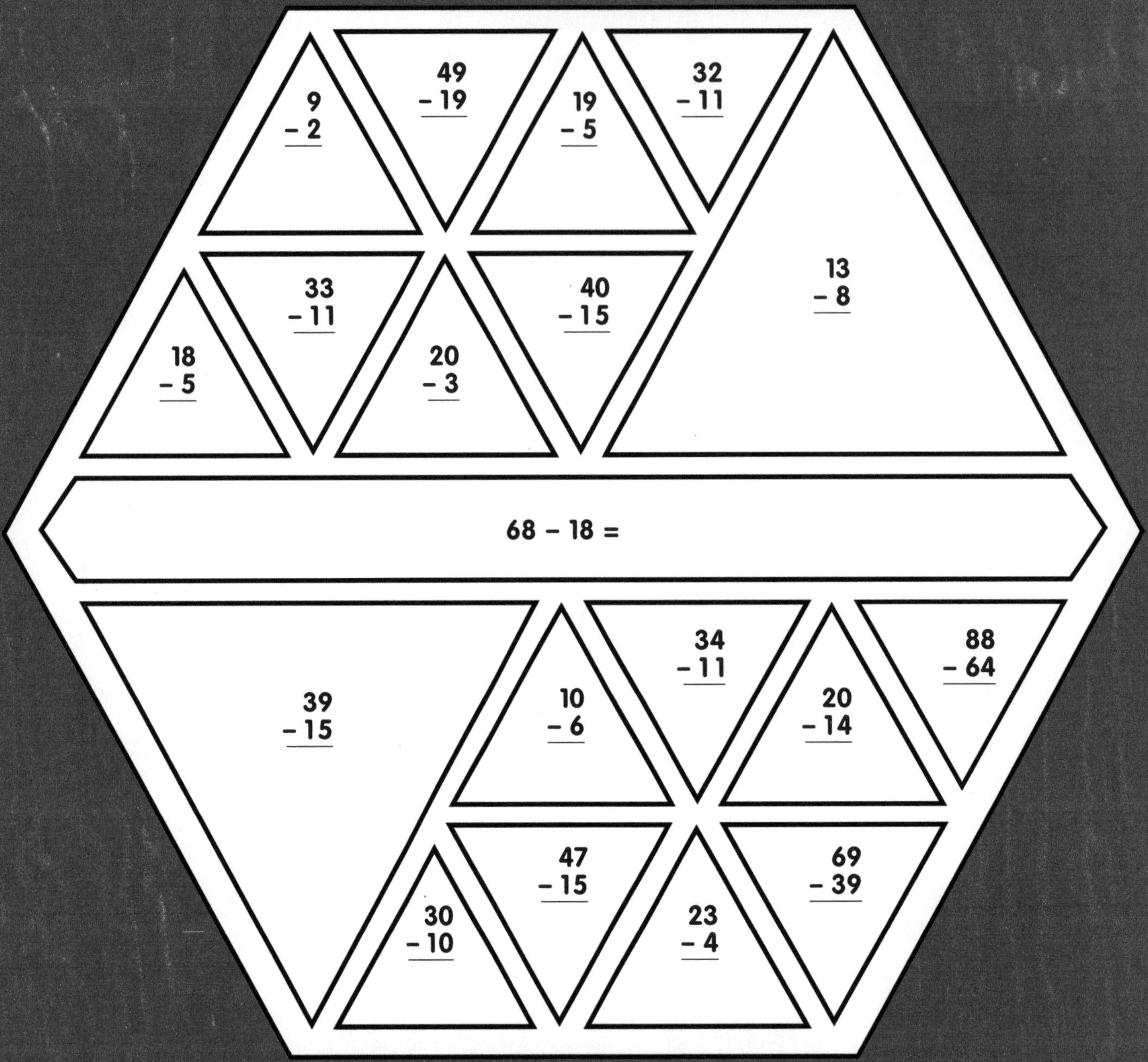
9 − 2
49 − 19
19 − 5
32 − 11
33 − 11
40 − 15
13 − 8
18 − 5
20 − 3
68 − 18 =
39 − 15
10 − 6
34 − 11
20 − 14
88 − 64
47 − 15
69 − 39
30 − 10
23 − 4

If the difference is between	Color the space
1 and 20	red
21 and 40	green
41 and 60	black

Fill in the other spaces with colors of your choice.

You're Getting Wiser

Read the clues. Write the words.
Start at the bottom and climb to the top.

opposite of *foolish*
change the third letter

a thin piece of metal
change the first vowel

past tense of *wear*
change the last letter

a combination of letters that has meaning
change the second vowel

furniture is made with this
change the first letter

what you eat
change the last letter

f o o l

What picture is missing?
Find the sticker on page 321. Add it to the pattern.

Draw your own pattern below.

Draw a poster for something you believe in.

Dynamically Different

Solve the crossword. Use the words in the Word Box.

Hint Each answer has the opposite meaning of the clue.

Word Box

ACROSS	DIRTY
FIRST	FOUND
FROWN	HAPPY
HARD	LEFT
LITTLE	NARROW
NORTH	OLD
OPEN	OVER
REMEMBER	SMOOTH
STOP	TALL

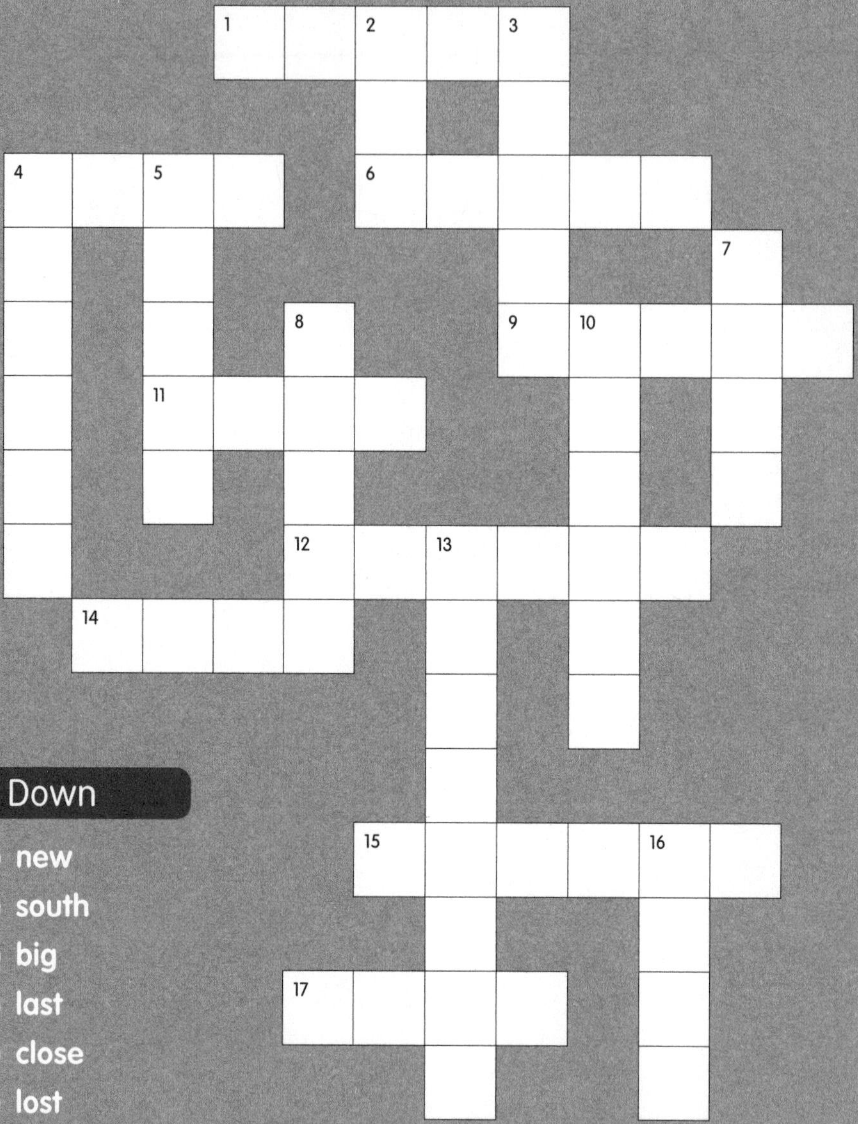

1
2
3
4
5
6
7
8
9
10
11
12
13
14
15
16
17

Across

1. smile
4. right
6. clean
9. sad
11. start
12. wide
14. soft
15. rough
17. under

Down

2. new
3. south
4. big
5. last
7. close
8. lost
10. down (puzzle)
13. forget
16. short

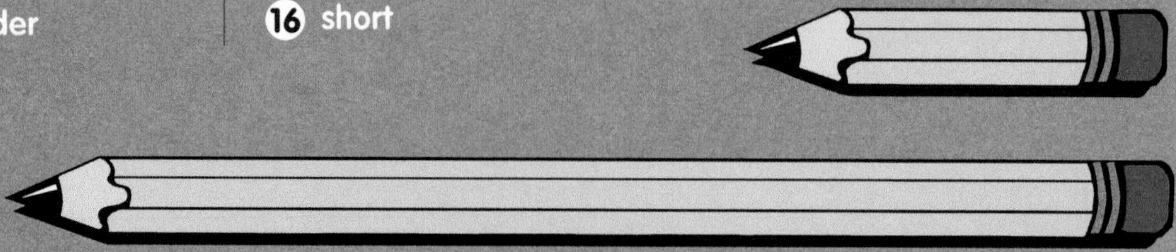

Skip count by 5 to connect the dots. Then color the picture.

10
5
60
20
50
15
55
25
45
35
30
40

Label each picture. Use the Word Box.
Match the pictures that use the same word.

Word Box			
BAT	GLASSES	PEN	SEAL

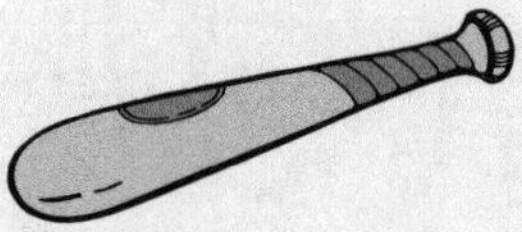

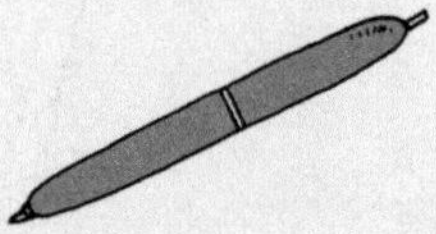

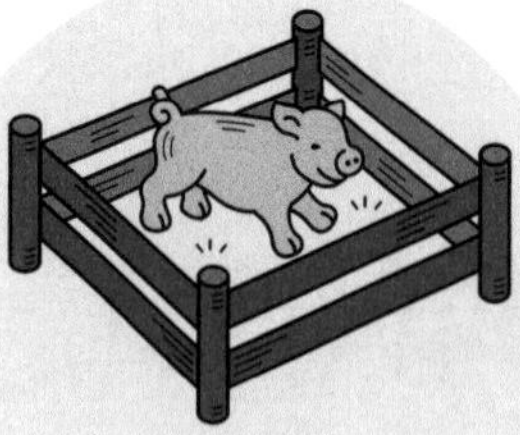

SEAL OF THE PRESIDENT OF THE UNITED STATES

Color the picture. Use the color key.

If the vowel matches the sound you hear in			STOP	
Color the space	orange	brown	red	yellow

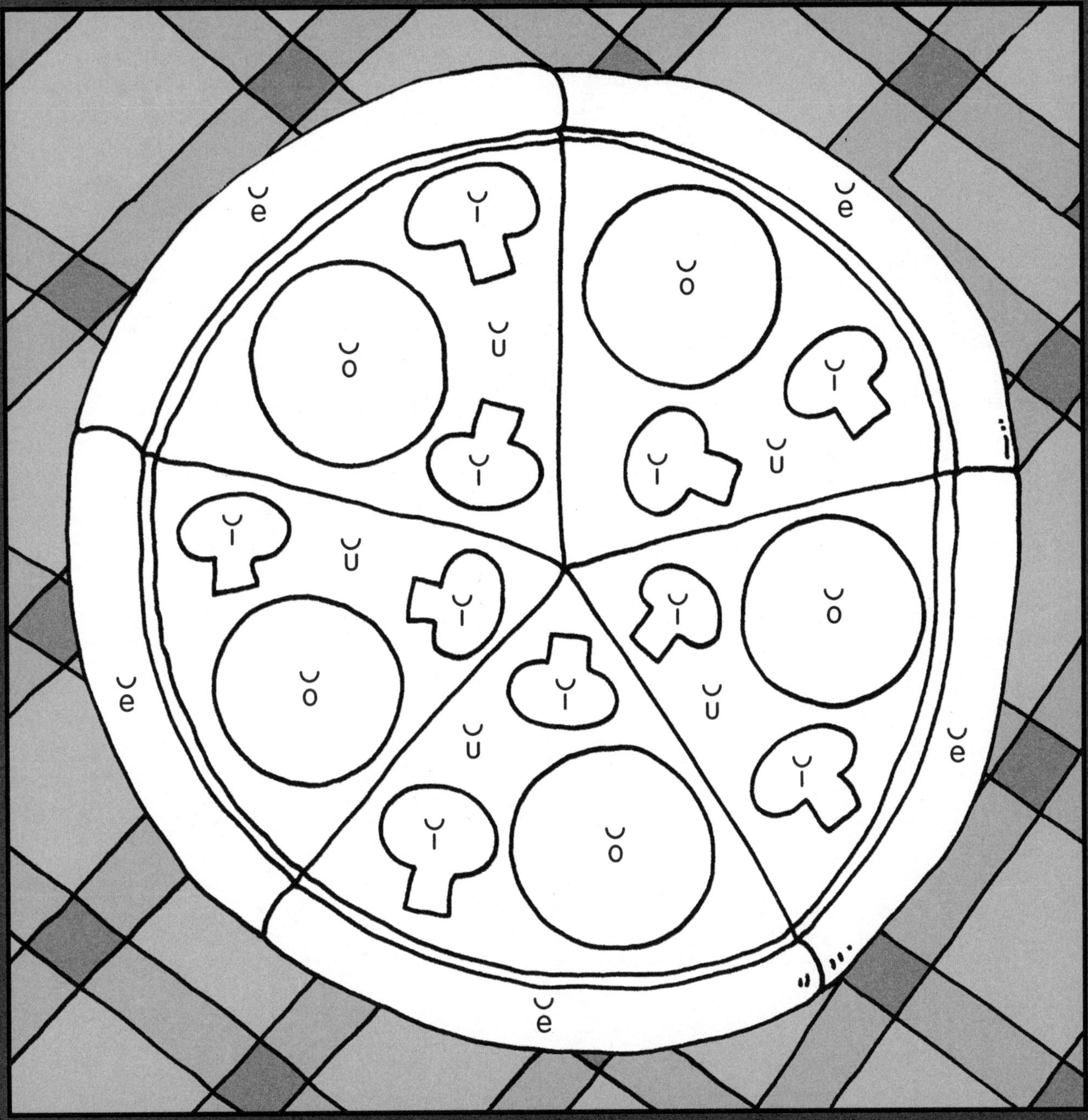

ĕ
ĭ
ĕ
ŏ
ŭ
ŏ
ĭ
ŭ
ĭ
ĭ
ĭ
ŭ
ĭ
ŏ
ĭ
ĕ
ŏ
ĭ
ŭ
ŭ
ĕ
ĭ
ĭ
ŏ
ĕ

Circle six differences.

Color the picture. Use the color key below.

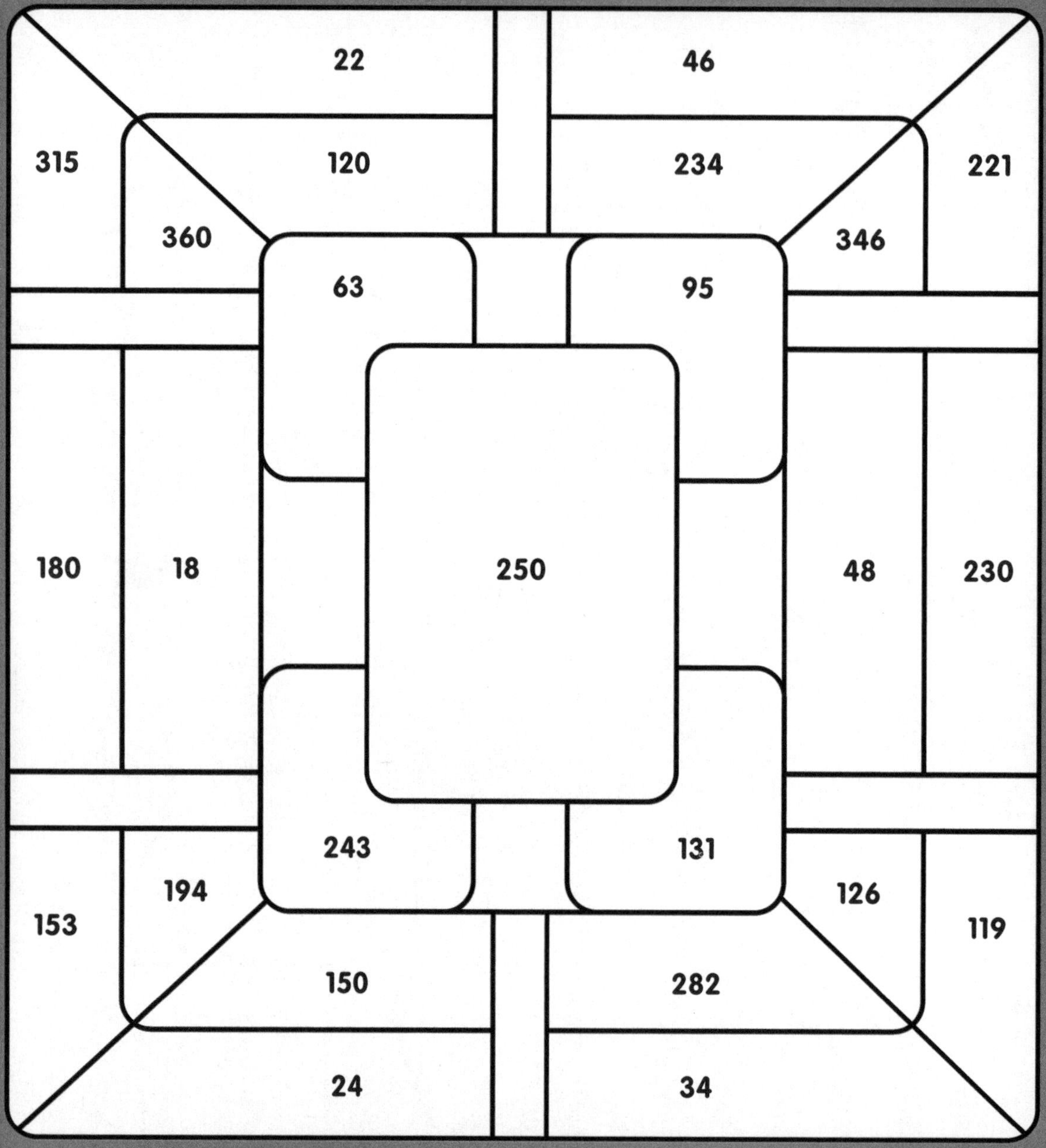
22
46
315
120
234
221
360
346
63
95
180
18
250
48
230
243
131
194
126
153
119
150
282
24
34

If the number is	Color the space
even and less than 50	red
odd and greater than 50	light gray
even and greater than 100	blue

Fill in the other spaces with colors of your choice.

Read the riddle. The answer is written in code.
Use the decoder to solve the riddle.

DECODER			
A	8	N	20
B	9	O	26
C	10	P	23
D	14	Q	1
E	2	R	3
F	25	S	18
G	5	T	24
H	6	U	4
I	13	V	21
J	15	W	12
K	17	X	16
L	7	Y	22
M	19	Z	11

OIL

Why did the little girl pour oil on her new pet mouse?

___ ___ ___ ___ ___ ___ ___   ___ ___   ___ ___ ___

9 2 10 8 4 18 2   13 24   12 8 18

___ ___ ___ ___ ___ ___ ___ ___ ___ !

18 1 4 2 8 17 13 20 5

The Southwest Scramble

Unscramble the name of each state.

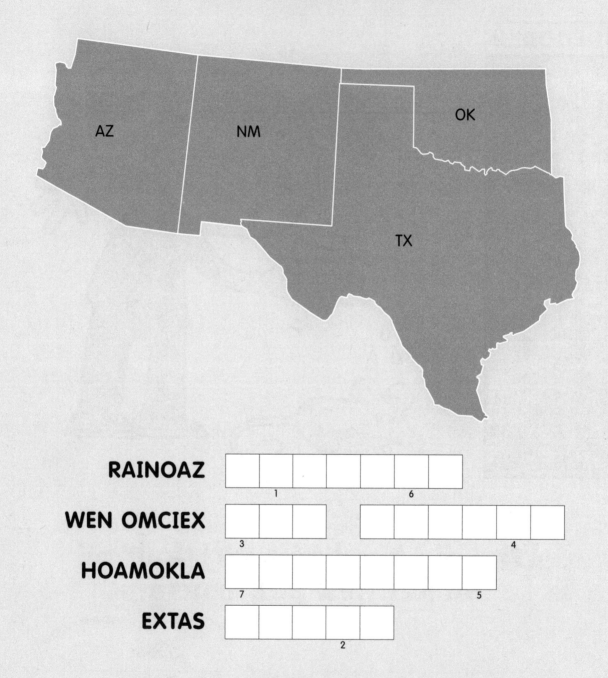

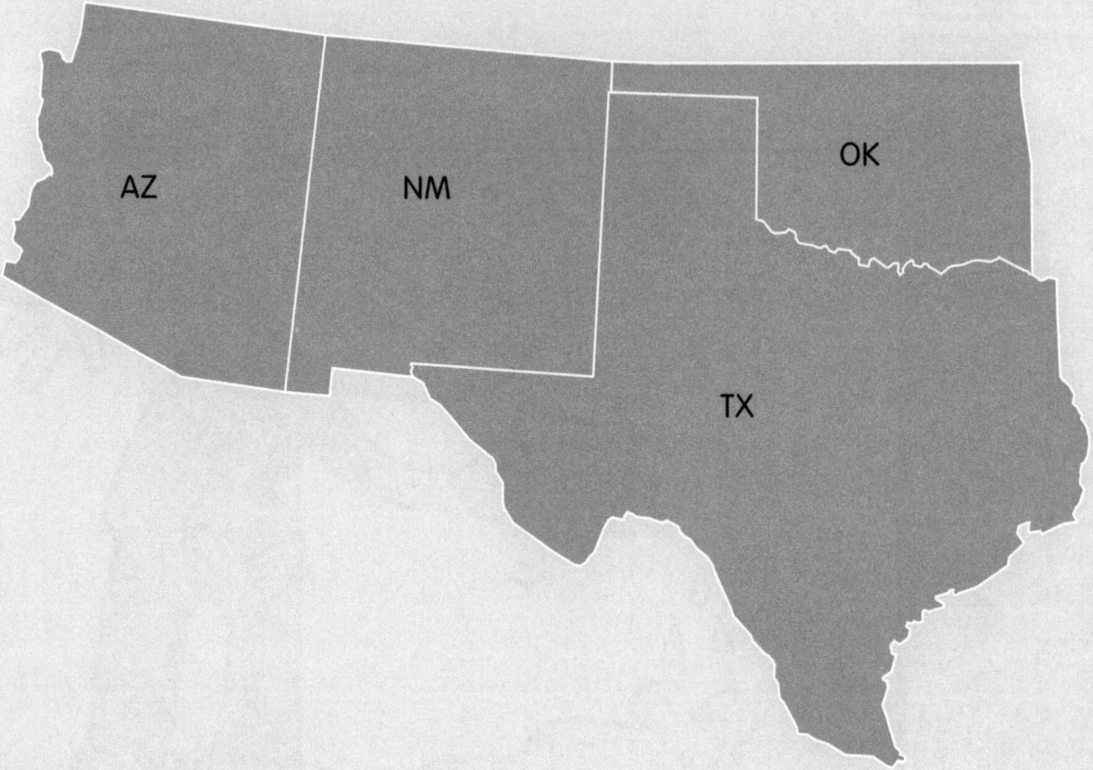
AZ
NM
OK
TX

RAINOAZ ☐☐☐☐☐☐☐ (1, 6)

WEN OMCIEX ☐☐☐ ☐☐☐☐☐☐ (3, 4)

HOAMOKLA ☐☐☐☐☐☐☐☐ (7, 5)

EXTAS ☐☐☐☐☐ (2)

Copy the letters in the numbered cells to answer the question.

Which national park in Arizona do nearly five million people visit every year?

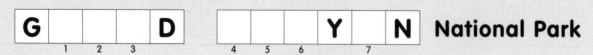

G _1 _2 _3 **D**   _4 _5 _6 **Y** _7 **N** **National Park**

Connect the dots from 50 to 120. Then color the picture.

50
51
52
53
54
55
56
57
58
59
60
61
62
63
64
65
66
67
68
69
70
71
72
73
74
75
76
77
78
79
80
81
82
83
84
85
86
87
88
89
90
91
92
93
94
95
96
97
98
99
100
101
102
103
104
105
106
107
108
109
110
111
112
113
114
115
116
117
118
119
120

Find and circle each item in the big picture.

W

WINTER

Magic Shapes

Follow the directions to complete each magic shape.

Write each of the numbers 1, 2, and 5 once in the boxes at the right so that the numbers in the row across and the column down **add up to 9**.

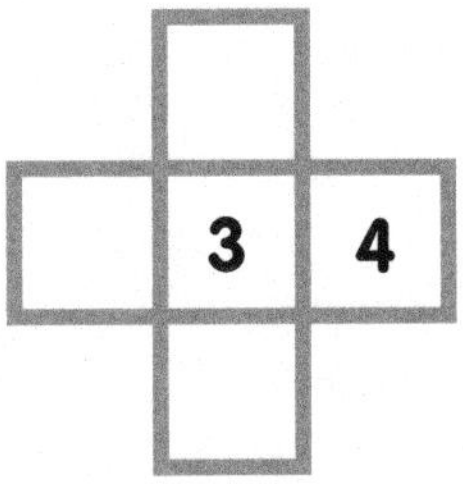
3
4

Write each of the numbers 1, 3, and 9 once in the boxes at the right so that the numbers in the row across and the column down **add up to 15**.

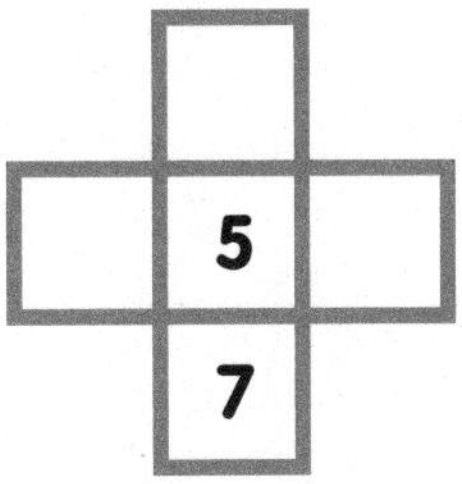
5
7

Write each of the numbers 3, 4, 6, and 7 once in the boxes at the right so that the numbers in the row across and the column down **add up to 15**.

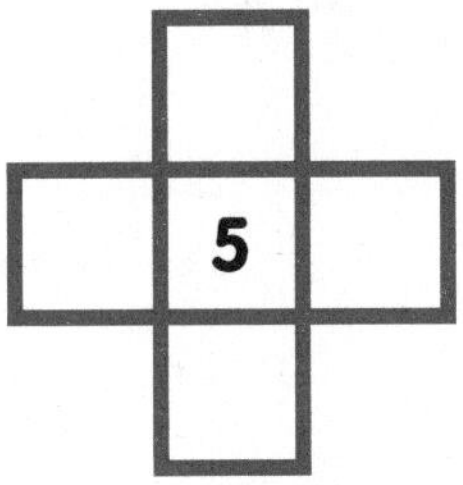
5

Write each of the numbers 2, 3, 5, and 6 once in the boxes at the right so that the numbers in the row across and the column down **add up to 12**.

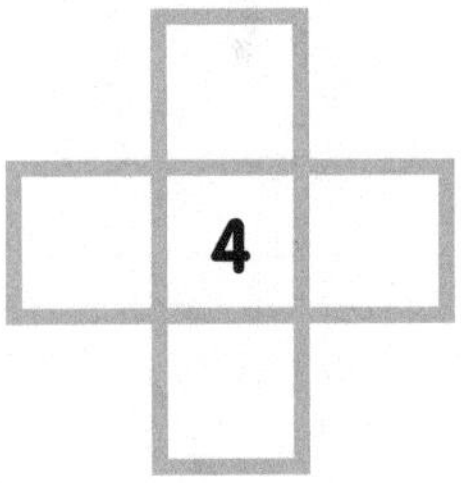
4

Write each of the numbers 2, 4, 8, and 10 once in the boxes at the right so that the numbers in the row across and the column down **add up to 18**.

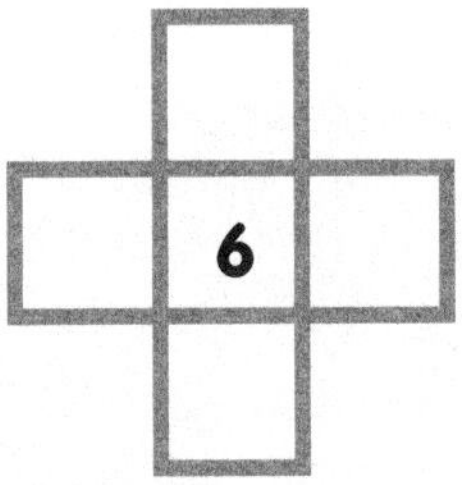
6

How many smaller words can you make using the letters in

independence?

1 ______ 16 ______
2 ______ 17 ______
3 ______ 18 ______
4 ______ 19 ______
5 ______ 20 ______
6 ______ 21 ______
7 ______ 22 ______
8 ______ 23 ______
9 ______ 24 ______
10 ______ 25 ______
11 ______ 26 ______
12 ______ 27 ______
13 ______ 28 ______
14 ______ 29 ______
15 ______ 30 ______

independence (in-di-PEN-duhnss) n. – freedom from outside control; the state of being independent

Bugs!

Solve the crossword. Use the Word Box and picture clues.

Across

2

3

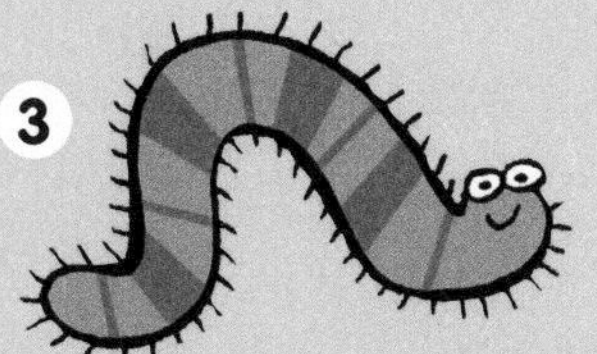

5

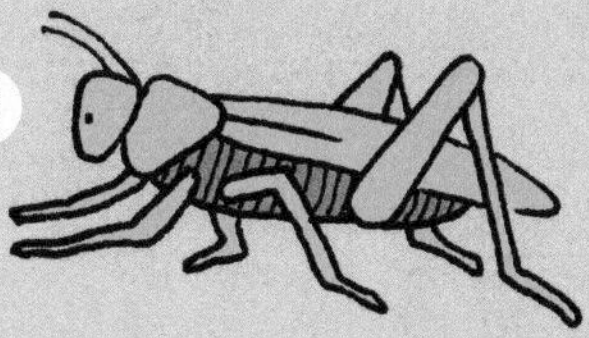

6

7

Down

1

2

4

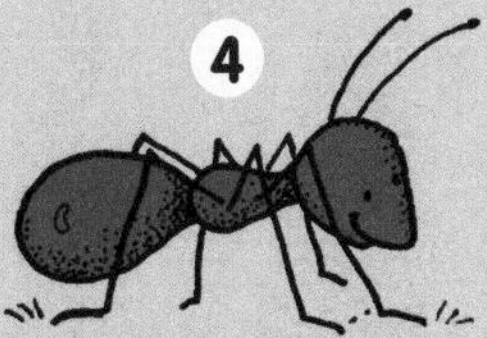

Word Box

- ANT
- BEE
- BEETLE
- BUTTERFLY
- CATERPILLAR
- FLY
- GRASSHOPPER
- LADYBUG

This is the painting I want in my bedroom.

What picture is missing?
Find the sticker on page 321. Add it to the pattern.

Draw your own pattern below.

Change tack into clock. Use the picture clues and letter tiles. Start at the bottom and climb to the top.

c k o s l t a

12
1
2
3
4
5
6
7
8
9
10
11

Color the word path each leaf follows to its basket. Use the color key.

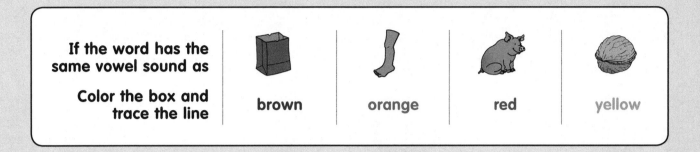

If the word has the same vowel sound as		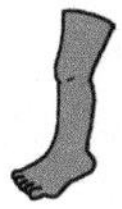		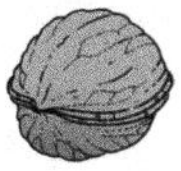
Color the box and trace the line	**brown**	**orange**	**red**	**yellow**

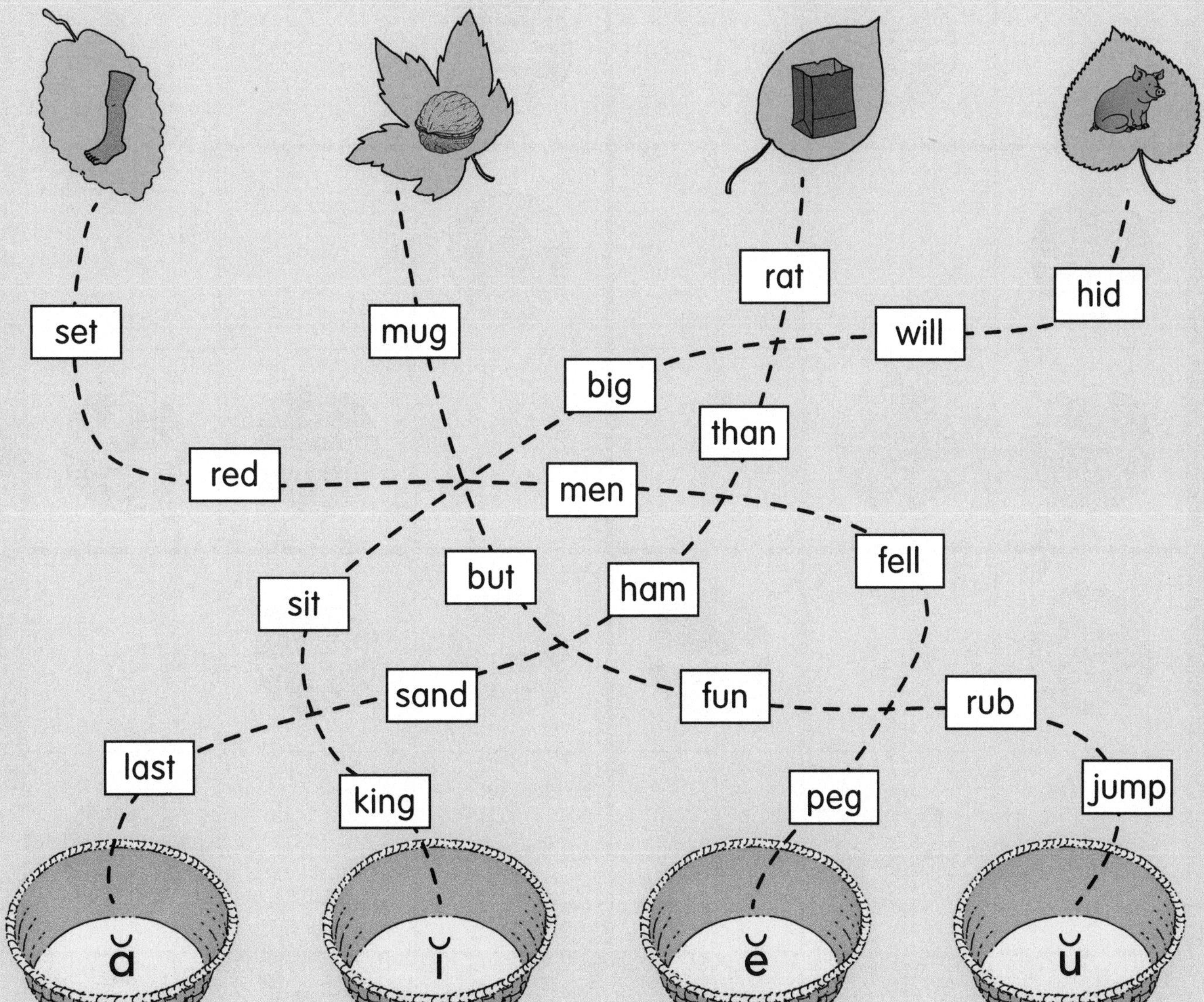
set
mug
rat
hid
will
big
than
red
men
fell
but
ham
sit
sand
fun
rub
last
king
peg
jump
ă
ĭ
ĕ
ŭ

Draw beachballs to complete the grid.
Each row, column, and minigrid should have one of each color.

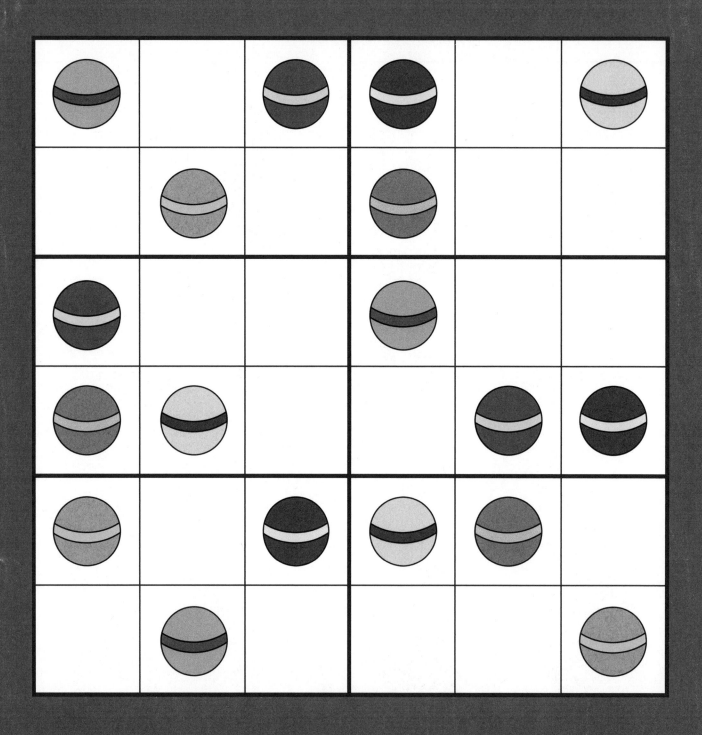

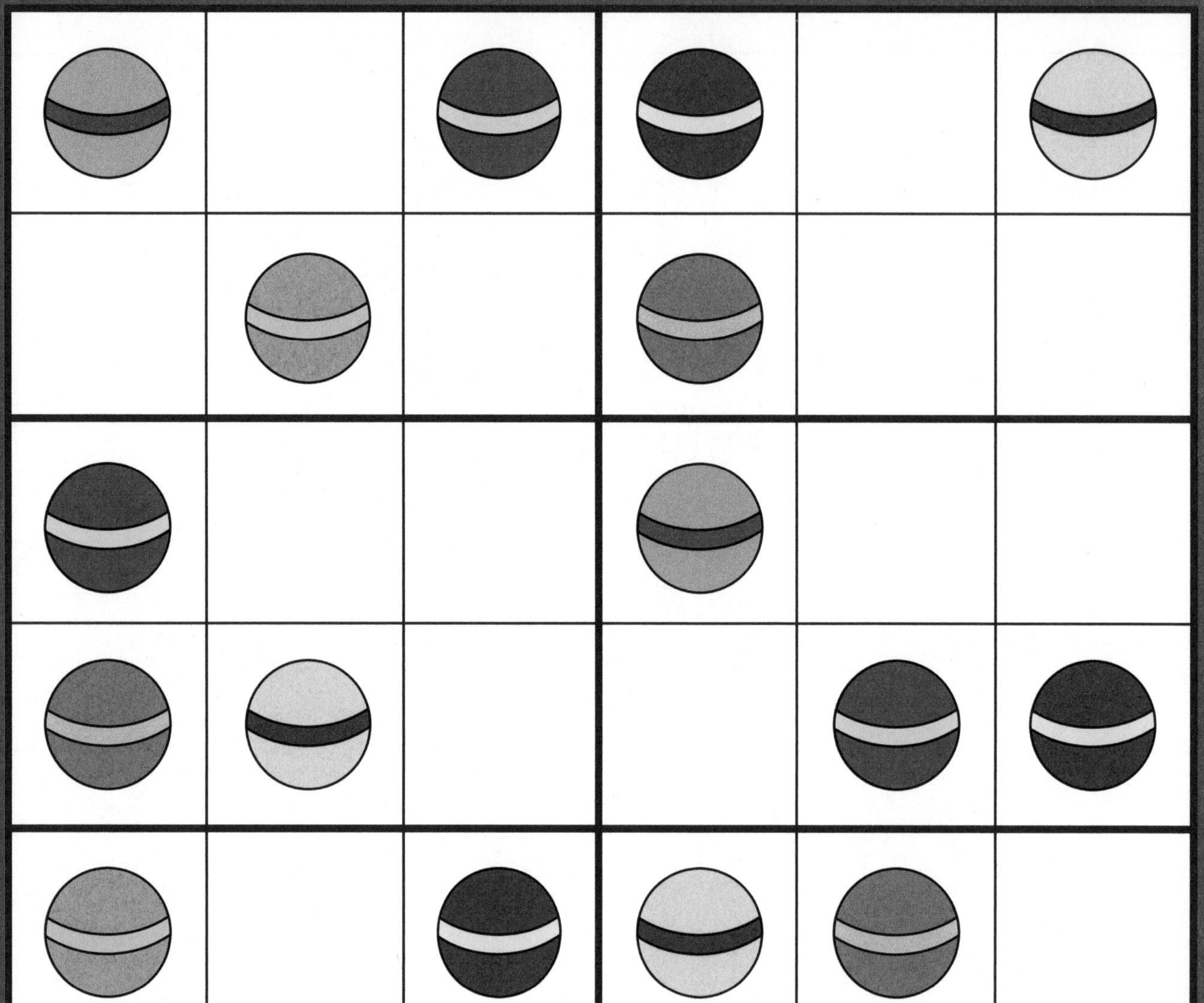

Find the child without a shadow.

Draw your dream vacation.

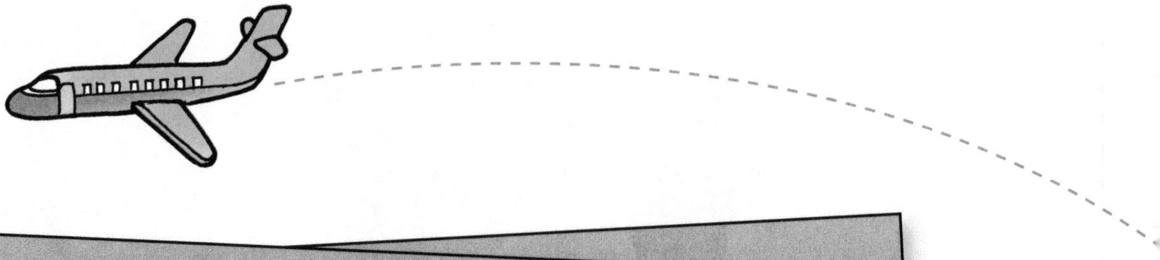

Fall Scramble

Unscramble each word. To help you get started, the first and last letter and some vowels are filled in.

ACNOR	A		O		N				
EPLPA	A				E				
SCOHOL	S			O		L			
NRCO	C			N					
STHARVE	H				E		T		
HYA	H		Y						
PIMPNKU	P						N		
SCREACWRO	S								W
SEWTAER	S			A			R		

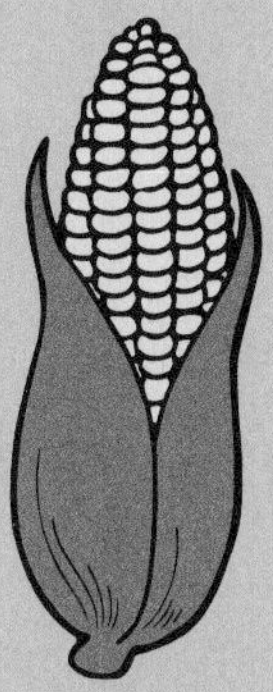

How many smaller words can you make using the letters in

ecosystem?

1 ______________________

2 ______________________

3 ______________________

4 ______________________

5 ______________________

6 ______________________

7 ______________________

8 ______________________

9 ______________________

10 ______________________

11 ______________________

12 ______________________

13 ______________________

14 ______________________

15 ______________________

16 ______________________

17 ______________________

18 ______________________

19 ______________________

20 ______________________

21 ______________________

22 ______________________

23 ______________________

24 ______________________

25 ______________________

26 ______________________

27 ______________________

28 ______________________

29 ______________________

30 ______________________

ecosystem (EE-koh-siss-tuhm) n. – a community of animals and plants interacting with their environment

Color the word path each chick follows to its mother. Use the color key.

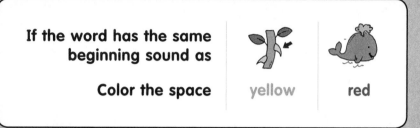

If the word has the same beginning sound as		
Color the space	yellow	red

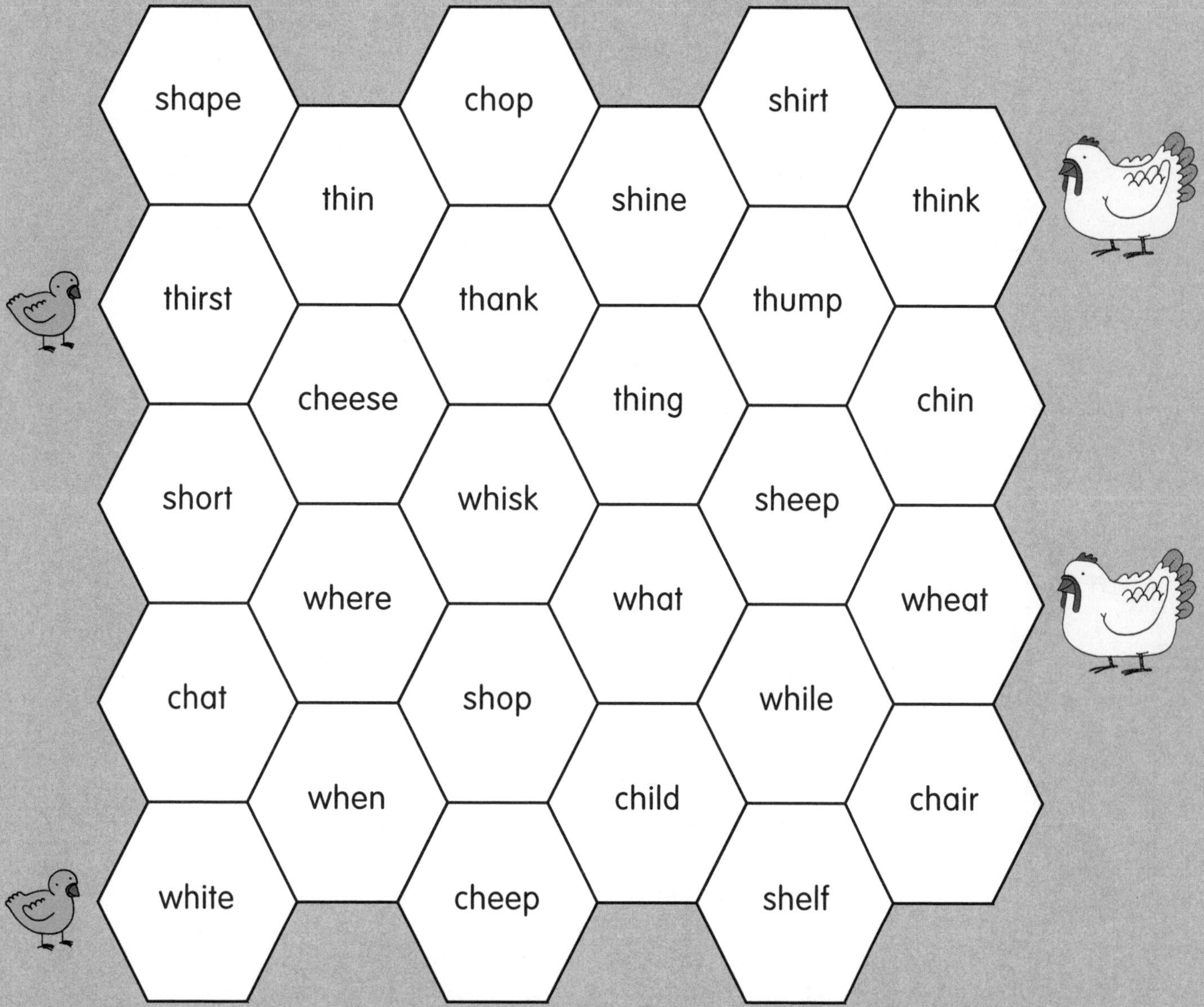
shape
chop
shirt
thin
shine
think
thirst
thank
thump
cheese
thing
chin
short
whisk
sheep
where
what
wheat
chat
shop
while
when
child
chair
white
cheep
shelf

CHEF ZACK
MACK

Circle six differences.

CHEF
ZACK

Fun Hobbies

Find the words below in the puzzle.
Words are hidden → and ↓.

BAKING	BIKING	COLLECTING	COLORING
COOKING	DANCING	DRAWING	GARDENING
PAINTING	READING	SINGING	WRITING

K	B	C	D	R	A	W	I	N	G
T	I	O	C	R	O	R	D	G	A
B	K	O	I	E	L	I	A	C	R
A	I	K	P	A	M	T	N	O	D
K	N	I	F	D	H	I	C	L	E
I	G	N	Z	I	V	N	I	O	N
N	P	G	W	N	G	G	N	R	I
G	S	I	N	G	I	N	G	I	N
C	O	L	L	E	C	T	I	N	G
P	N	S	G	L	C	A	T	G	J
O	P	A	I	N	T	I	N	G	B

Connect the dots from A to Z. Then color the picture.

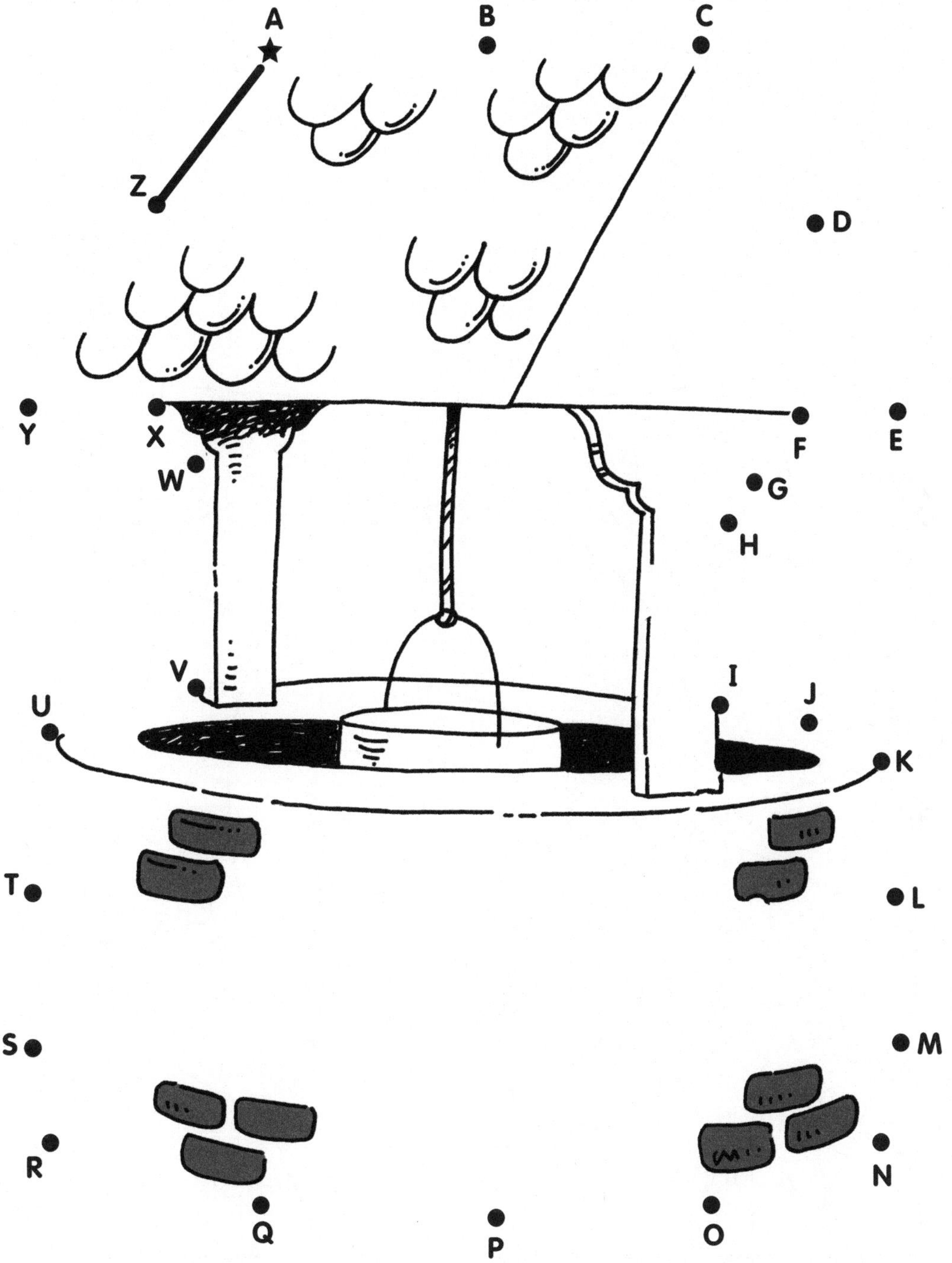
A
B
C
D
E
F
G
H
I
J
K
L
M
N
O
P
Q
R
S
T
U
V
W
X
Y
Z

Find each space with cold, fast, its, off, or, and use.
Color those spaces blue. Then color the rest of the picture.

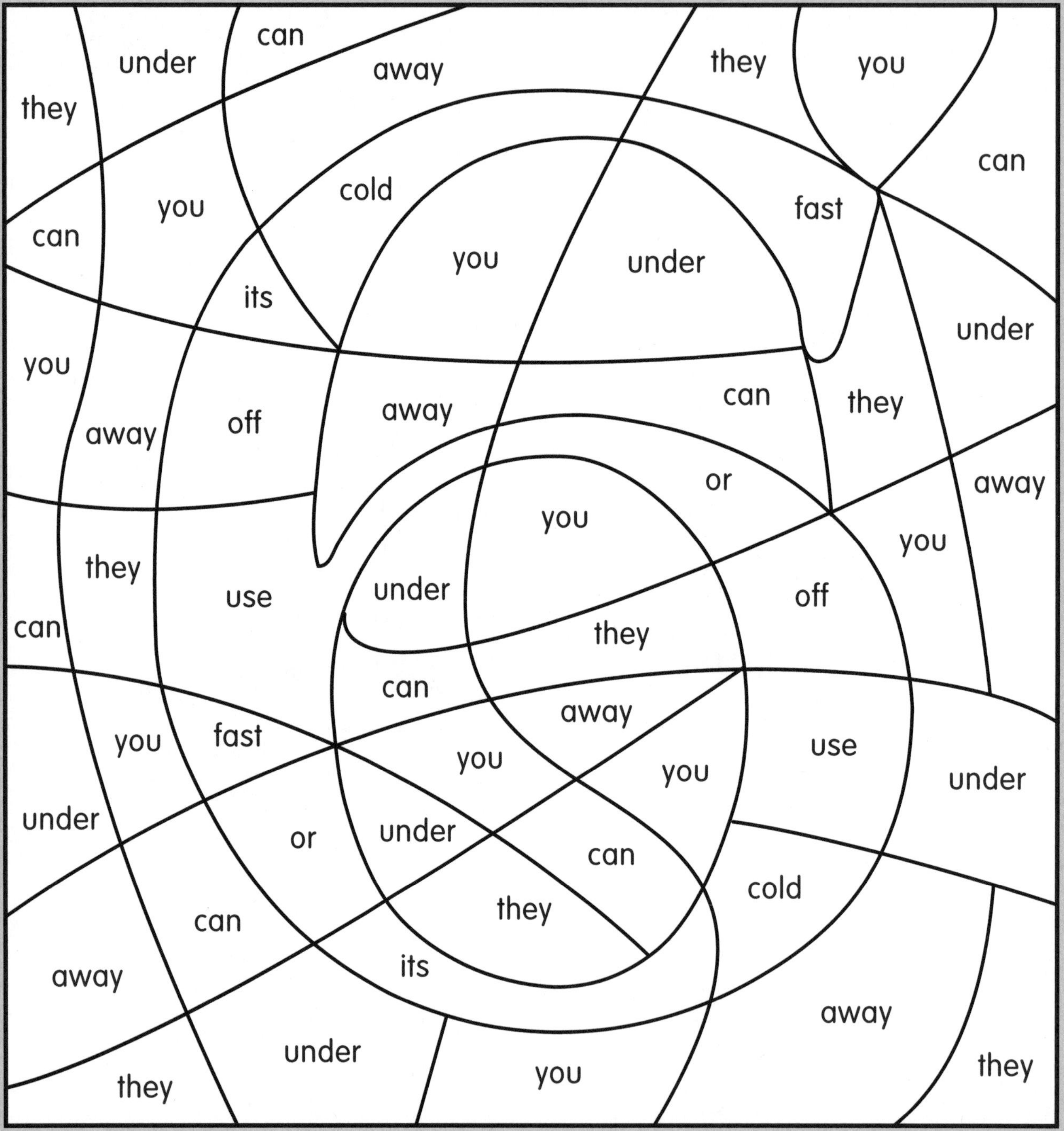

can
under
away
they
you
they
can
can
you
cold
fast
you
under
its
under
you
off
away
can
they
away
or
you
you
they
under
use
off
can
they
can
away
you
fast
use
you
under
you
under
or
under
can
cold
can
they
away
its
away
under
you
they
they

The Call of the Wild

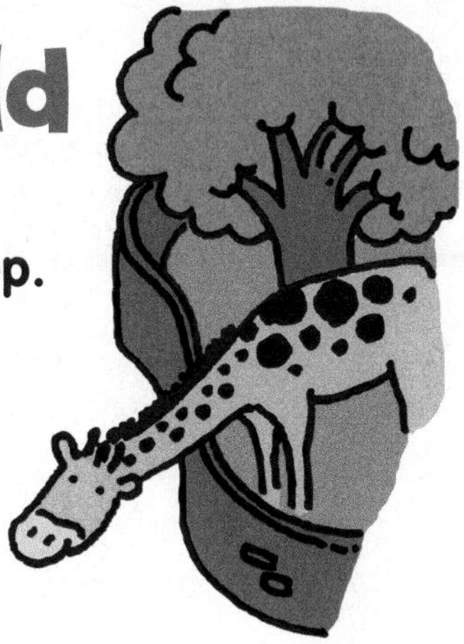

Read the clues. Write the words.
Start at the bottom and climb to the top.

opposite of *tame*
change the first letter

___ ___ ___ ___

lightly flavored
change the last letter

___ ___ ___ ___

a unit of distance
change the first letter

___ ___ ___ ___

covering for a bathroom floor or wall
change the third letter

___ ___ ___ ___

what a clock tells
change the first vowel

___ ___ ___ ___

t a m e

Add. Color the picture. Use the color key below.

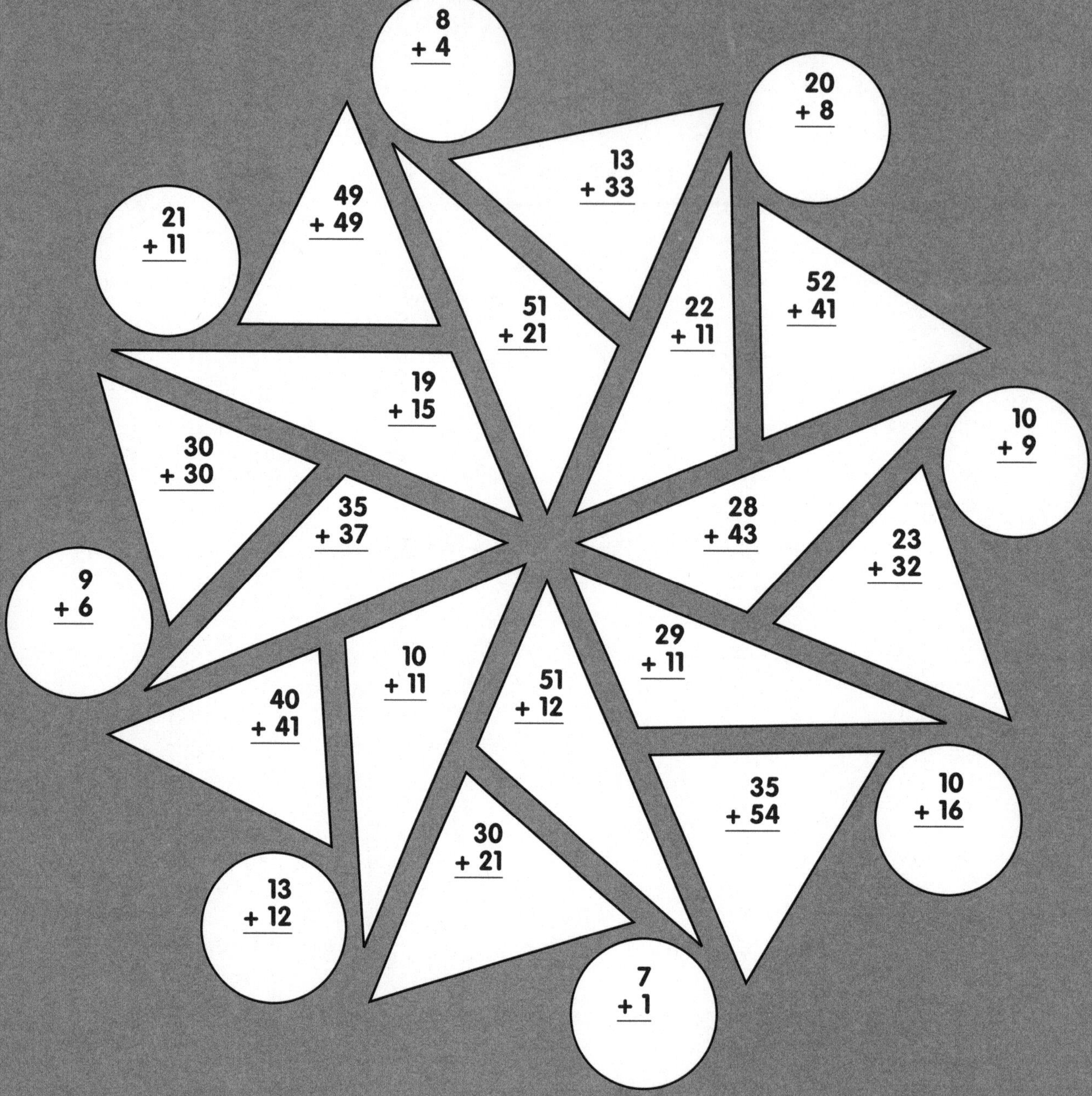
8 + 4
20 + 8
21 + 11
49 + 49
13 + 33
51 + 21
22 + 11
52 + 41
19 + 15
10 + 9
30 + 30
35 + 37
28 + 43
23 + 32
9 + 6
29 + 11
10 + 11
51 + 12
40 + 41
35 + 54
10 + 16
30 + 21
13 + 12
7 + 1

If the sum is between	Color the space
1 and 20	yellow
21 and 40	blue
41 and 60	purple
61 and 80	pink
81 and 100	orange

The Rescue

Read the story.
Number the sentences on the ladder in the order they happen.

Mia's grey cat climbed to the top of a telephone pole and couldn't get down. "Come down, Spooky!" cried Mia. Mia thought hard. What could she do? She went across the street to ask Mr. Carson for help. He was a firefighter before he retired. "What's the matter, Mia?" asked Mr. Carson when he saw Mia's tears. "My cat is up on that pole, and I can't get her down!" Mr. Carson hugged Mia and said, "I'll call my buddies at the fire station. They will come and help." A few minutes later, Mia saw the fire truck coming. The firefighters parked near the pole and raised a long ladder to the top. A firefighter climbed the ladder and reached out for Spooky. Just then, Spooky jumped to a nearby tree limb, climbed down the tree, and ran into the backyard. Mia said, "Spooky! You naughty cat!" Mr. Carson and the firefighters laughed and laughed.

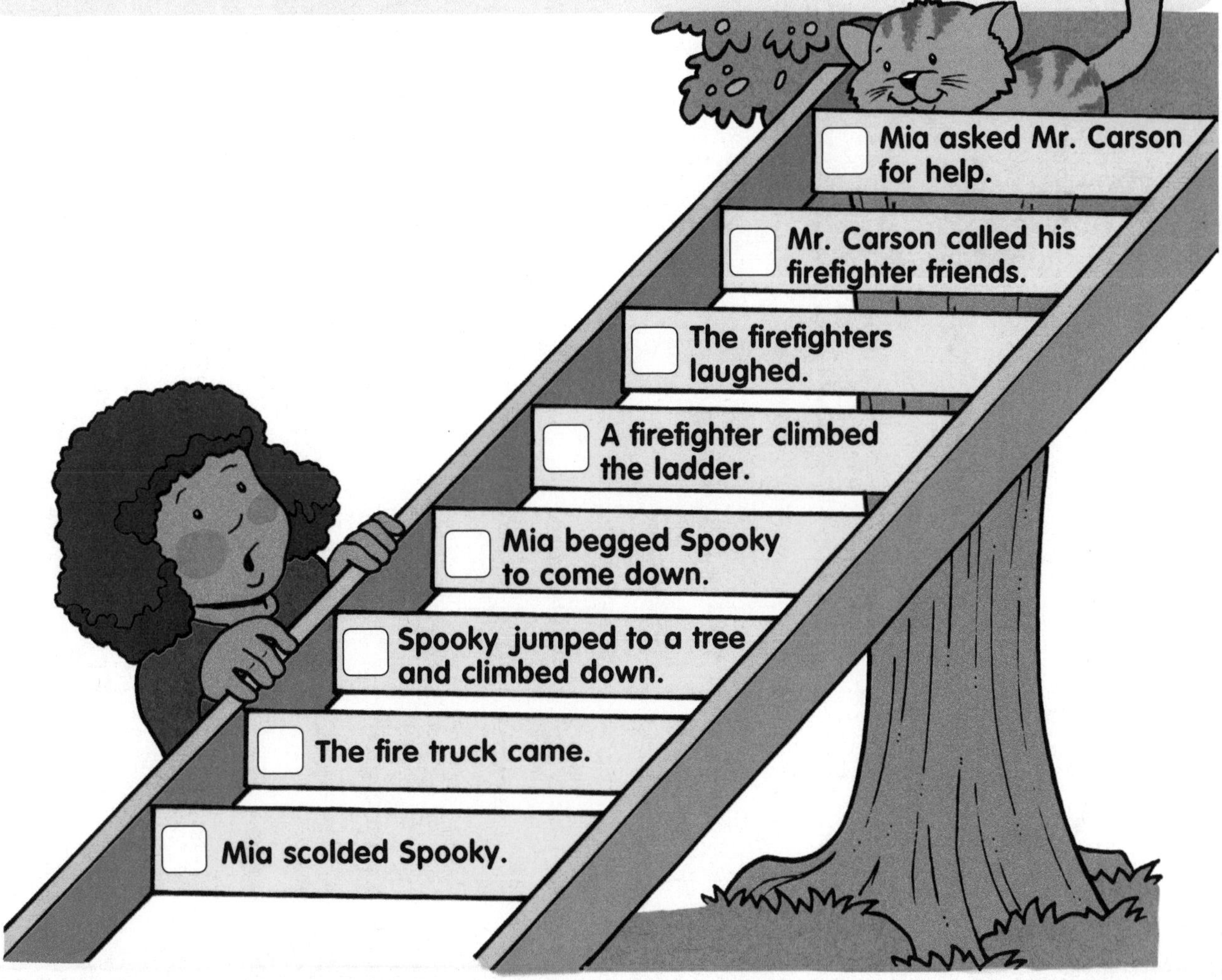

☐ Mia asked Mr. Carson for help.
☐ Mr. Carson called his firefighter friends.
☐ The firefighters laughed.
☐ A firefighter climbed the ladder.
☐ Mia begged Spooky to come down.
☐ Spooky jumped to a tree and climbed down.
☐ The fire truck came.
☐ Mia scolded Spooky.

Change pear into beach. Use the picture clues and letter tiles. Start at the bottom and climb to the top.

r e c h p b d k a

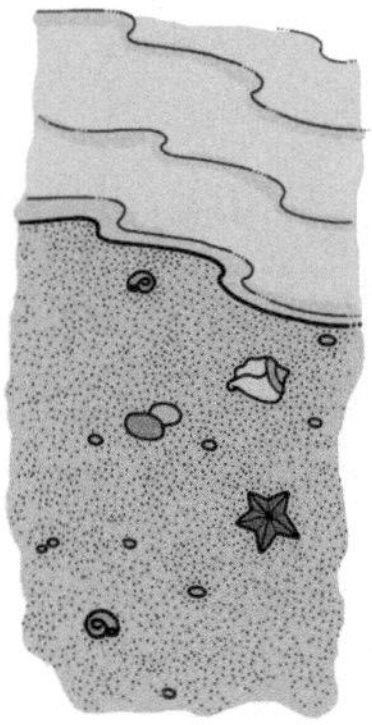

___ ___ ___ ___ ___

___ ___ ___ ___

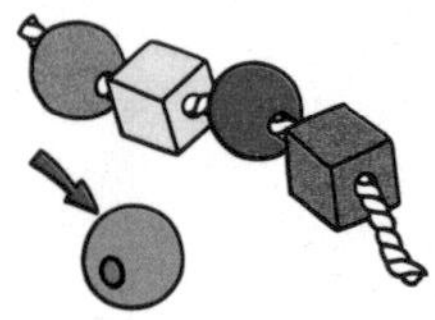

___ ___ ___ ___

___ ___ ___ ___

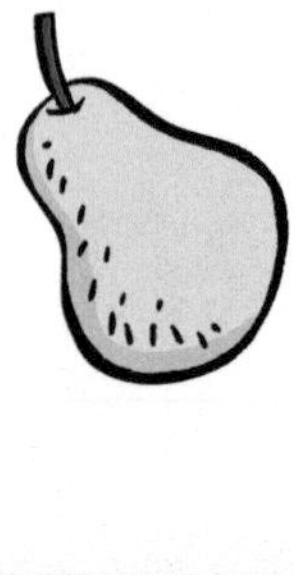

___ ___ ___ ___

Find and circle each item in the big picture.

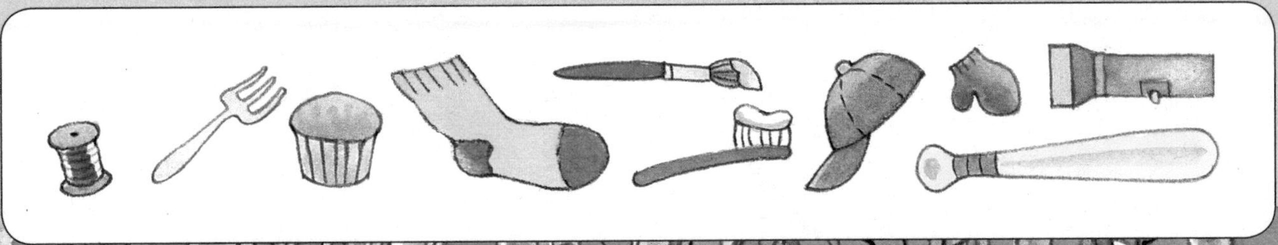

How many items did you find? ________

This is my role model.

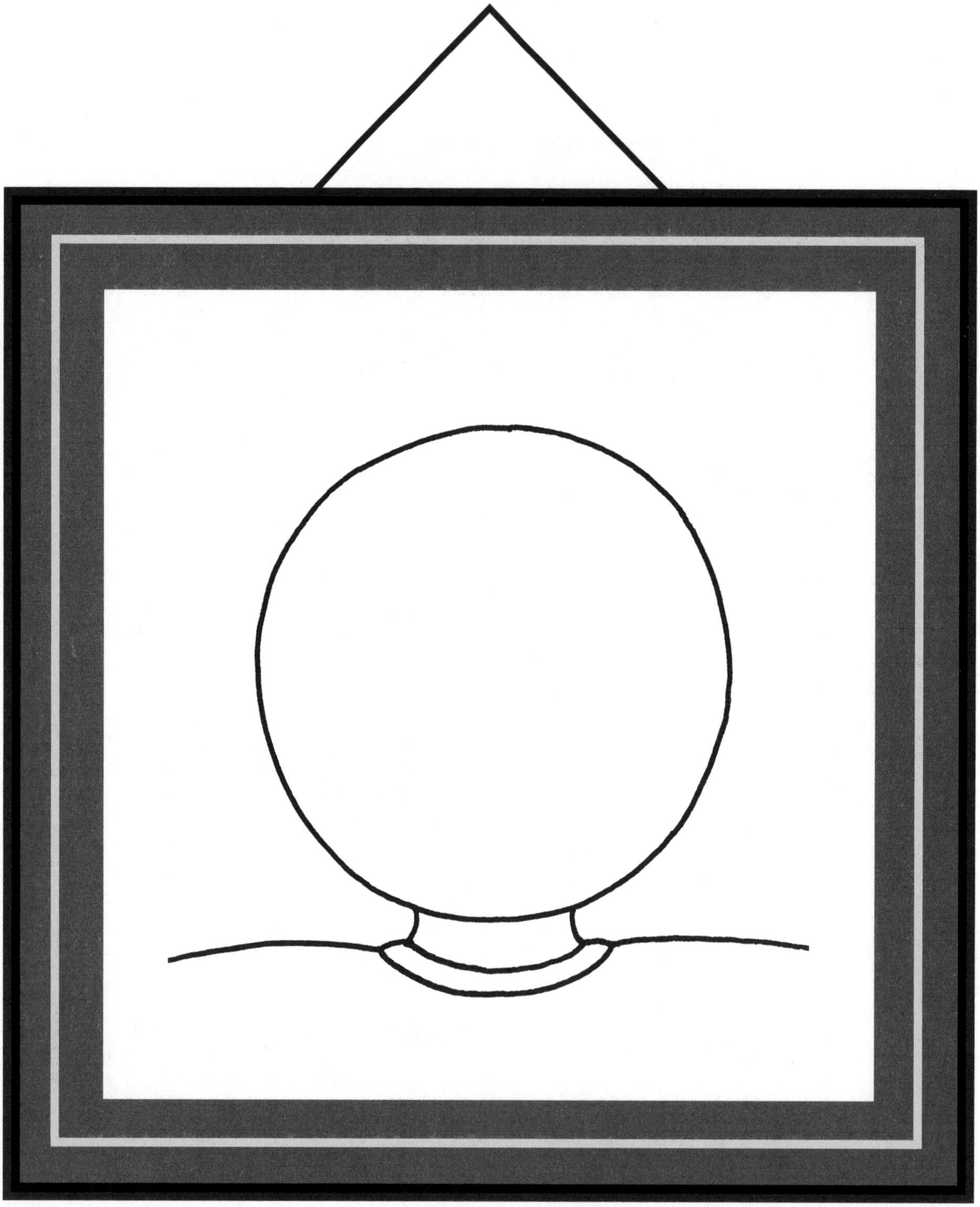

Help the ants carry the bread out of the maze.

Numbers

Solve the crossword. Use the Word Box and picture clues.

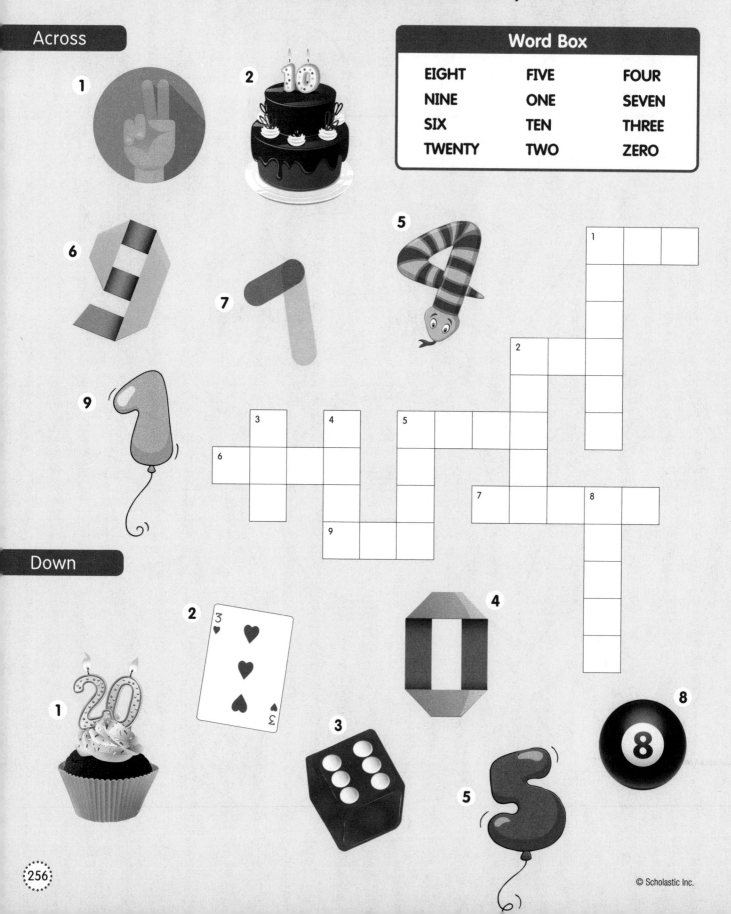

Across

1

2

Word Box

EIGHT	FIVE	FOUR
NINE	ONE	SEVEN
SIX	TEN	THREE
TWENTY	TWO	ZERO

6

7
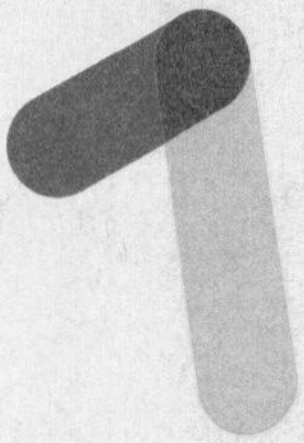

5

9
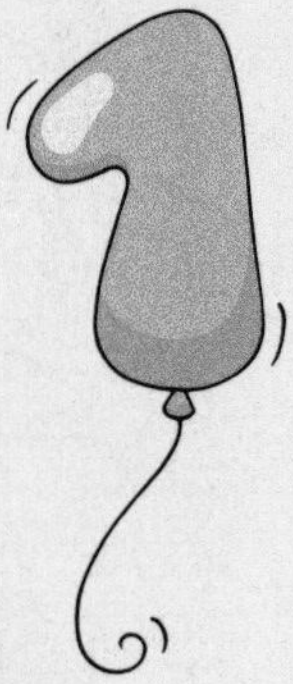

Down

2

4

1

3
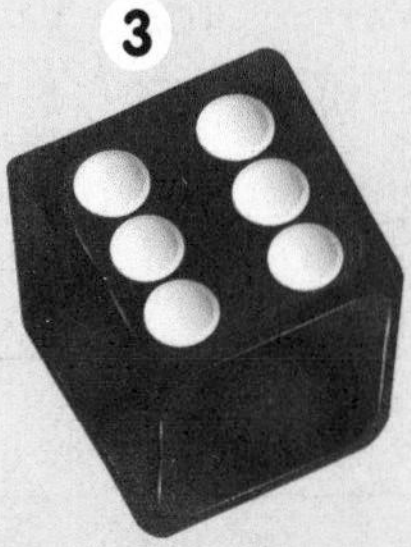

8

5
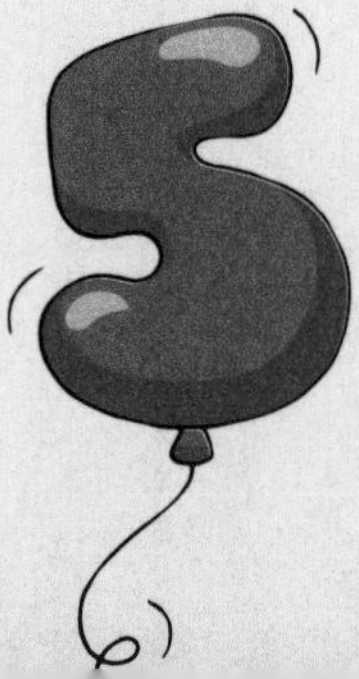

Connect the dots from A to Z. Then color the picture.

A
B
C
D
E
F
G
H
I
J
K
L
M
N
O
P
Q
R
S
T
U
V
W
X
Y
Z

Circle the two clocks that do not have a match.

Winter Scramble

Unscramble each word. To help you get started,
the first and last letter and some vowels are filled in.

LODC	C			D					
BEERECMD	D			E				R	
RFEYBARU	F	E			U			Y	
ZEGNERFI	F			E		I		G	
CEI	I		E						
YURANJA	J			U	A		Y		
WNOS	S			W					
SNFLOKEAW	S		O				A		E
ONSMAWN	S		O			A	N		

How many smaller words can you make using the letters in

magnificent?

1 ______________________

2 ______________________

3 ______________________

4 ______________________

5 ______________________

6 ______________________

7 ______________________

8 ______________________

9 ______________________

10 ______________________

11 ______________________

12 ______________________

13 ______________________

14 ______________________

15 ______________________

16 ______________________

17 ______________________

18 ______________________

19 ______________________

20 ______________________

21 ______________________

22 ______________________

23 ______________________

24 ______________________

25 ______________________

26 ______________________

27 ______________________

28 ______________________

29 ______________________

30 ______________________

magnificent (mag-NIF-i-sent) adj. – very impressive or beautiful

Subtract. Color the picture. Use the color key below.

51 − 40
92 − 70
86 − 11
64 − 14
86 − 32
39 − 20
89 − 23
65 − 34
99 − 24
64 − 30
99 − 10
98 − 12
85 − 60
89 − 67
76 − 35
79 − 32
78 − 50
48 − 25

If the difference is between	Color the space
1 and 30	yellow
31 and 60	blue
61 and 90	purple

Fill in the other spaces with colors of your choice.

THRILLING & AMAZING TOURS OF BORING
GUS
SR

Circle six differences.

THRILLING &
AMAZING
TOURS OF
BORING
GUS
SR

Buggy Creatures

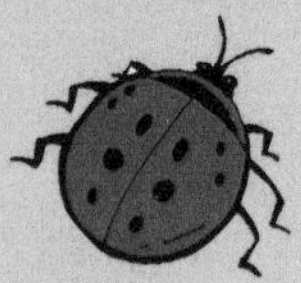

Find the words below in the puzzle.
Words are hidden →, ↓, ↘ and ↗.

ANT	BUTTERFLY	CATERPILLAR	CRICKET
GRASSHOPPER	HONEY BEE	LADYBUG	MOSQUITO
MOTH	PRAYING MANTIS	ROACH	WASP

F	J	C	N	M	O	S	Q	U	I	T	O	C
B	A	Z	L	A	D	Y	B	U	G	R	D	R
O	V	A	I	Z	H	B	D	G	W	Z	H	I
P	J	A	M	Y	S	U	T	P	F	C	A	C
P	L	A	O	E	T	L	I	Q	A	C	B	K
W	A	L	T	P	N	A	S	O	I	R	K	E
R	F	B	H	L	A	T	R	A	S	L	I	T
P	R	A	Y	I	N	G	M	A	N	T	I	S
C	A	T	E	R	P	I	L	L	A	R	U	T
Z	W	R	O	B	U	Z	X	J	D	Q	N	F
X	D	A	O	T	E	F	G	Z	C	A	J	H
A	C	S	S	I	I	P	Y	W	M	P	R	L
N	L	A	S	P	H	O	N	E	Y	B	E	E
B	U	T	T	E	R	F	L	Y	H	J	O	A
Z	K	G	R	A	S	S	H	O	P	P	E	R

What picture is missing?

Find the sticker on page 321. Add it to the pattern.

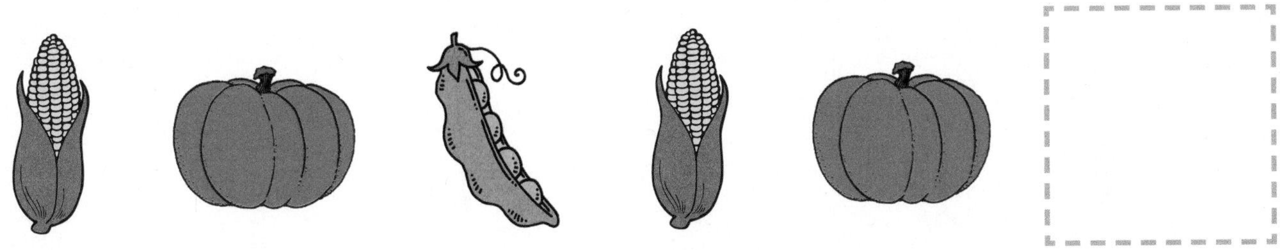

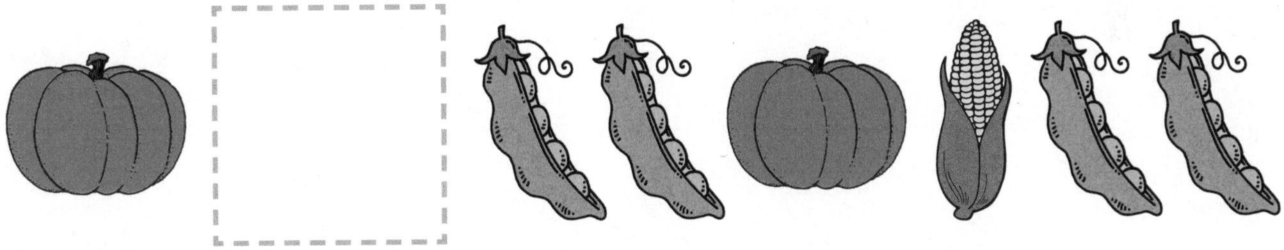

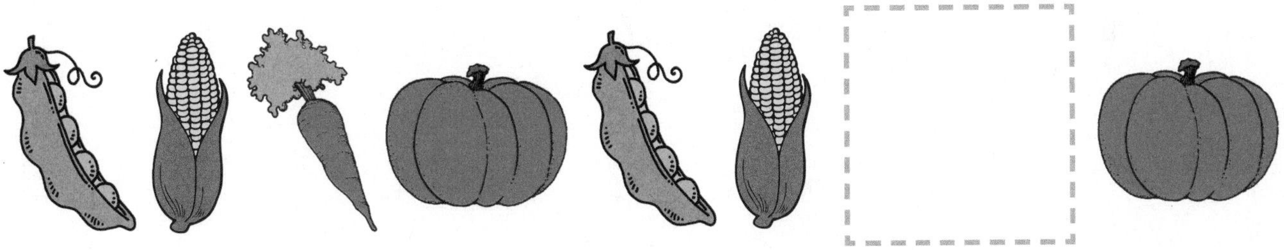

Draw your own pattern below.

Circle 10 pieces of litter.

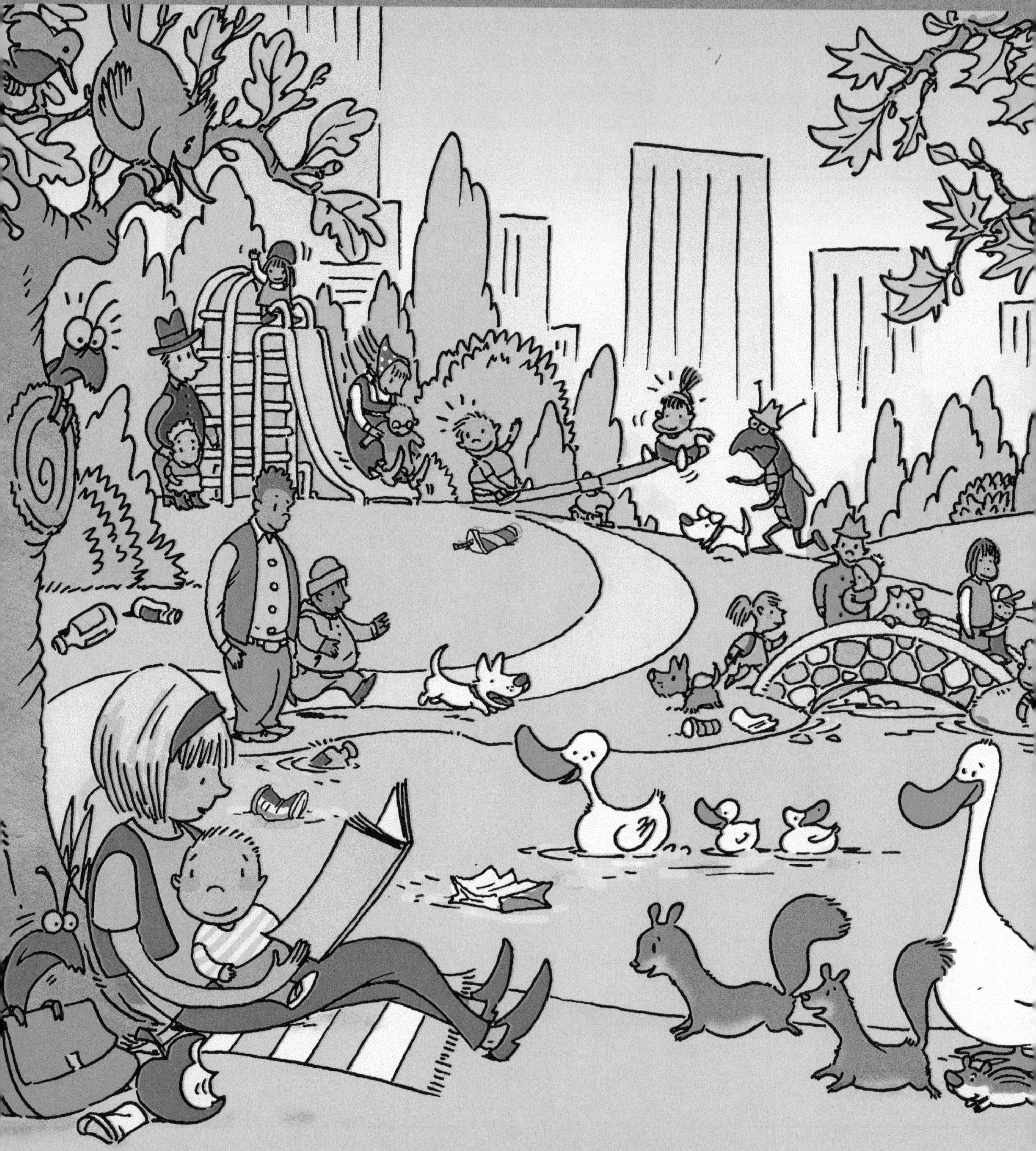

I'm Ready to Play!

Read the clues. Write the words.
Start at the bottom and climb to the top.

area of public land **change the last letter**

___ ___ ___ ___

a portion **change the third letter**

___ ___ ___ ___

to breathe hard and quickly **add a letter to the end**

___ ___ ___ ___

used to cook with **change the first letter**

___ ___ ___

synonym of *able to* **change the last letter**

___ ___ ___

worn at a game **change the first letter**

___ ___ ___

n a p

Color the picture. Use the color key.

If the word has the same vowel sound as	 **and** 	 **and** 
Color the space	yellow	blue

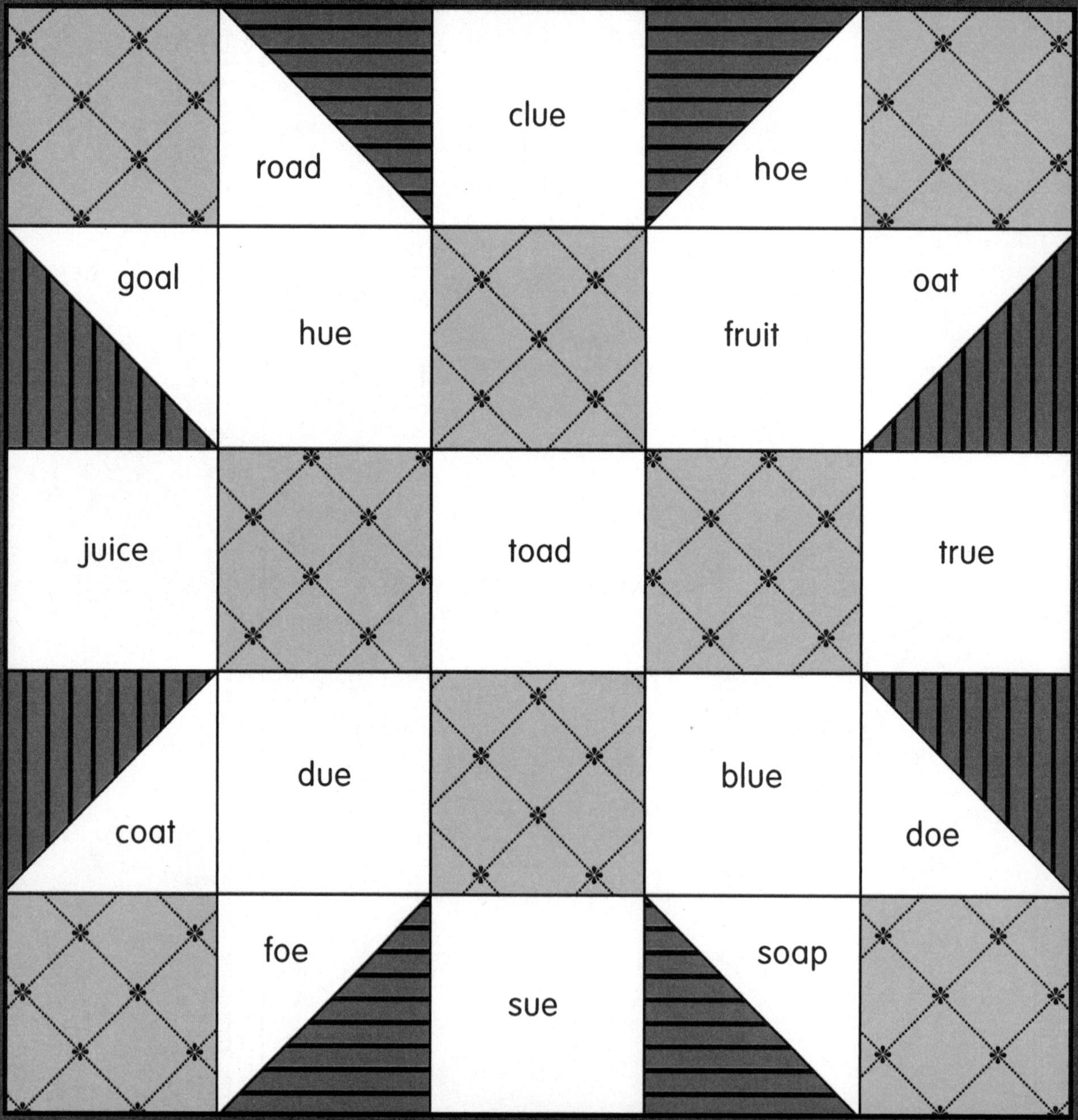

road
clue
hoe
goal
hue
fruit
oat
juice
toad
true
due
blue
coat
doe
foe
sue
soap

Skip count by 2 to connect the dots. Then color the picture.

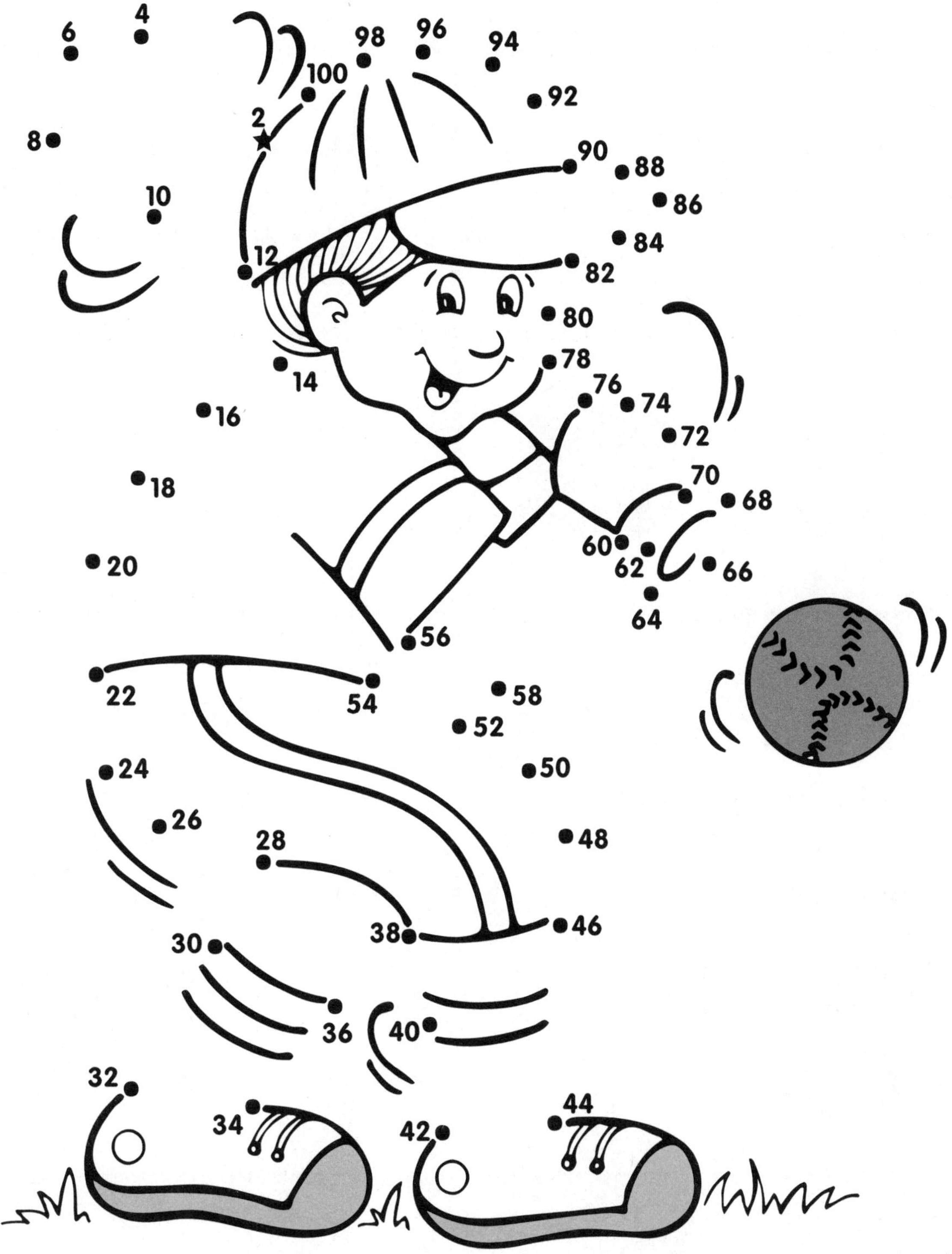

2
4
6
8
10
12
14
16
18
20
22
24
26
28
30
32
34
36
38
40
42
44
46
48
50
52
54
56
58
60
62
64
66
68
70
72
74
76
78
80
82
84
86
88
90
92
94
96
98
100

Draw fruit to complete the grid.
Each row, column, and minigrid should have one of each kind.

Read the riddle. The answer is written in code.
Use the decoder to solve the riddle.

DECODER
A B C D E F G H I J K L M
N O P Q R S T U V W X Y Z

What do you call an ant that lives with your great uncle?

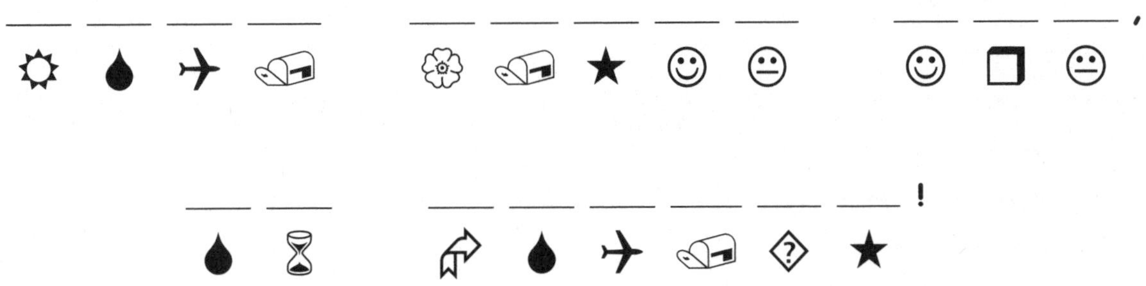

Gorillas

Read the story. Then solve the crossword.

Gorillas are the largest apes. They live in the rain forests of Africa. Every morning, they wake up and eat a breakfast of leaves, fruit, and bark. During most of the day, the adult gorillas take naps. Meanwhile, young gorillas play. They wrestle and chase each other. They swing on vines. When the adults wake up, everyone eats again. When there is danger, gorillas stand up on their hind legs, scream, and beat their chests. Every night before it gets dark, the gorillas build a new nest to sleep in. They break off leafy branches to make their beds, either on the ground or in the trees. Baby gorillas snuggle up to their mothers to sleep.

1
2
3
4
5
6
7
8

Across

1 **During the day, adult gorillas ______.**

3 **Gorillas eat leaves, bark, and ______.**

5 **The largest apes are ______.**

7 **When there's danger, gorillas beat their ______.**

8 **Young gorillas swing on ______.**

Down

2 **The continent where gorillas live is ______.**

4 **When young gorillas play, they ______ and chase each other.**

6 **Baby gorillas snuggle up to their mothers to ______.**

Subtract. Color the picture. Use the color key below.

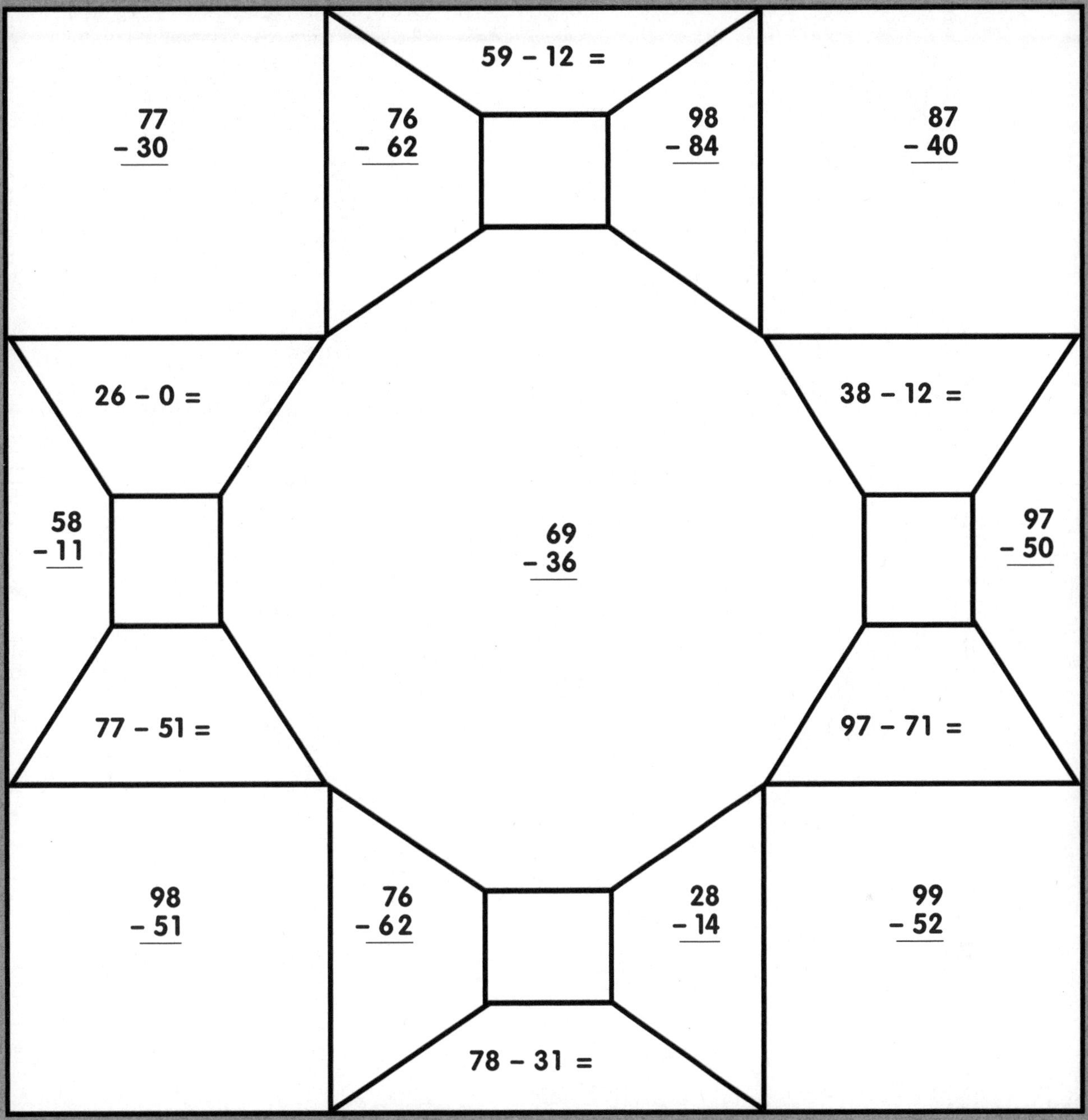
59 – 12 =
77 – 30
76 – 62
98 – 84
87 – 40
26 – 0 =
38 – 12 =
58 – 11
69 – 36
97 – 50
77 – 51 =
97 – 71 =
98 – 51
76 – 62
28 – 14
99 – 52
78 – 31 =

If the difference is	Color the space
14	red
26	purple
33	blue
47	yellow

Fill in the other spaces with colors of your choice.

LIVE CONCERT AT 8 O'CLOCK
BROCK'S FLOCK

Circle six differences.

LIVE CONCERT AT 8 O'CLOCK
BROCK'S FLOCK

© Scholastic Inc.

Help the bird find its nest.

Add the missing numbers, letters, or symbols to each pattern.

1. ZYX WVU _____ QPO _____ KJI HGF

2. ★ _____ ✜ ✜ ★ ★ ❍ ❍ ★ ★ ✜ ✜ ★ ★ _____ ❍

3. 5 20 35 _____ 65 80 95 110 125 _____

4. 12 24 36 48 60 _____ 84 96 _____ 120

5. ❍ ◆ ■ ★ ___ ◆ ■ ★ ❍ ◆ ___ ★ ❍ ◆ ■ ★

6. ac _____ gi jl mo _____ su vx

7. 2 4 6 10 16 _____ 42 _____ 110 178

8. ✔✔ ✖✖ ❑❑ _____ ✖✖ ❑❑ ✔✔ _____ ❑❑

Design a costume for this superhero.

Sudoku

The numbers 1 through 4 go in each row and in each column. The numbers can't be repeated in any row or column. Fill in the missing numbers in the puzzles below.

TIP

- Begin in a row or column in which only one number is missing.
- If you have a row in which two boxes are missing numbers, figure out which two numbers are missing in the row.
- Then look above and/or below to see which numbers won't repeat.
- If you have a column in which two boxes are missing numbers, figure out which two numbers are missing in the column.
- Then look to the right and/or the left to see which numbers won't be repeats.

Example

4	3	1	2
1	4	2	3
3	2	4	1
2	1	3	4

	1	2	3
3		1	
	4		2
2	3	4	

1		2	
	2	3	1
	1	4	
	4		3

2	1	4	
4			2
1			4
	4	2	

1	2		3
	4		
	1	3	
		1	2

Label each picture. Use the Word Box.
Match the pictures that use the same word.

Word Box			
FALL	SHAKE	TIE	WAVE

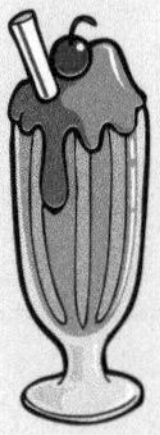

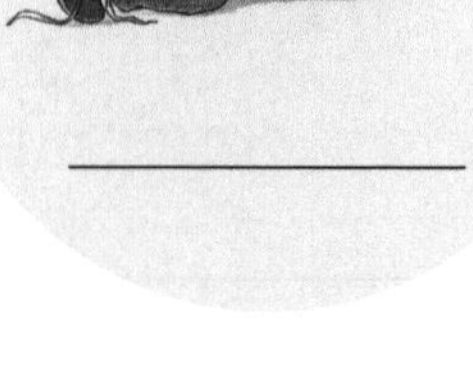

Color the picture. Use the color key.

If the word has the same vowel sound as	 and 	 and 
Color the space	purple	orange

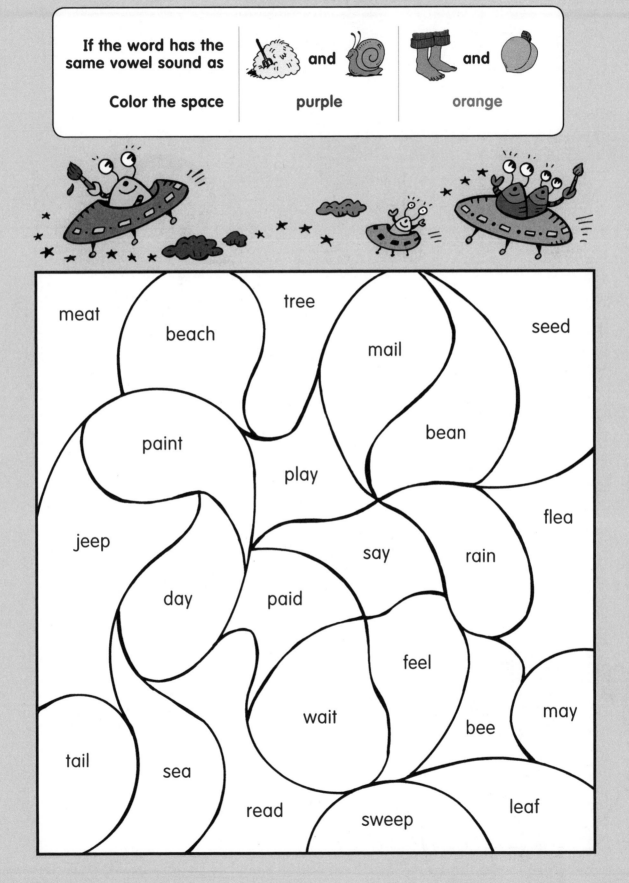

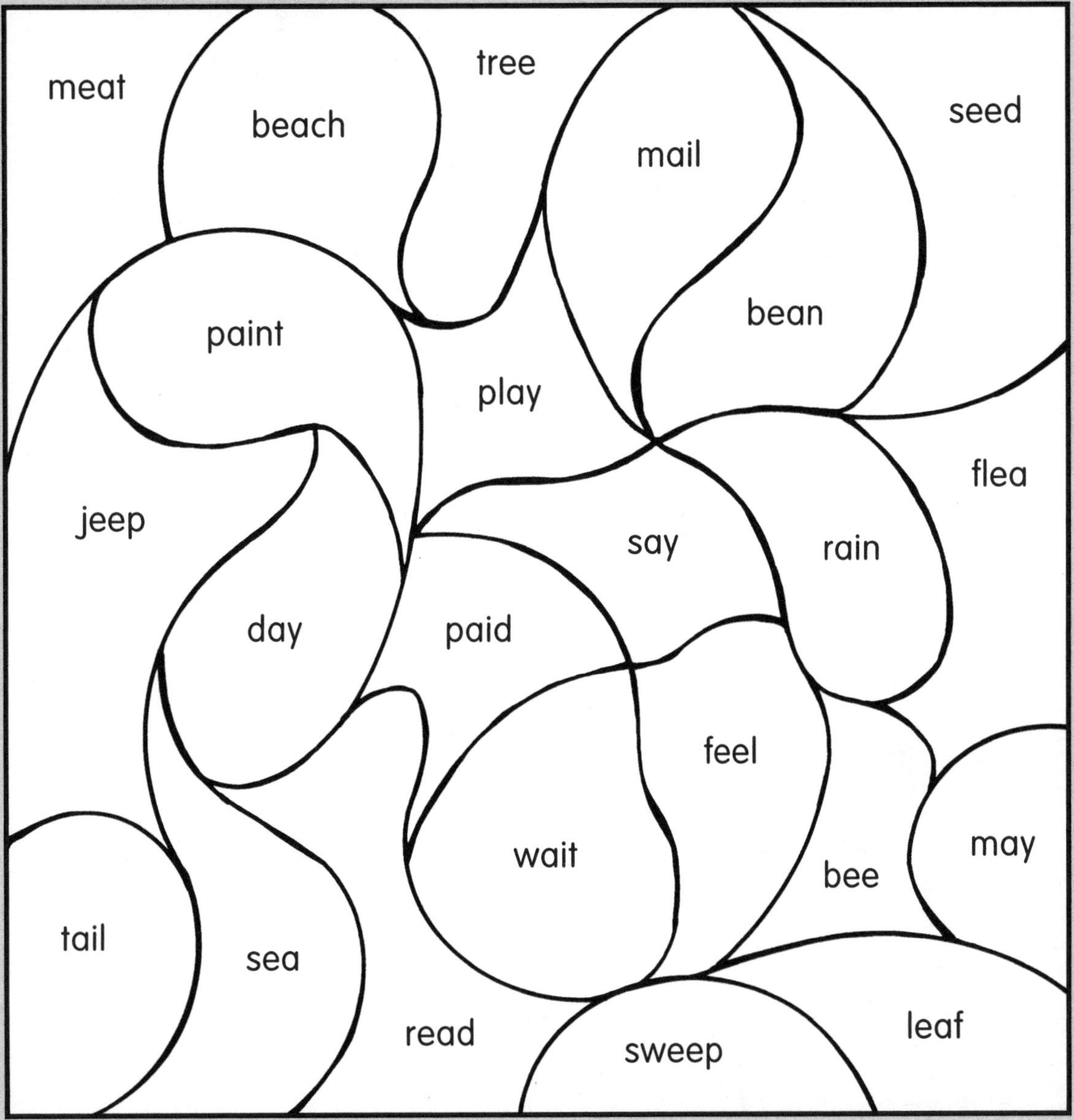
meat
beach
tree
mail
seed
bean
paint
play
jeep
flea
say
rain
day
paid
feel
wait
bee
may
tail
sea
read
sweep
leaf

Yesterday's Crossword

Solve the crossword.

Hint Each clue gives an action in the present tense. Each answer is the same action in the past tense.

Across

1 buy
3 bark
5 say
6 draw
9 drive
10 take
11 understand

Down

1 build
2 hear
3 break
4 ride
7 watch
8 cook

Change rain into hair. Use the picture clues and letter tiles. Start at the bottom and climb to the top.

n r d s h i t a

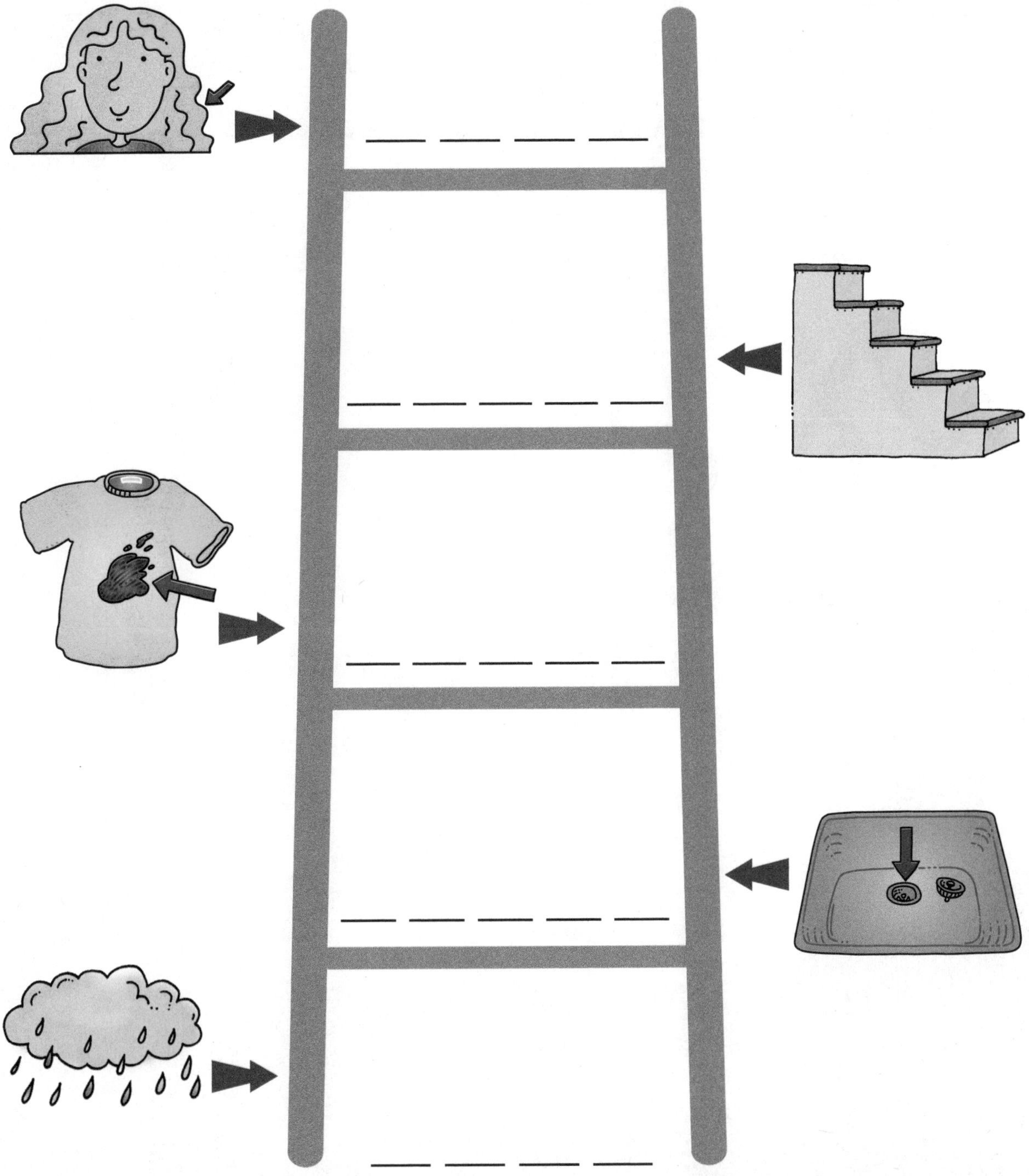

Help the rocket get to the moon.

Math Tic-Tac-Toe

Add or subtract. Draw a line through the three problems in a row with the same answer. The row can go →, ↓, ↘ or ↗.

13 + 22	50 − 25	18 + 2
35 − 4	9 + 22	53 − 22
12 + 18	44 − 16	33 + 16

49 − 18	18 + 36	42 − 9
56 + 33	120 − 20	19 + 14
25 − 19	72 + 16	65 − 32

92 − 16	56 + 5	88 − 25
63 + 22	88 − 12	65 + 15
49 + 15	22 − 18	52 + 24

49 + 18	62 − 18	77 + 23
68 + 25	95 − 51	82 + 8
95 − 62	17 + 27	58 − 14

Out in Space

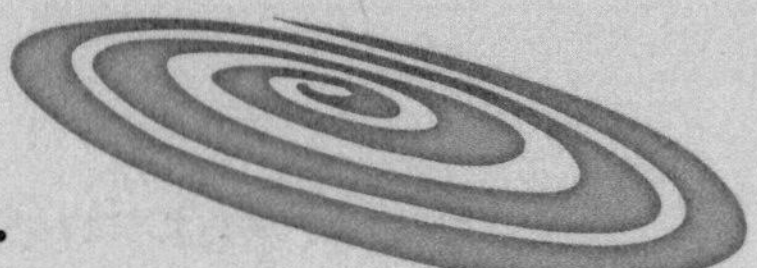

**Find the words below in the puzzle.
Words are hidden → and ↓.**

ASTEROID	BLACK HOLE	COMET	EARTH
GALAXY	METEOR	MOON	NEBULA
ORBIT	PLANET	STAR	SUN

C	B	C	O	Z	W	T	A	Y	D
L	P	T	S	N	R	D	M	N	B
Z	N	X	M	E	T	E	O	R	L
F	E	A	R	T	H	P	O	A	A
O	B	U	S	U	N	M	N	S	C
R	U	G	J	C	O	M	E	T	K
B	L	P	L	A	N	E	T	E	H
I	A	R	Z	S	L	X	U	R	O
T	M	I	A	T	V	B	N	O	L
C	G	A	L	A	X	Y	L	I	E
O	H	T	F	R	Q	K	H	D	J

Connect the dots from 50 to 120. Then color the picture.

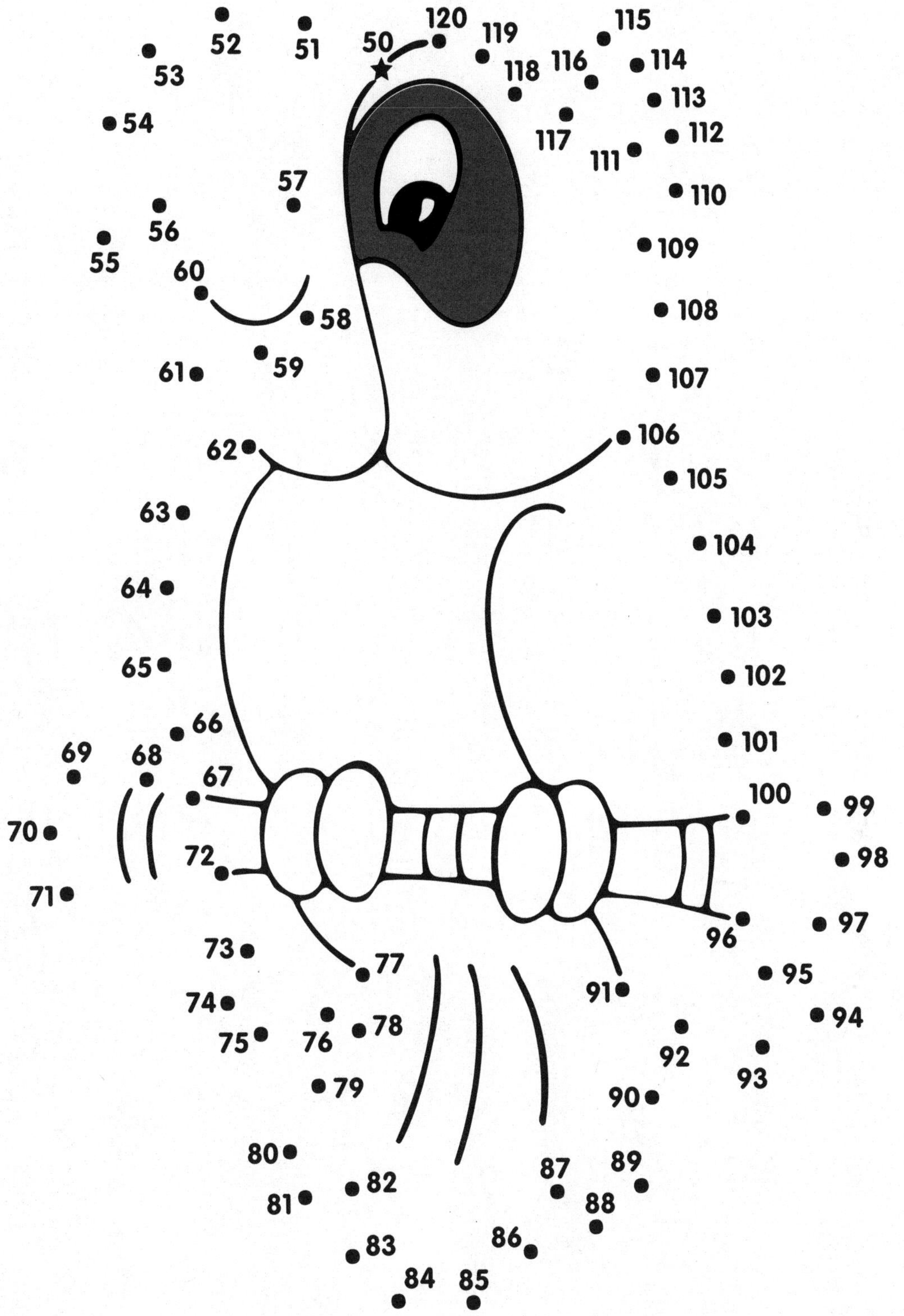
50
51
52
53
54
55
56
57
58
59
60
61
62
63
64
65
66
67
68
69
70
71
72
73
74
75
76
77
78
79
80
81
82
83
84
85
86
87
88
89
90
91
92
93
94
95
96
97
98
99
100
101
102
103
104
105
106
107
108
109
110
111
112
113
114
115
116
117
118
119
120

OPPOSITE
DOGGIE
TREATS

Circle six differences.

DOGGIE
TREATS

Time to Study!

Read the clues. Write the words.
Start at the bottom and climb to the top.

synonym
of *exam*
change the first letter

better than
the rest
change the third letter

worn around
the waist
change the vowel

a flash
of lightning
change the second vowel

keeps foot
warm in snow
change the last letter

b o o k

SPACE

Find each letter and number pair on the graph. Draw a star for each. The first one has been done for you.

1. (F, 10)
2. (G, 2)
3. (B, 9)
4. (A, 4)
5. (D, 8)
6. (G, 6)
7. (I, 9)
8. (K, 11)
9. (D, 5)
10. (C, 1)
11. (J, 5)
12. (K, 2)

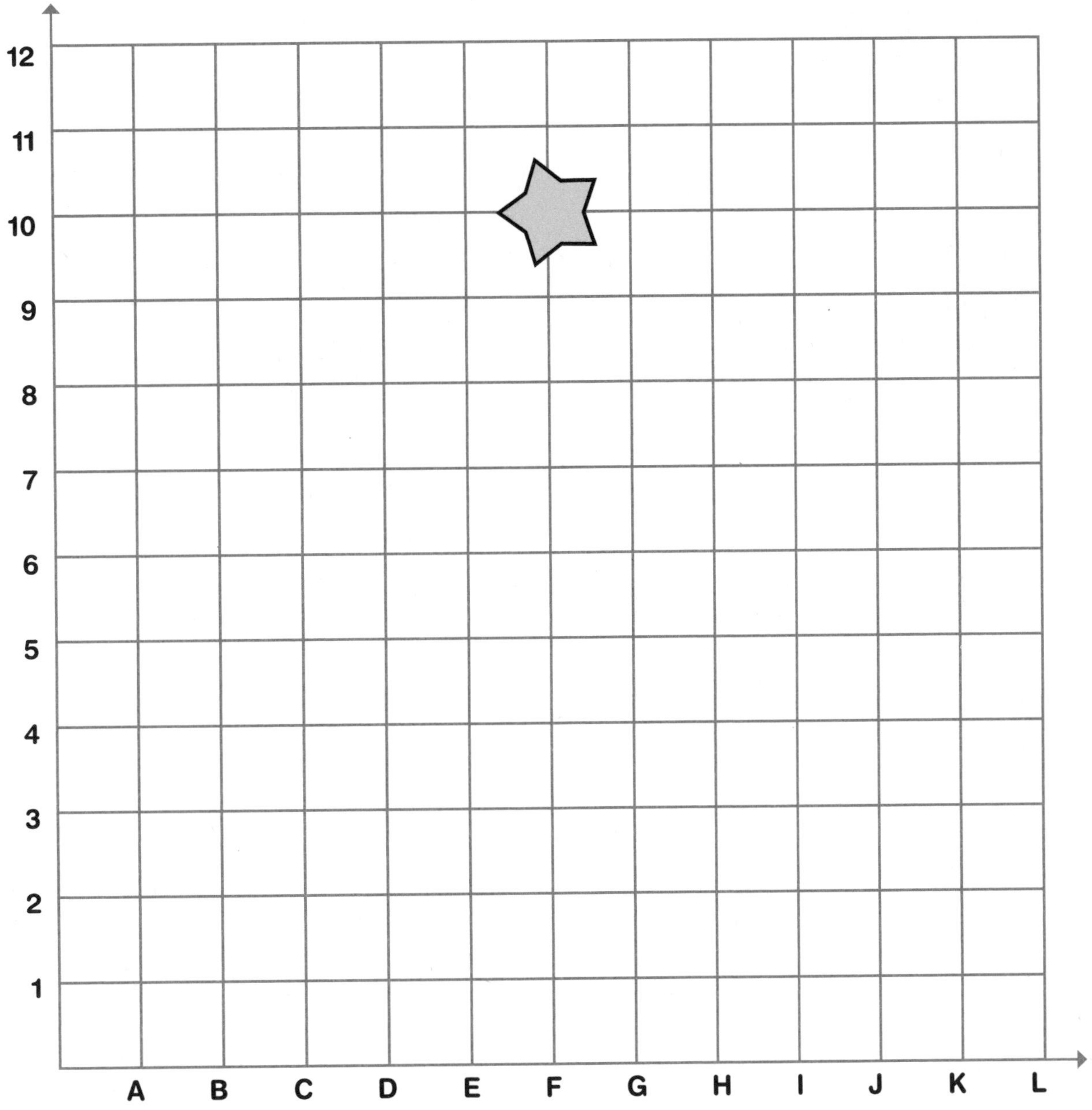

12
11
10
9
8
7
6
5
4
3
2
1
A
B
C
D
E
F
G
H
I
J
K
L

Read the riddle. The answer is written in code.
Use the decoder to solve the riddle.

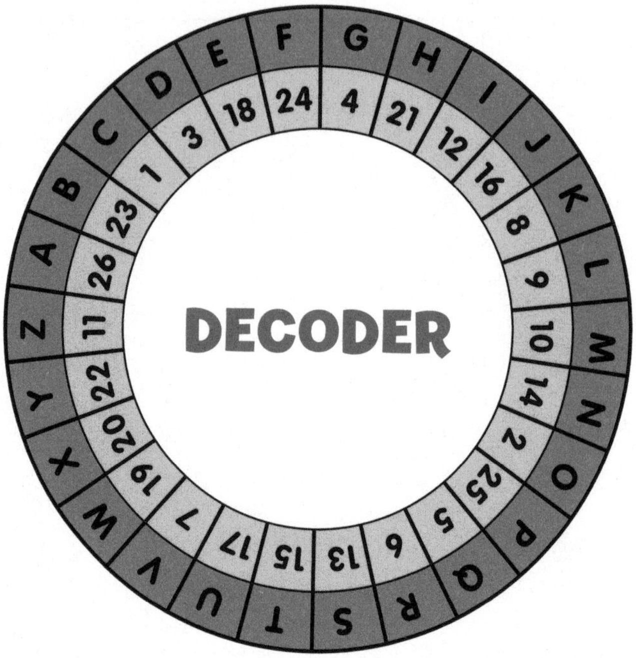
DECODER
A 26
B 23
C 1
D 3
E 18
F 24
G 4
H 21
I 12
J 16
K 8
L 9
M 10
N 14
O 2
P 25
Q 5
R 6
S 13
T 15
U 17
V 7
W 19
X 20
Y 22
Z 11

What is black and white and red all over?

___   ___ ___ ___ ___   ___ ___ ___ ___ ___ ___ ___ ___ ___ ___ ___

26   7 18 6 22   18 10 23 26 6 6 26 13 13 18 3

___ ___ ___ ___ ___ !

11 18 23 6 26

Places Everyone!

Solve the crossword.

Hint The place value clues may not go in order from highest to lowest place.

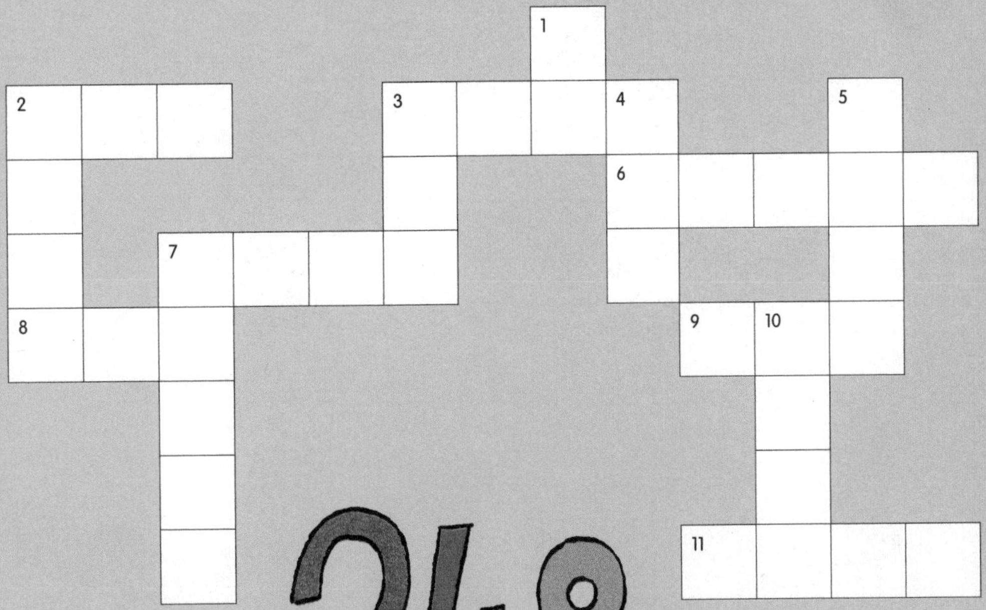
1
2
3
4
5
6
7
8
9
10
11

Across

2 seven hundreds, five tens, and six ones

3 three thousands, nine tens, zero hundreds, and nine ones

6 sixty thousands, two tens, seven ones, and five hundreds

7 six hundreds, seven thousands, two tens, and nine ones

8 zero ones, five hundreds, and one ten

9 five hundreds, seven tens, and eight ones

11 zero hundreds, two ones, six tens, and five thousands

Down

1 nine ones and eight tens

2 seven thousands, three hundreds, four tens, and five ones

3 nine ones, three hundreds, and two tens

4 nine hundreds, six tens, and zero ones

5 two hundreds, eight ones, six tens, and one thousand

7 seventy thousands, four ones, eight hundreds, and six tens

10 zero ones, zero hundreds, seven thousands, and seven tens

Find and circle each item in the big picture.

Sunscreen
SPF
50
waterproof

Sea Creatures
Sunscreen
SPF
50
waterproof

Riddle Fun

Read the riddle. Use the clues on the horse to find the answers. Write the letters on the lines above the matching numbers.

What kind of food does a racehorse like to eat?

___ ___ ___ ___   ___ ___ ___ ___

11 5 10 3   11 9 9 2

What does a rose sleep in at night?

___ ___ ___ ___ ___ ___   ___ ___ ___

11 1 9 4 8 7   6 8 2

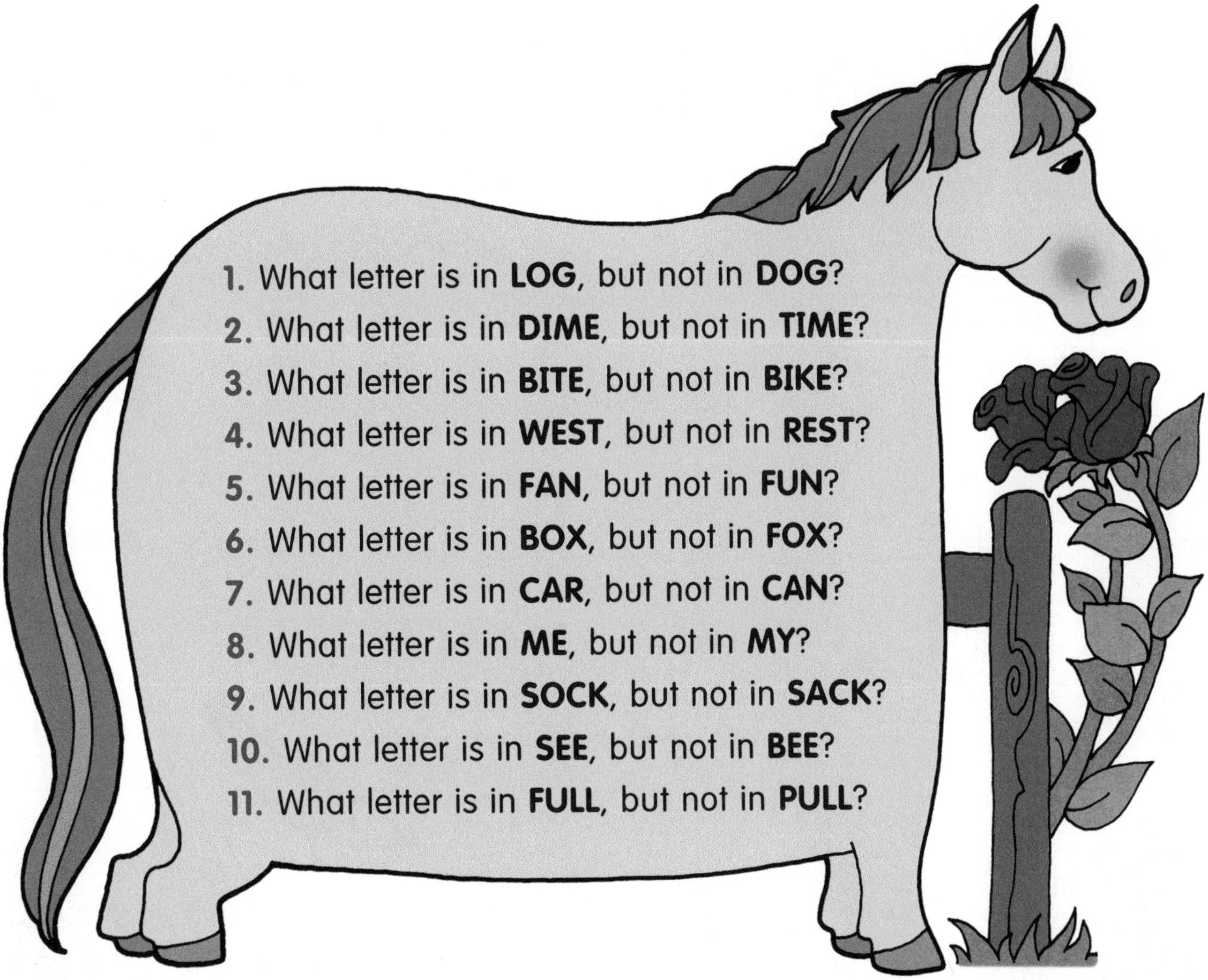

1. What letter is in **LOG**, but not in **DOG**?
2. What letter is in **DIME**, but not in **TIME**?
3. What letter is in **BITE**, but not in **BIKE**?
4. What letter is in **WEST**, but not in **REST**?
5. What letter is in **FAN**, but not in **FUN**?
6. What letter is in **BOX**, but not in **FOX**?
7. What letter is in **CAR**, but not in **CAN**?
8. What letter is in **ME**, but not in **MY**?
9. What letter is in **SOCK**, but not in **SACK**?
10. What letter is in **SEE**, but not in **BEE**?
11. What letter is in **FULL**, but not in **PULL**?

Draw the submarine of the future.

Color the picture. Use the color key.

If the word begins with a blend like the one in				
Color the space	**red**	**green**	**blue**	**yellow**

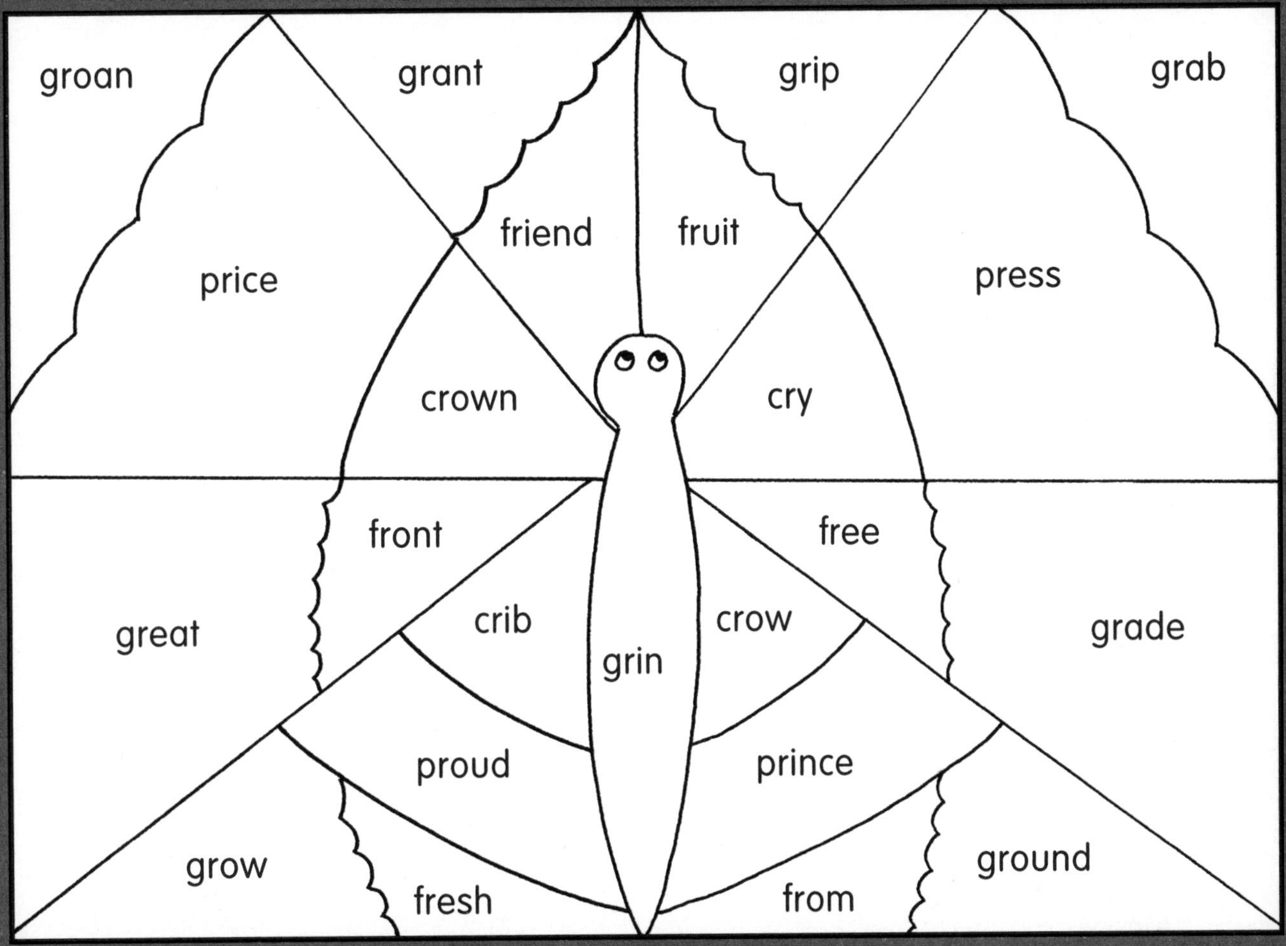
groan
grant
grip
grab
friend
fruit
price
press
crown
cry
front
free
great
crib
crow
grade
grin
proud
prince
grow
fresh
from
ground

How many smaller words can you make using the letters in

metamorphosis?

1 ____________________
2 ____________________
3 ____________________
4 ____________________
5 ____________________
6 ____________________
7 ____________________
8 ____________________
9 ____________________
10 ____________________
11 ____________________
12 ____________________
13 ____________________
14 ____________________
15 ____________________
16 ____________________
17 ____________________
18 ____________________
19 ____________________
20 ____________________
21 ____________________
22 ____________________
23 ____________________
24 ____________________
25 ____________________
26 ____________________
27 ____________________
28 ____________________
29 ____________________
30 ____________________

metamorphosis (met-uh-MOR-fuh-siss) adj. – the series of changes some animals go through as they develop from eggs to adults

Help the bee find the center of the flower.

The West Scramble

Unscramble the name of each state.

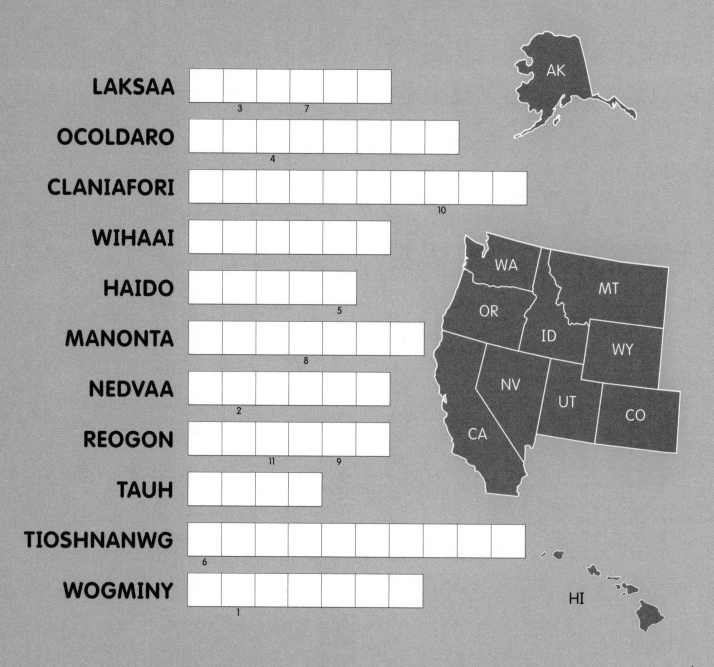

Scrambled word	Numbered cells
LAKSAA	3, 7
OCOLDARO	4
CLANIAFORI	10
WIHAAI	
HAIDO	5
MANONTA	8
NEDVAA	2
REOGON	11, 9
TAUH	
TIOSHNANWG	6
WOGMINY	1

AK

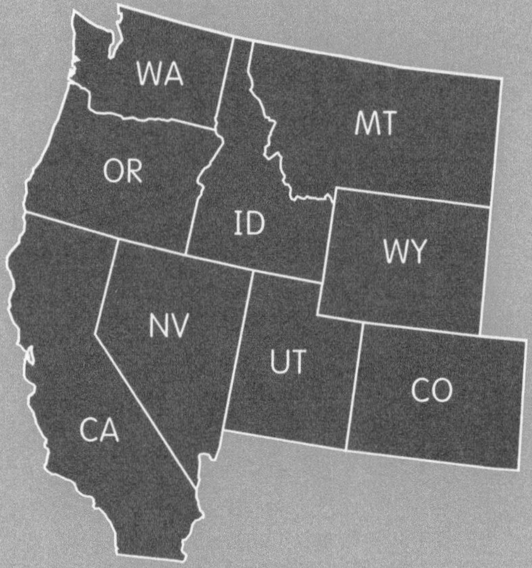
WA
MT
OR
ID
WY
NV
UT
CO
CA

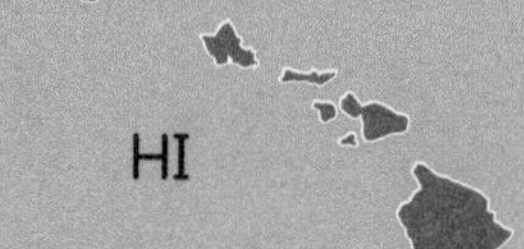
HI

Copy the letters in the numbered cells to answer the question.

Which was America's first National Park?

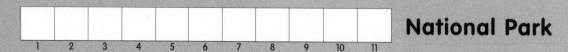

1 2 3 4 5 6 7 8 9 10 11 **National Park**

Skip count by 5 to connect the dots. Then color the picture.

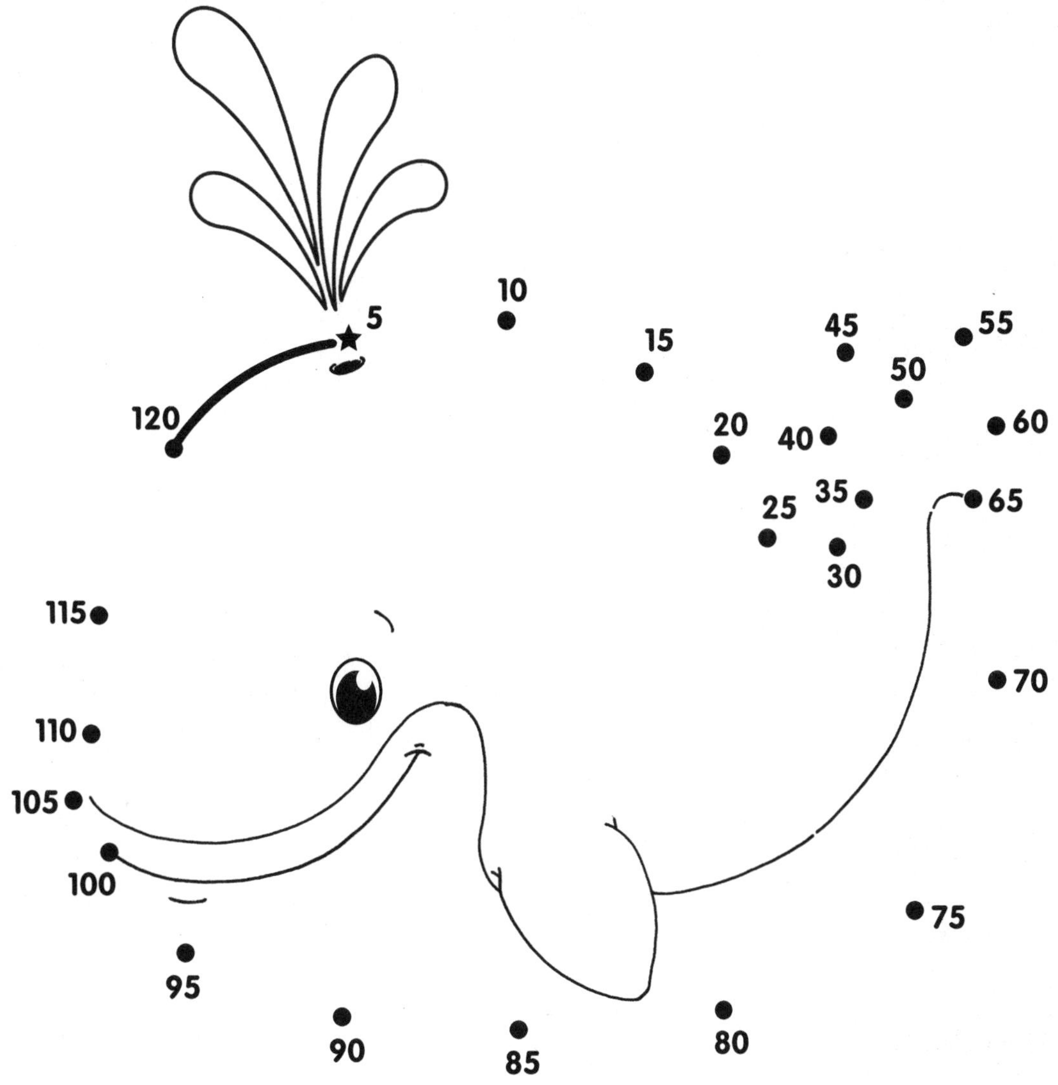
5
10
15
20
25
30
35
40
45
50
55
60
65
70
75
80
85
90
95
100
105
110
115
120

These are the things I like to think about . . .

What picture is missing?
Find the sticker on page 321. Add it to the pattern.

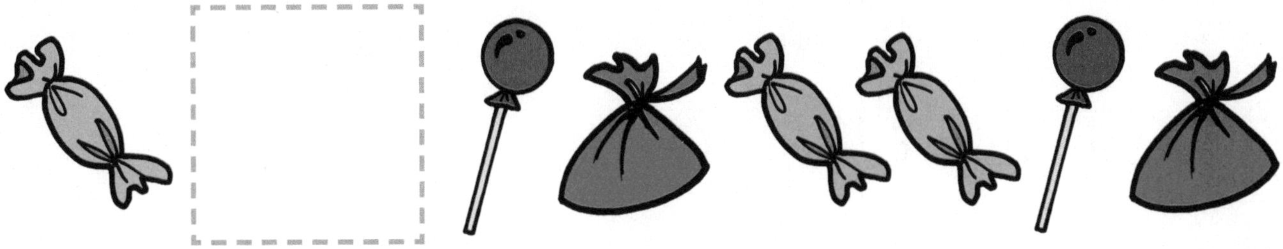

Draw your own pattern below.

We Like to Read

Find the words below in the puzzle.
Words are hidden → and ↓.

ADVENTURE	ANIMALS	BIOGRAPHY	COMICS
FABLE	FANTASY	FICTION	HUMOR
MAGAZINES	NONFICTION	SCI FI	SPORTS

B	I	O	G	R	A	P	H	Y	F
R	F	A	B	L	E	A	M	J	I
P	A	I	M	P	P	D	A	Y	C
W	H	T	F	C	A	V	G	L	T
F	U	B	V	O	A	E	A	S	I
A	M	W	K	M	S	N	Z	P	O
N	O	N	F	I	C	T	I	O	N
T	R	O	S	C	T	U	N	R	U
A	V	L	D	S	A	R	E	T	J
S	C	I	F	I	D	E	S	S	P
Y	A	N	I	M	A	L	S	W	Z

Can You Tell the Difference?

Read the clues. Write the words.
Start at the bottom and climb to the top.

___ ___ ___ ___

not real
change the first letter

opposite of *give*
change the third letter

___ ___ ___ ___

___ ___ ___ ___

synonym of *story*
change the last letter

opposite of *short*
change the vowel

___ ___ ___ ___

___ ___ ___ ___

present tense of *told*
change the first letter

to offer something for sale
change the second vowel

___ ___ ___ ___

___ ___ ___ ___

to close something firmly
change the first letter

r e a l

Circle the two chairs that do not have a match.

Help the girl find the treasure chest.

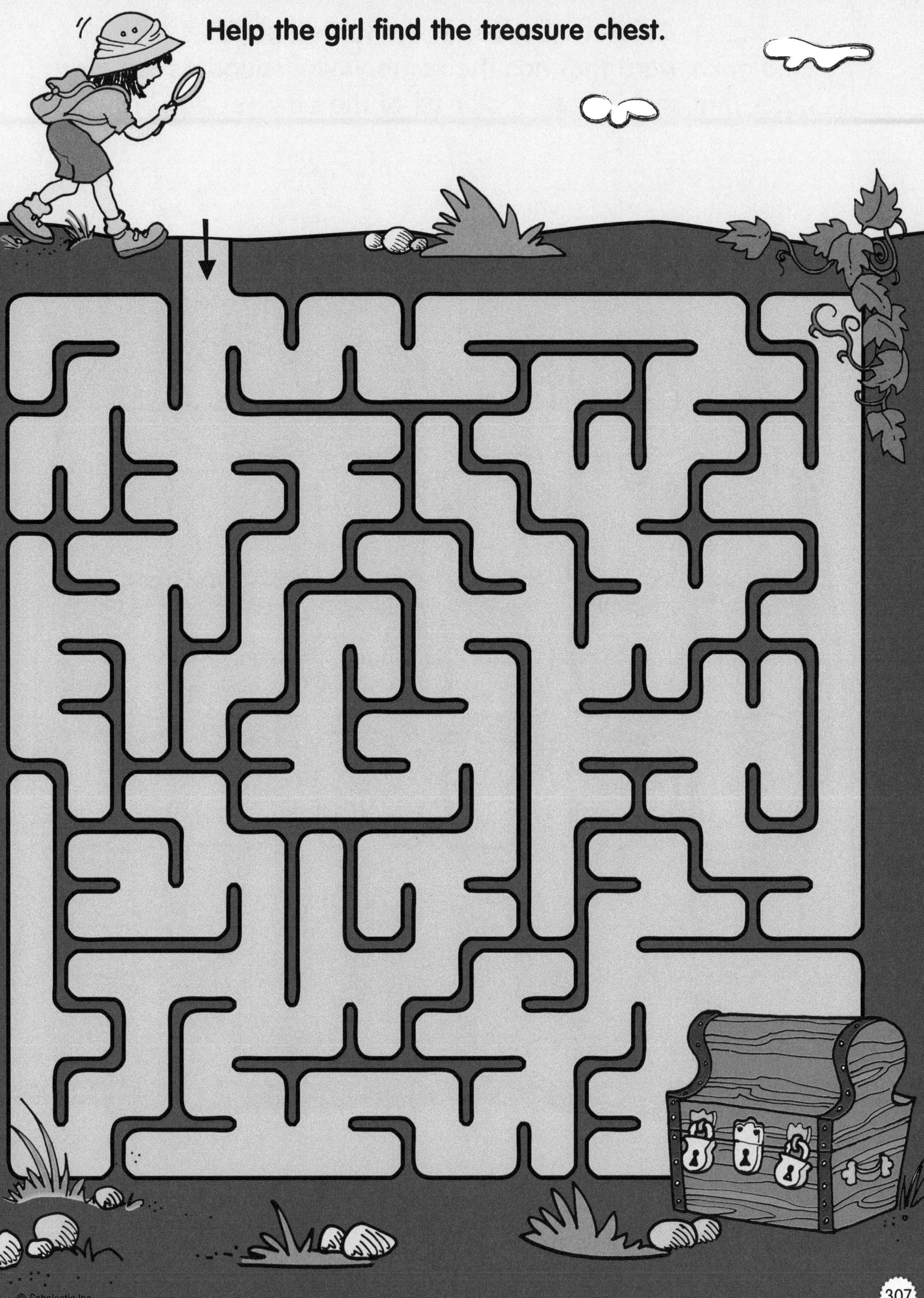

Color the scales on the turtle's shell.
Find each word that has the same vowel sound as *square*
Color that scale green. Color all of the other scales brown.

pear
dart
chair
spare
shark
care
dare
hard
pair
wear
swear
stair
mark
hair
far
air
harm
stare
bear
scare
flare
share
fair
card

Draw shapes to complete the grid.
Each row, column, and minigrid should have one of each shape.

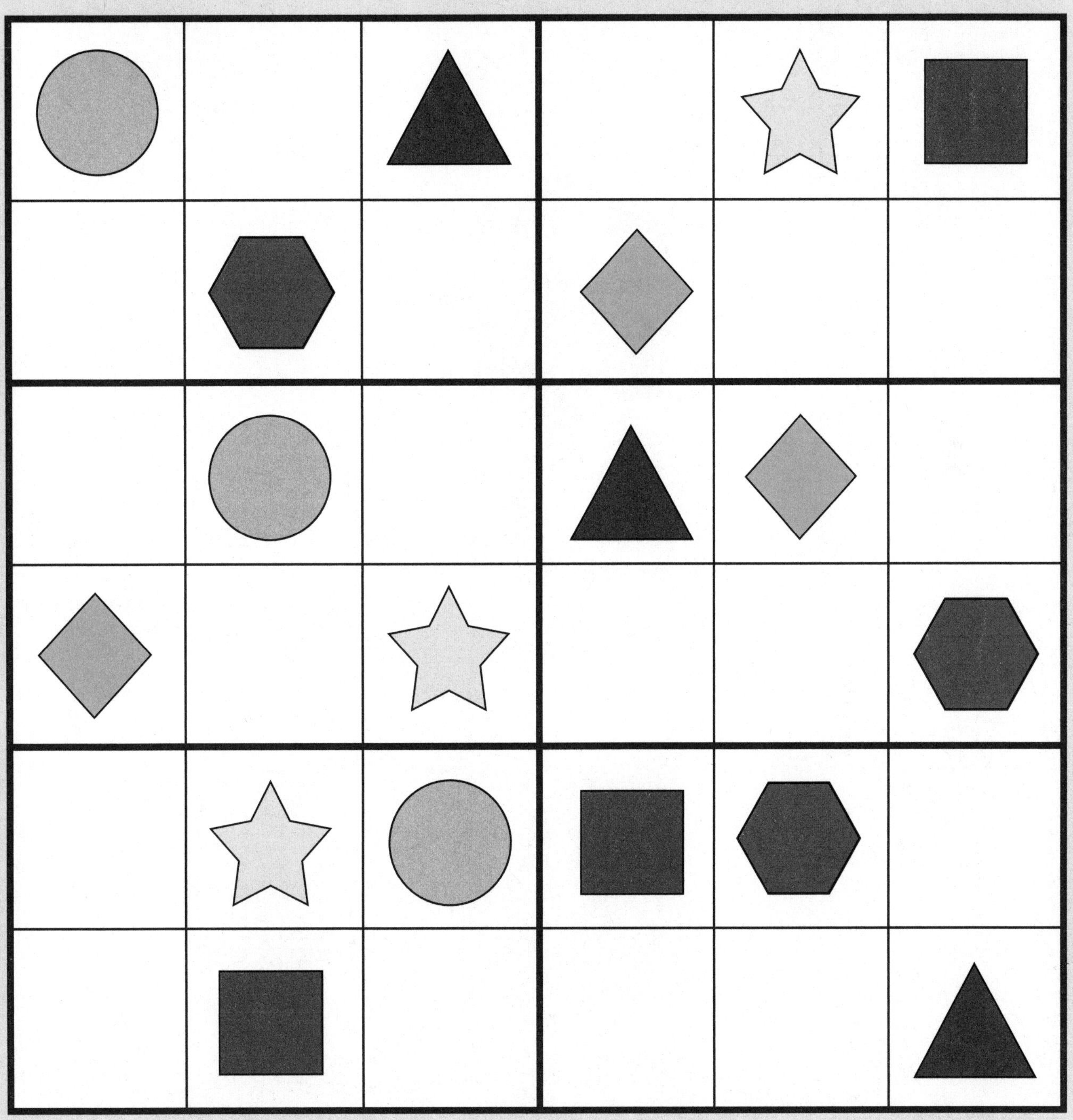

ANSWER KEY

For pages not listed, please check your child's work.

p. 7

Because you might step in a poodle!

p. 9

p. 10

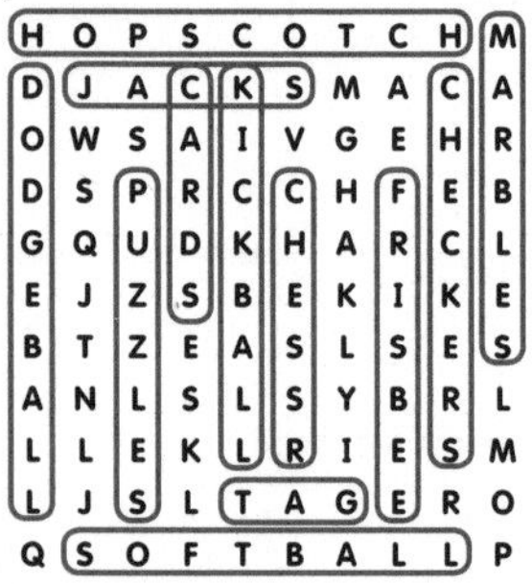

p. 11

The scarecrows are in the first row on the left and the last row on the right.

p. 12

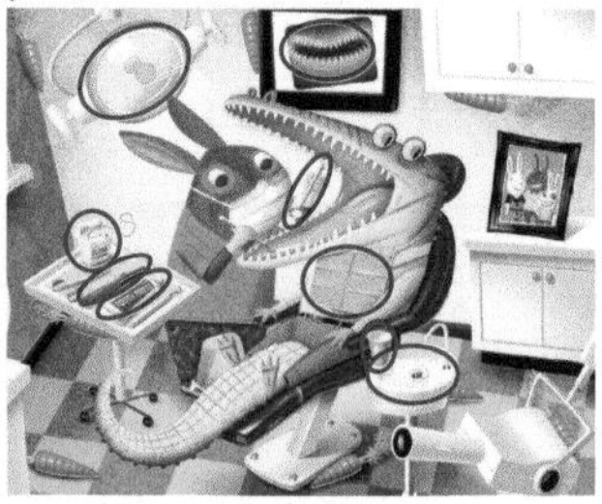

There are 8 hidden carrots.

p. 13

Sample answers: even, ever, germ, go, gone, got, green, meet, men, met, more, move, net, none, not, note, on, one, or, oven, over, rent, teen, ten, to, toe, ton, tree, vote, voter

p. 15

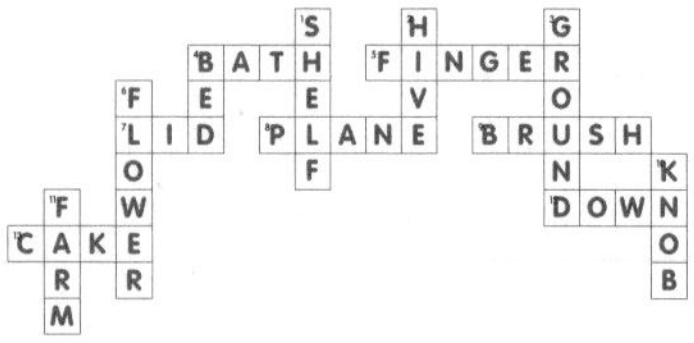

p. 17

fan, man, mat, bat, cat, cap

p. 18

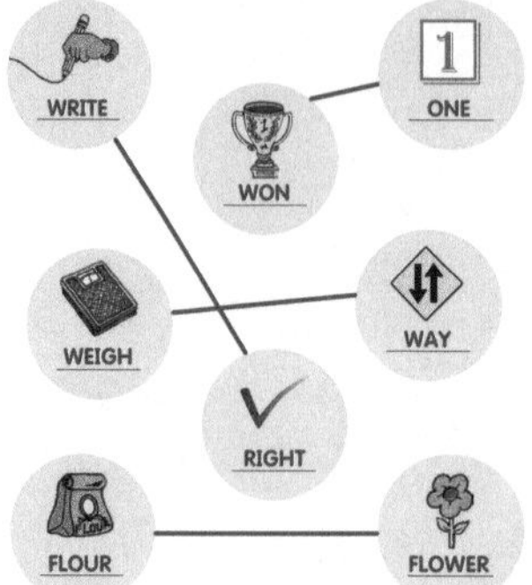
WRITE
ONE
WON
WEIGH
WAY
RIGHT
FLOUR
FLOWER

p. 19

p. 24

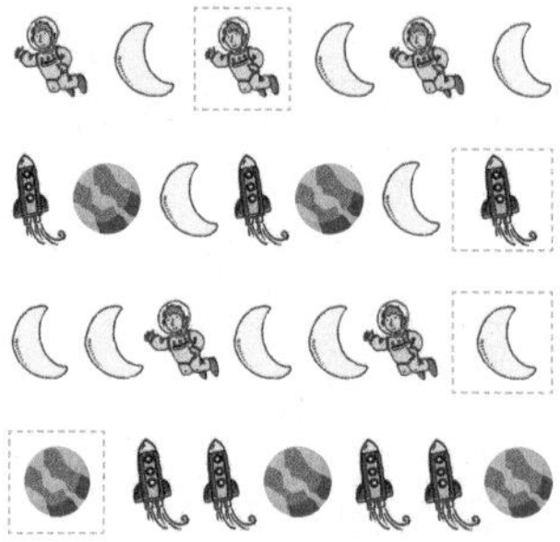

p. 25

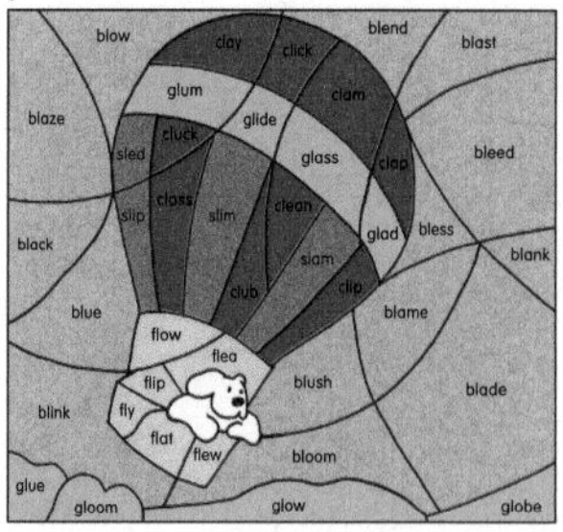

p. 26

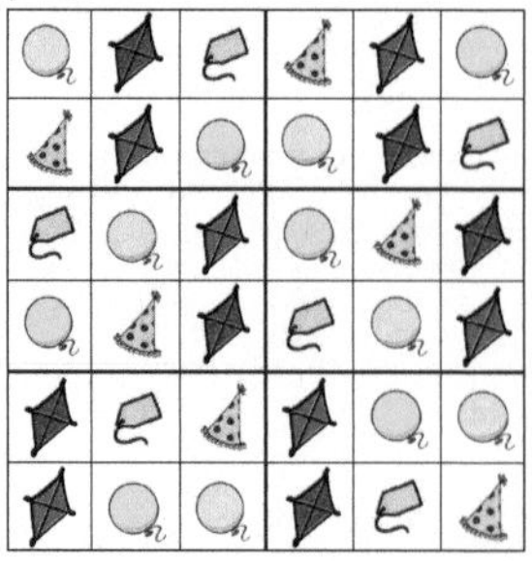

p. 27

"Polly want a quacker!"

p. 28

man, pan, pane, pine, pie

p. 29

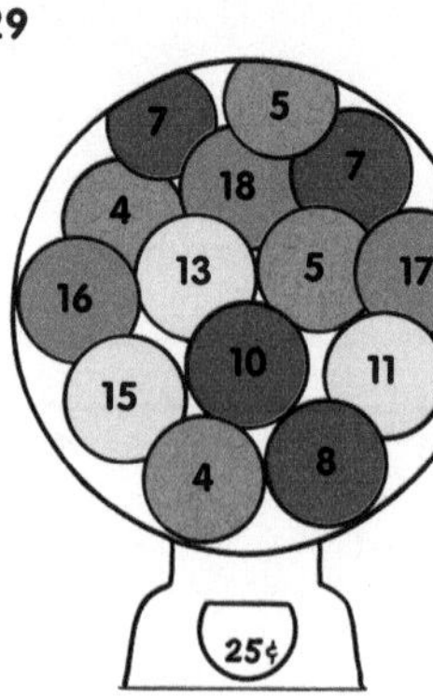

p. 30

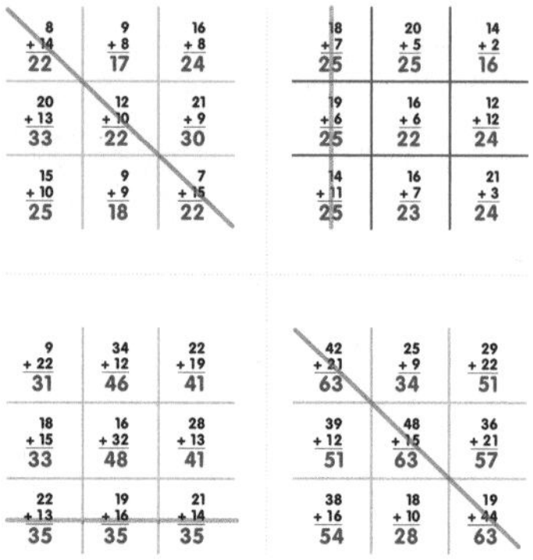

p. 32

Delaware, Maryland, New Jersey, New York, Pennsylvania; Washington D.C.

p. 34

The monsters are in the first row on the left and the second row on the right.

p. 35

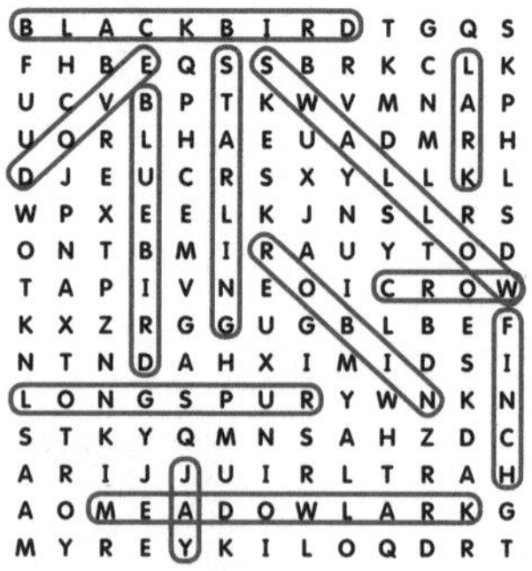

p. 36

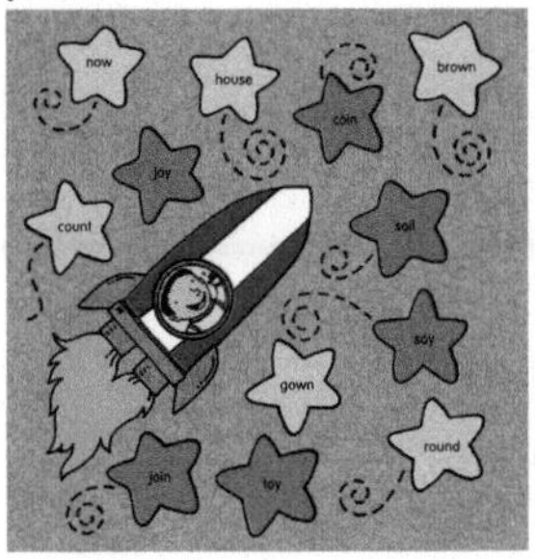

p. 37

Sample answers: acorn, action, air, ant, any, art, can, candy, cat, city, coat, coin, crayon, cry, day, diary, dirty, dot, dry, into, not, rain, rat, toad, today, toy, train, tray, try, yard

p. 39

p. 41

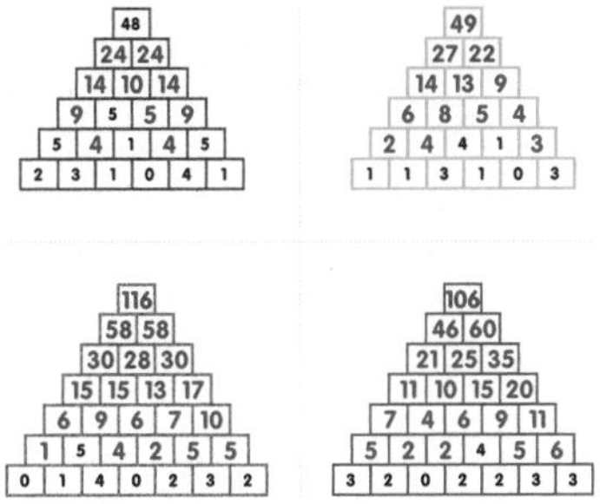

p. 42

p. 43

fall, tall, toll, told, cold

p. 44

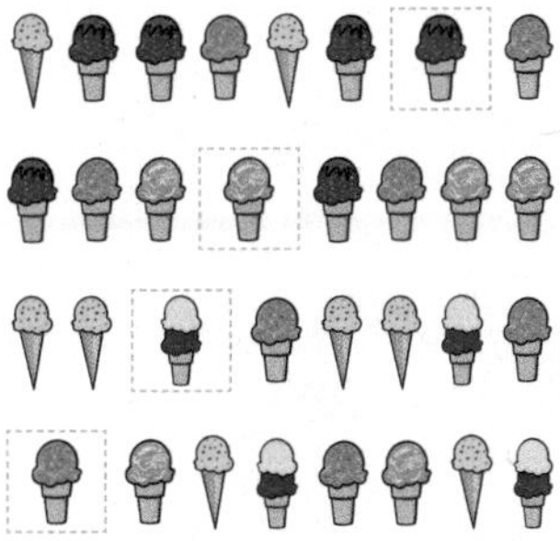

p. 45

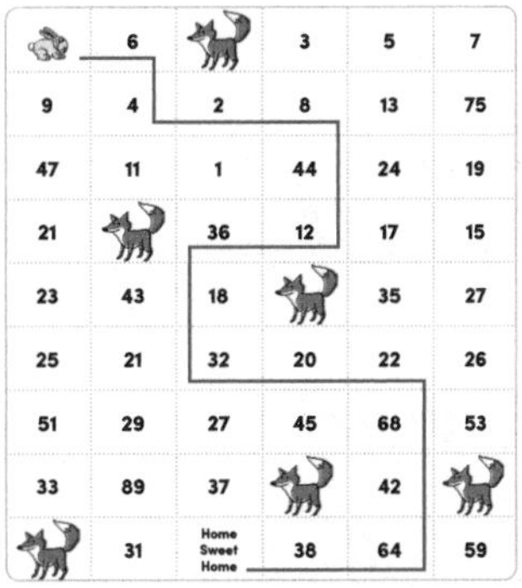

p. 46

p. 47

wig, pig, pill, bill, bell

p. 50

butterfly, caterpillar, flowers, grass, kite, ladybug, rainbow, umbrella, rain

p. 52

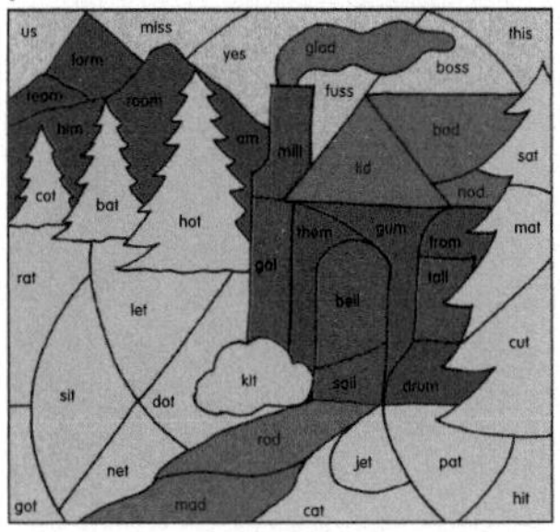

p. 53

1. 50, 2. 33, 3. 4, 4. 8, 5. 60, 6. 3, A. 3, B. 33, C. 60, D. 50, E. 8, F. 4

p. 55

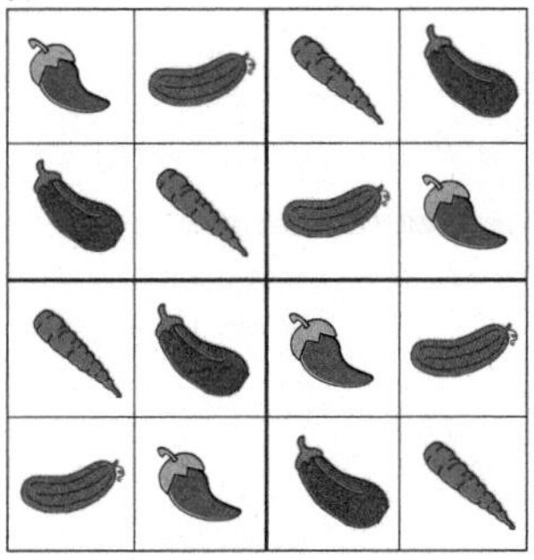

p. 56

The hats are in the middle column, second row and right column, last row.

p. 58

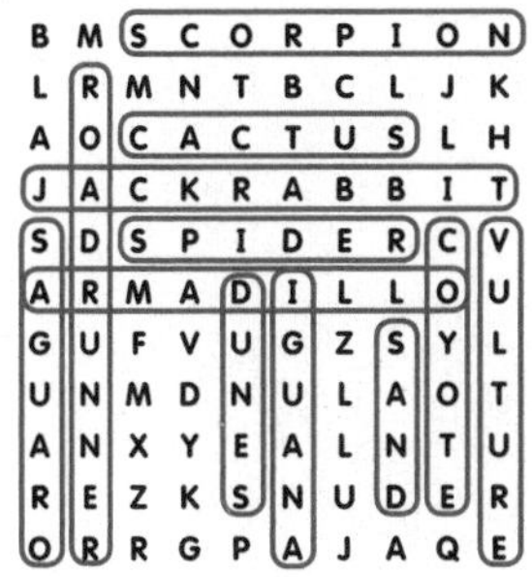

p. 60

cat, cot, dot, dog, fog, frog

p. 61

p. 62

He wanted to improve his bite!

p. 64

stop, pop, hop, hip, hill

p. 65

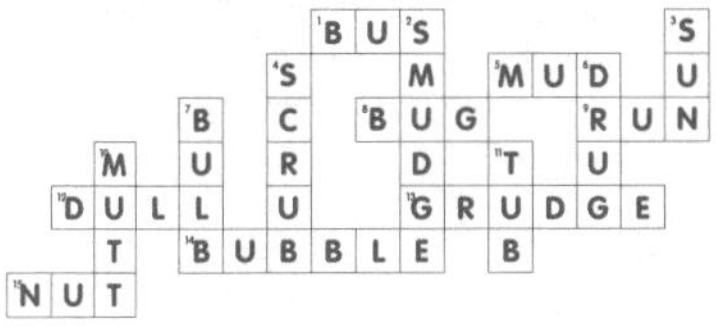

p. 66

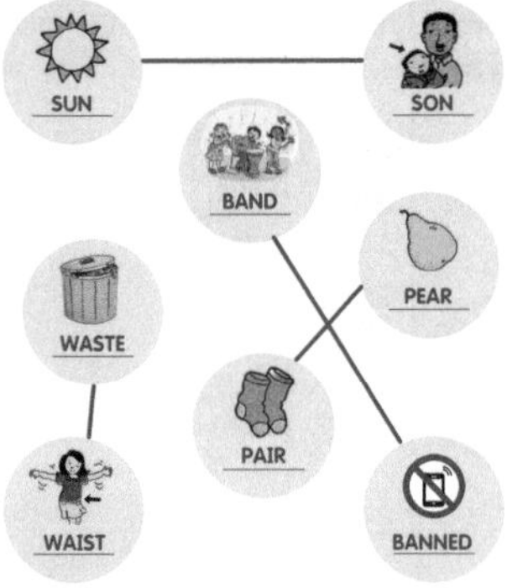
SUN
SON
BAND
PEAR
WASTE
PAIR
WAIST
BANNED

p. 69

p. 71

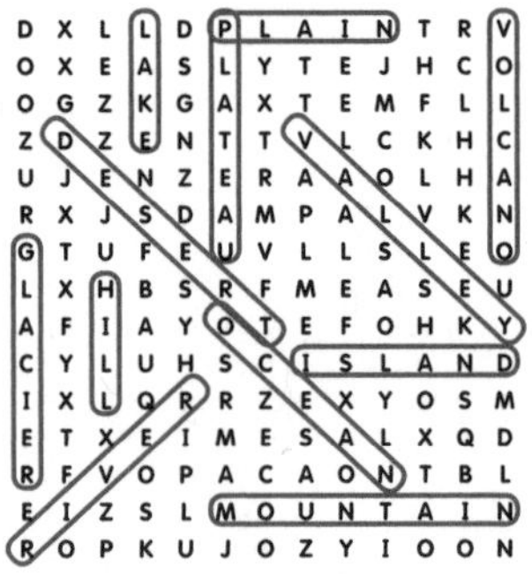

p. 72

4	9	2
3	5	7
8	1	6

5	6	1
0	4	8
7	2	3

10	5	6
3	7	11
8	9	4

5	10	3
4	6	8
9	2	7

p. 75

p. 77

Alabama, Florida, Georgia, Kentucky, Arkansas, Louisiana, Mississippi, North Carolina, South Carolina, Tennessee, Virginia, West Virginia; Mississippi River

p. 79

p. 81

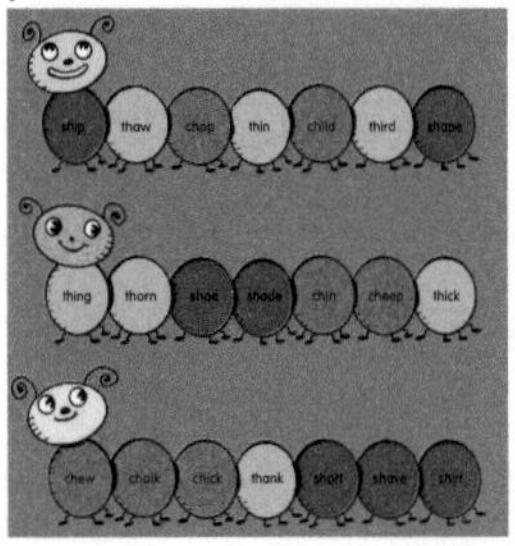

p. 82

hand, land, lane, late, fate, fade, made

p. 83

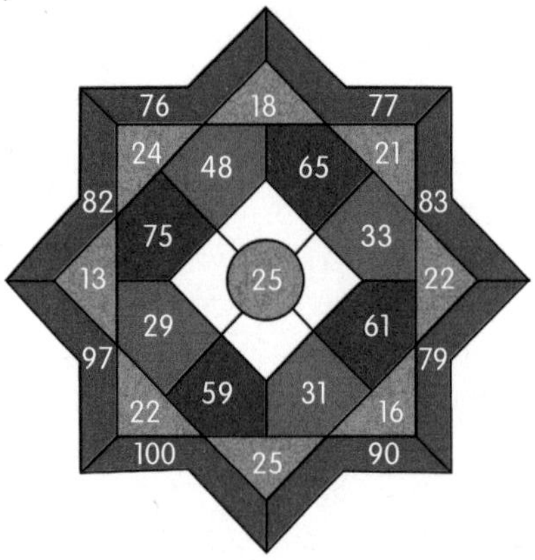
76
18
77
24
48
65
21
82
83
75
33
13
25
22
29
61
97
79
59
31
22
16
100
25
90

p. 84

jar, car, can, cane, crane

p. 85

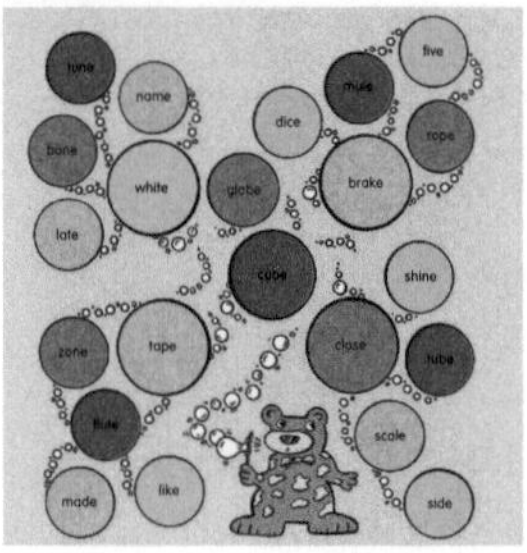

p. 86

p. 87

p. 88

Sample answers: ant, ape, eat, hat, heat, heel, help, lane, leap, let, neat, pal, pale, pan, path, pea, pen, pet, petal, plan, plane, planet, plant, plate, tape, tea, teen, ten, than, then

p. 90

Because they love to hang out with their friends!

p. 91

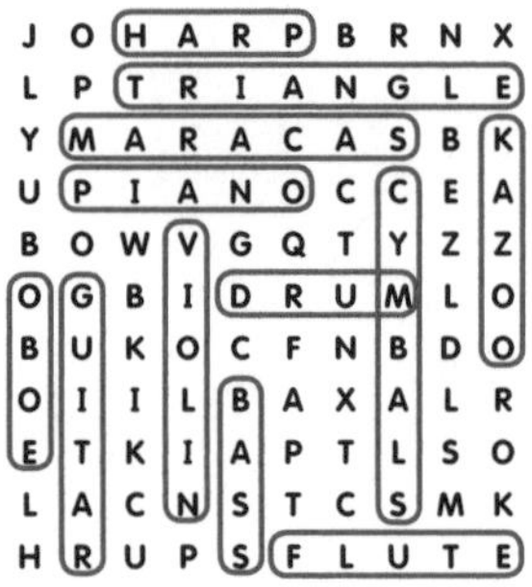

p. 92

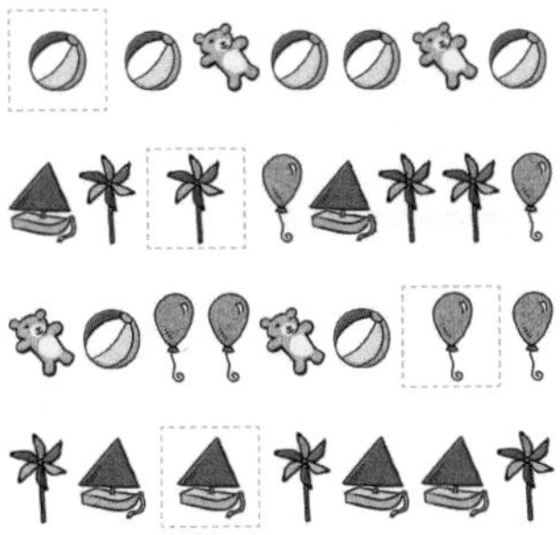

p. 95

6 + 2 = 8; 4 + 3 = 7; 2 + 1 = 3;
4 + 1 = 5; 11 + 3 = 14; 8 + 2 = 10;
7 + 5 = 12; 9 + 2 = 11; 6 + 3 = 9;
11 + 4 = 15; 5 + 13 = 18; 9 + 4 = 13;
A PIANO

p. 96

Because he could not fit inside the elevator!

p. 97

Six things should be circled.

p. 99

p. 100

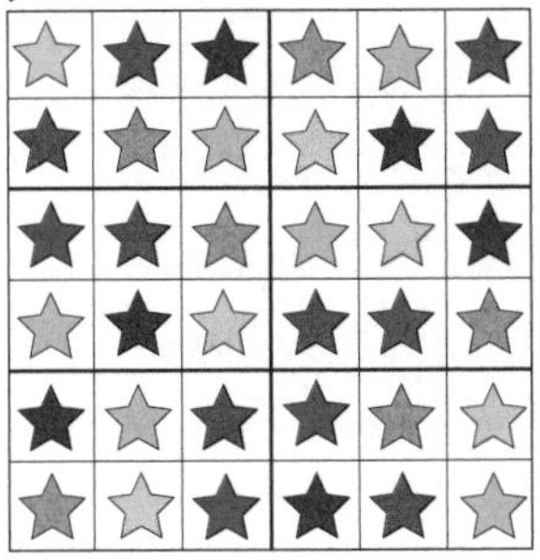

p. 101

fin, fan, ran, rain, train

p. 103

p. 104

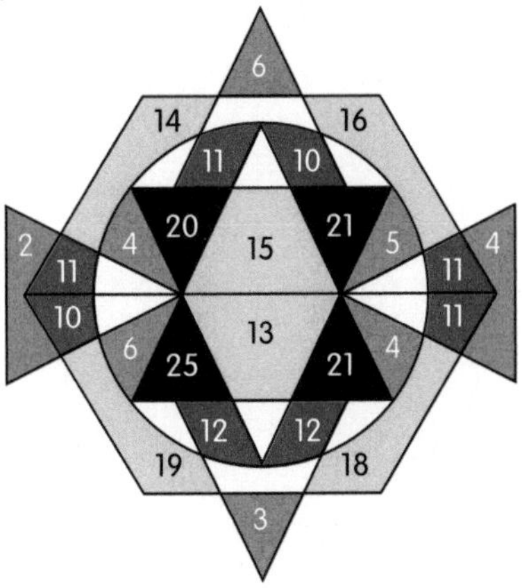

p. 105

tie, tip, rip, hip, ship

p. 107

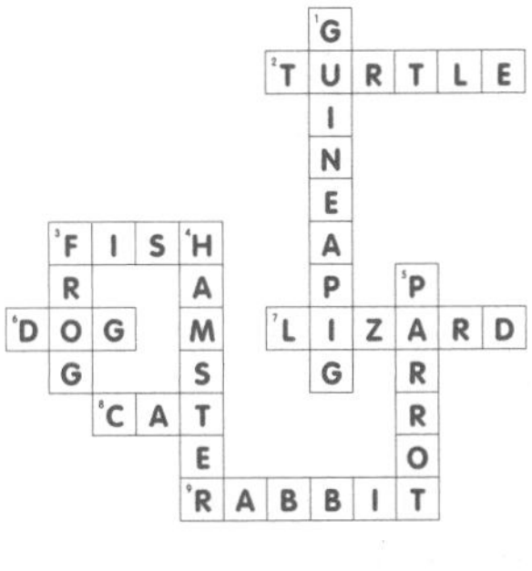
GUINEA PIG
TURTLE
FISH
HAMSTER
FROG
DOG
LIZARD
PARROT
CAT
RABBIT

p. 108

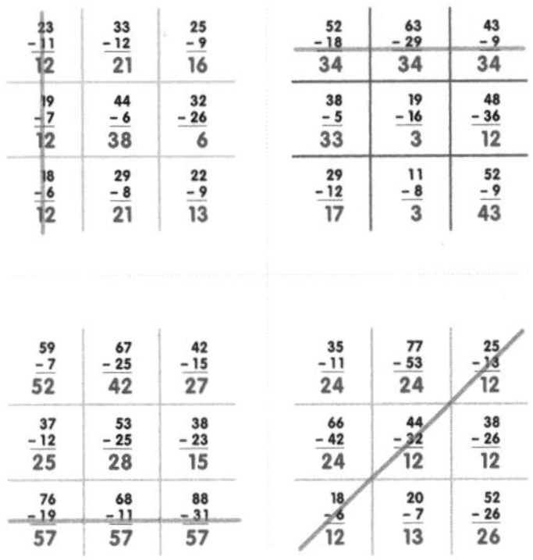

p. 109

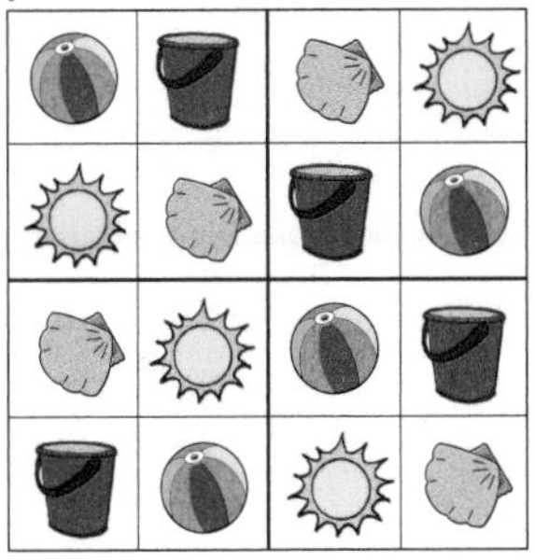

p. 110

The drawings are in the second row, far right and far left column.

p. 111

Connecticut, Maine, Massachusetts, New Hampshire, Rhode Island, Vermont; Boston

p. 113

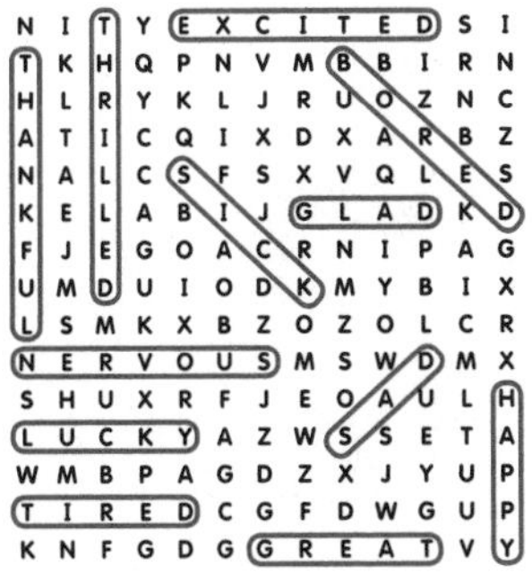

p. 115

king, wing, wig, pig, pin

p. 116

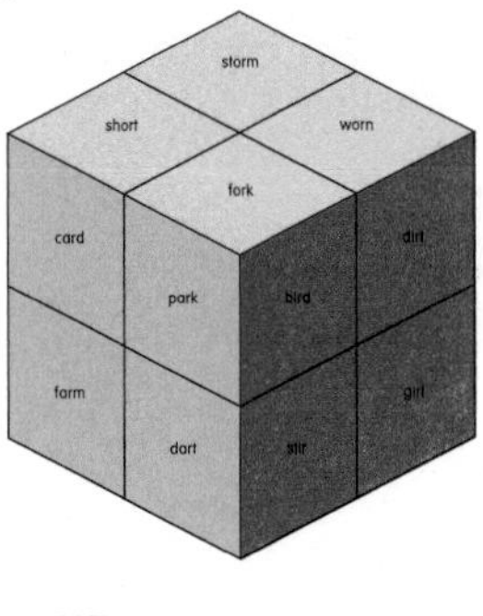
storm
short
worn
fork
card
park
bird
dirt
farm
dart
stir
girl

p. 117

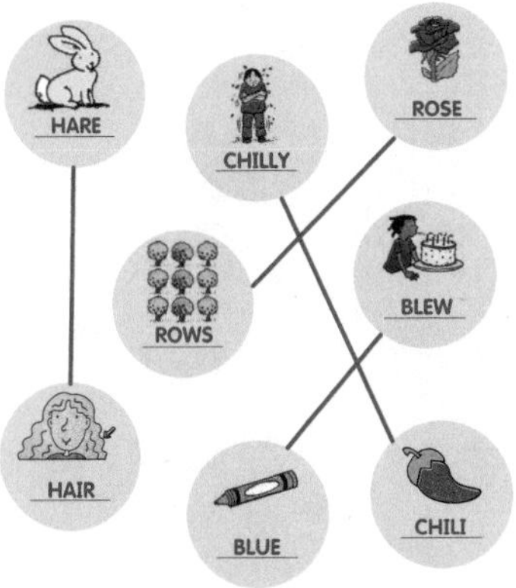
HARE
CHILLY
ROSE
ROWS
BLEW
HAIR
BLUE
CHILI

p. 118

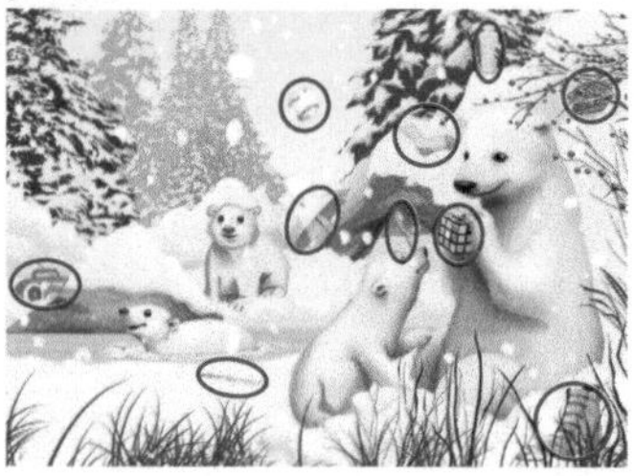

p. 119

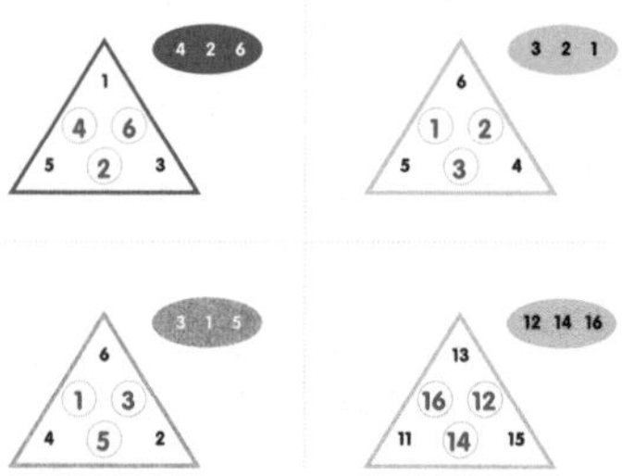

p. 121

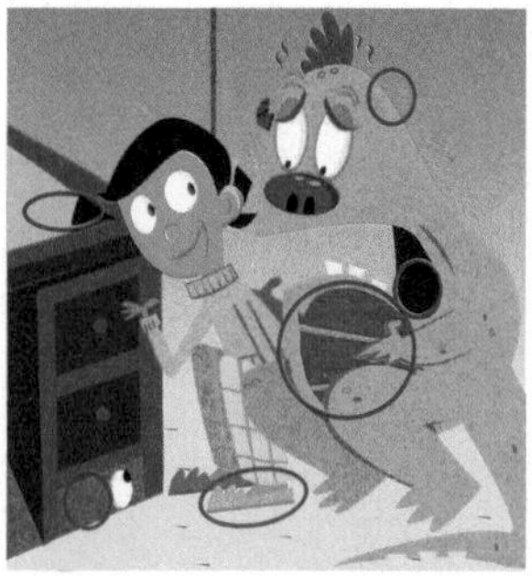

p. 122

Sample answers: air, alien, alone, ant, are, ate, ear, learn, let, lion, nail, national, near, neat, nine, none, not, one, otter, rain, rat, real, tail, ten, tent, tire, toe, torn, train, treat

p. 124

p. 127

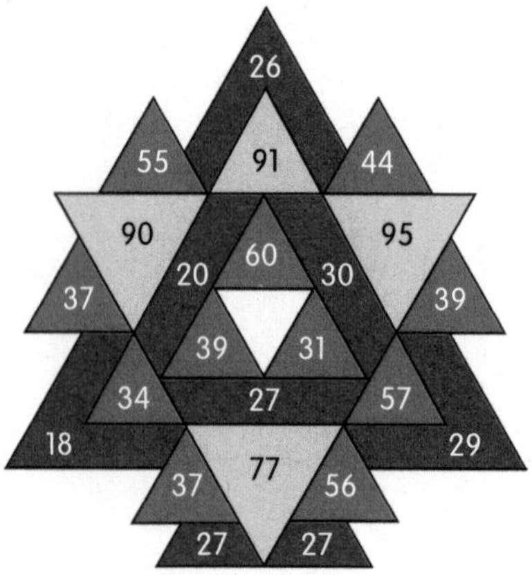

p. 129

He wanted to get to the other slide!

p. 130

p. 131

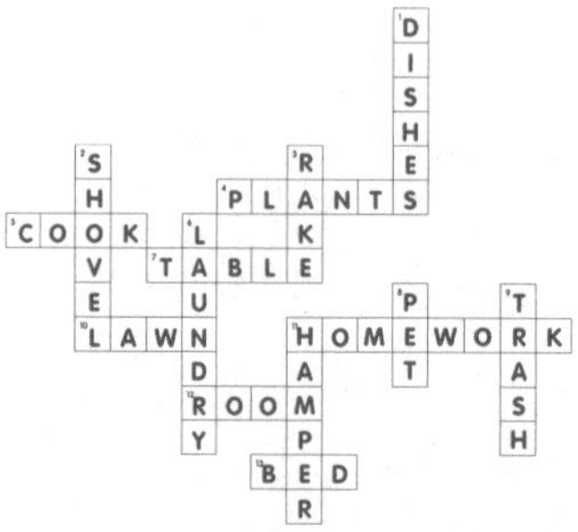

p. 132

sail, fail, fall, ball, bell, belt, bolt, boat

p. 133

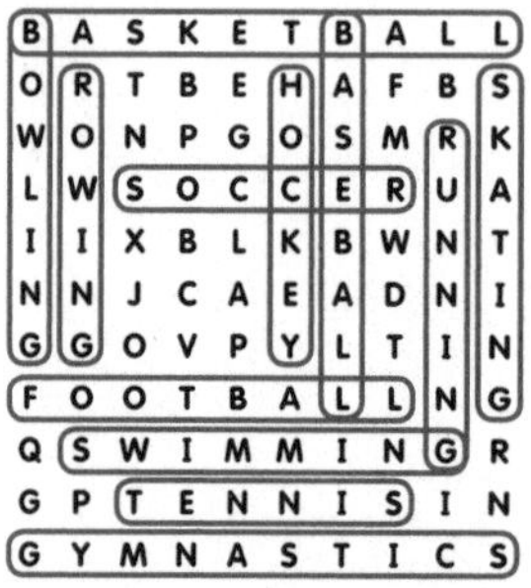

p. 134

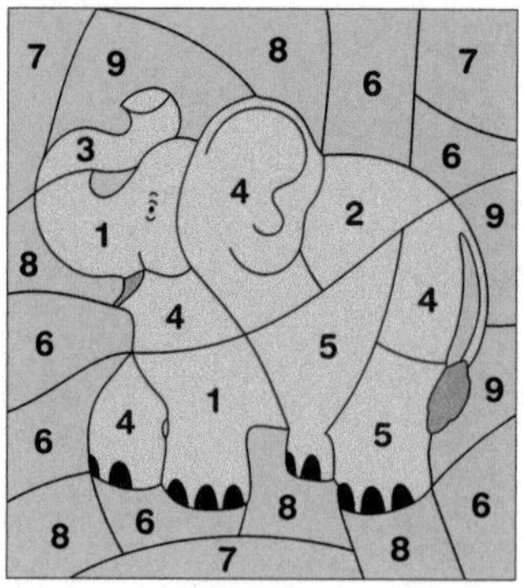

p. 135

clay, tray, hay, pay, pan

p. 137

The totem poles are top right and lower left.

p. 139

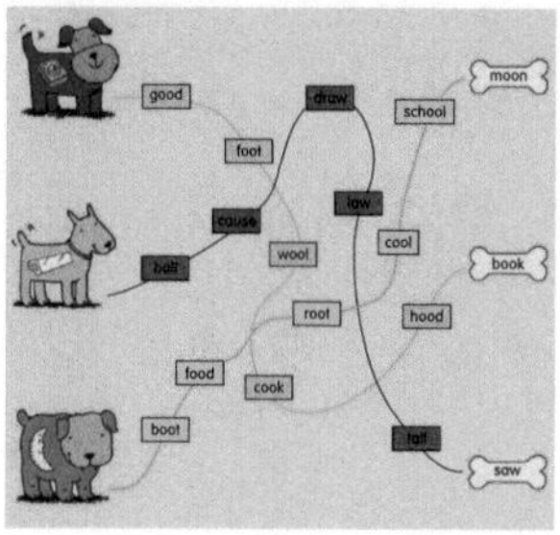
good
draw
school
moon
foot
cause
law
ball
wool
cool
book
root
hood
food
cook
boot
fall
saw

p. 140

good, gold, bold, bolt, belt, best

p. 142

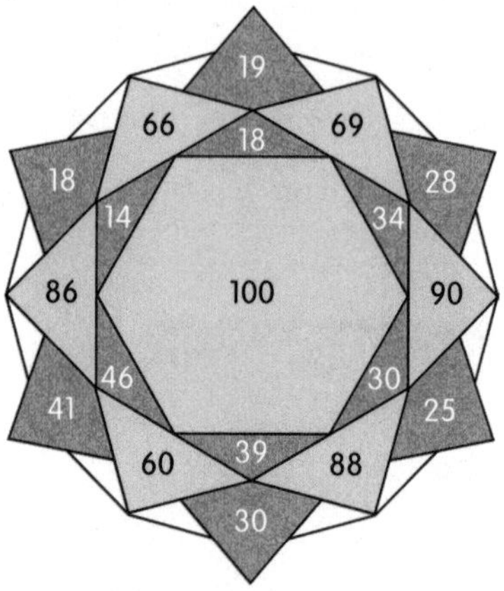

p. 143

coat, boat, bowl, bow, snow

p. 144

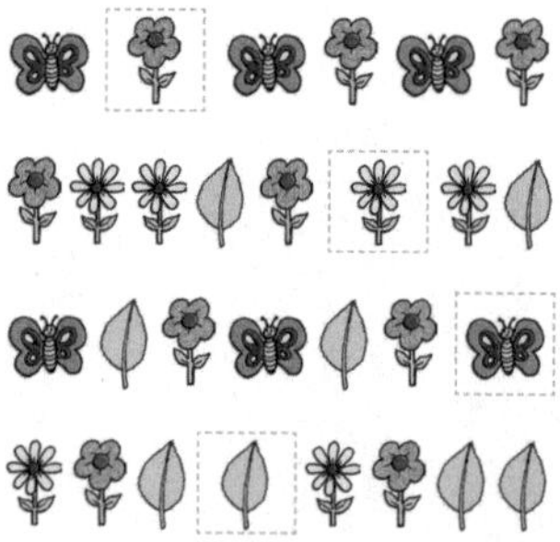

p. 145

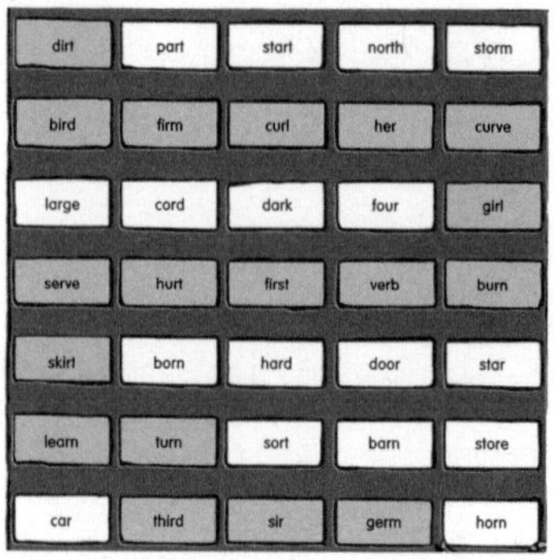
dirt
part
start
north
storm
bird
firm
curl
her
curve
large
cord
dark
four
girl
serve
hurt
first
verb
burn
skirt
born
hard
door
star
learn
turn
sort
barn
store
car
third
sir
germ
horn

p. 146

Clowns can do funny tricks.

p. 149

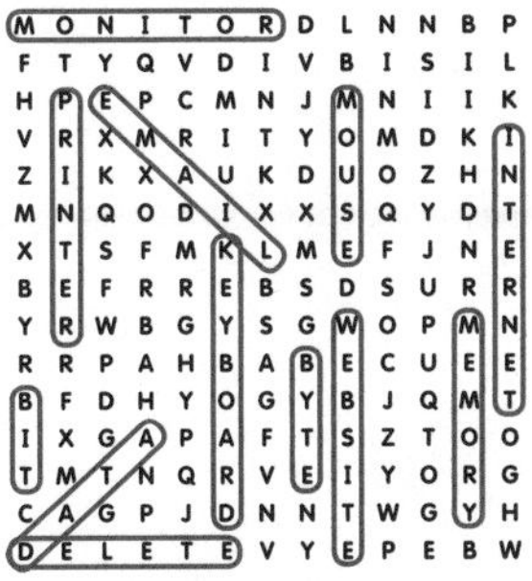

p. 151

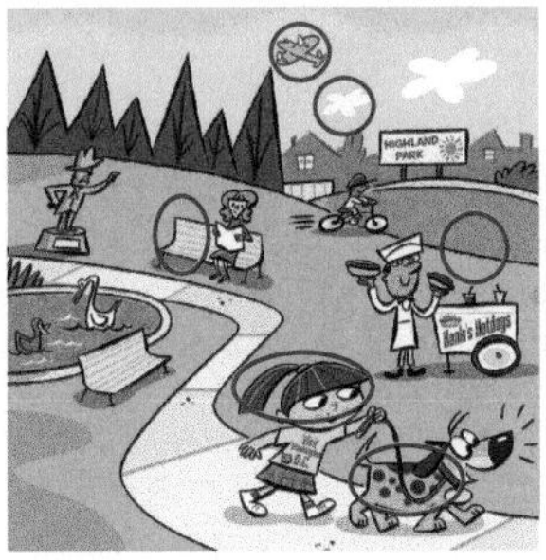

p. 153

p. 154

1. 10, 2. 30, 3. 12, 4. 5, 5. 40, 6. 400, A. 12, B. 400, C. 10, D. 5, E. 40, F. 30

p. 155

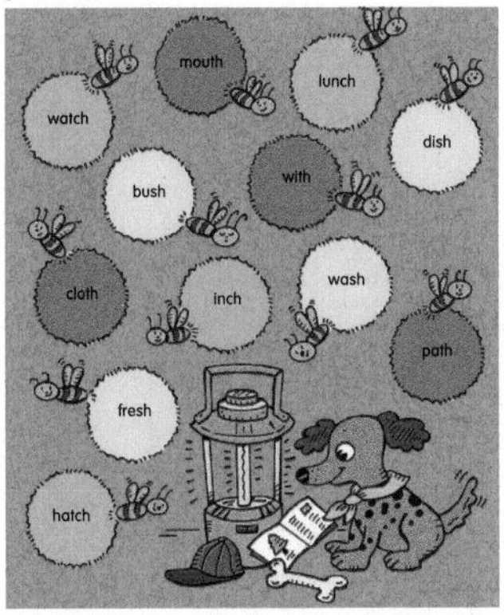
mouth
lunch
watch
dish
bush
with
cloth
inch
wash
path
fresh
hatch

p. 159

Ohio, Iowa, Kansas, Indiana, Illinois, Minnesota, Missouri, Nebraska, North Dakota, Michigan, South Dakota, Wisconsin; breadbasket

p. 161

Because they can never remember all of the words!

p. 162

beach, firefly, fireworks, ice cream, lake, picnic, sandals, swim, watermelon

p. 163

Sample answers: giant, goat, has, his, hot, nation, night, nothing, now, own, saw, show, sing, sit, snow, song, sting, than, thin, things, this, town, twin, two, wait, was, wash, what, who, with

p. 164

cup, cop, mop, mow, bow, bowl

p. 165

How many of each animal did you find?
4 1 6 3 2

p. 166

The unique pattern is in the last row, left column.

p. 167

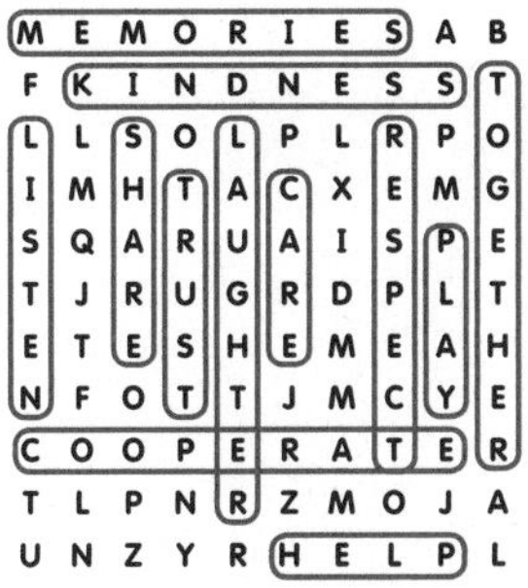

p. 168

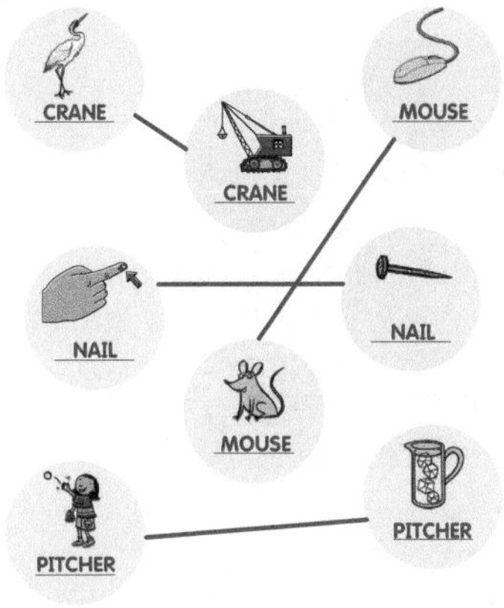
CRANE
CRANE
MOUSE
NAIL
NAIL
MOUSE
PITCHER
PITCHER

p. 169

p. 171

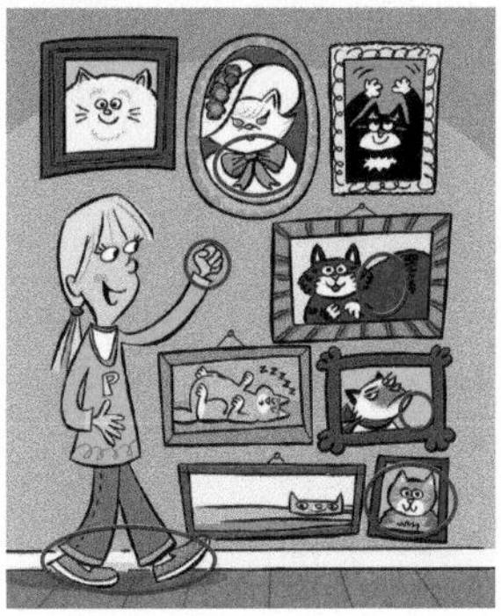

p. 172

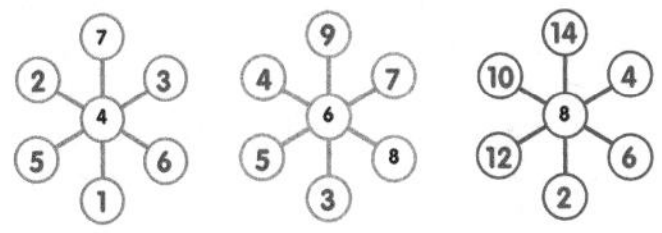

p. 174

bell, ball, tall, tail, mail

p. 177

"Excuse me, I am a little horse."

p. 178

p. 181

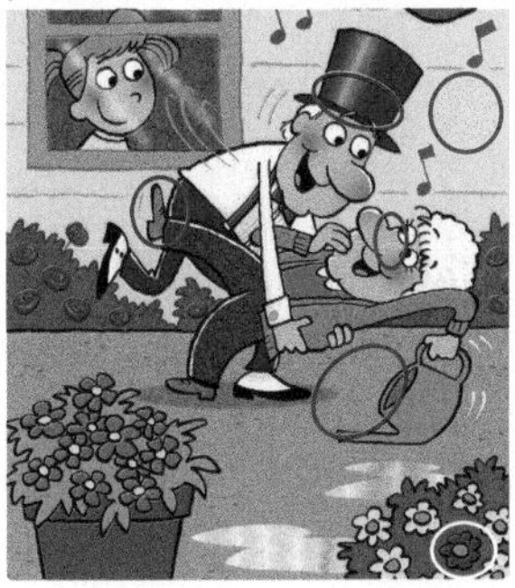

p. 182

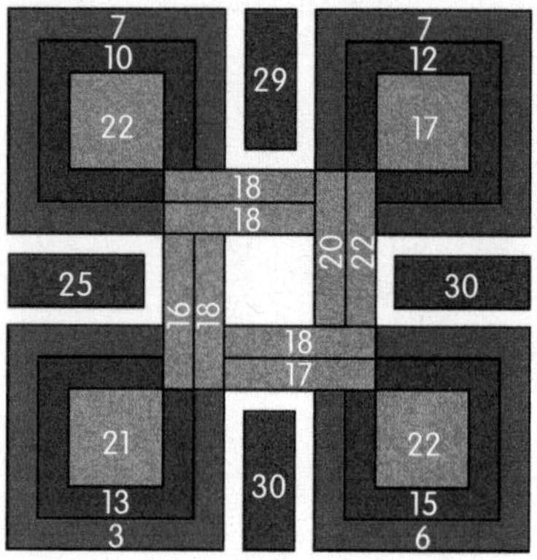

p. 183

hand, band, bond, fond, food, foot

p. 184

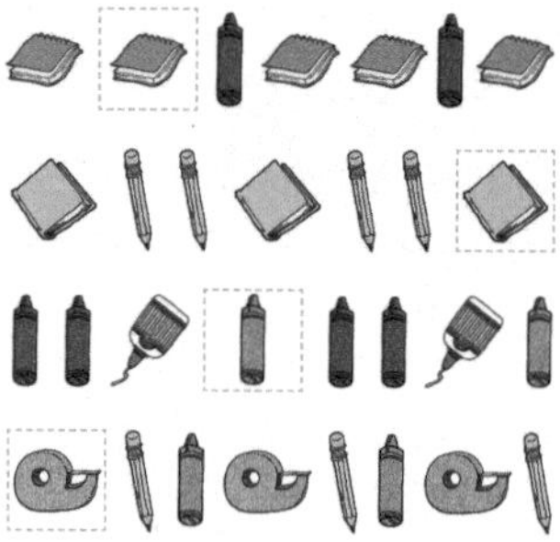

p. 185

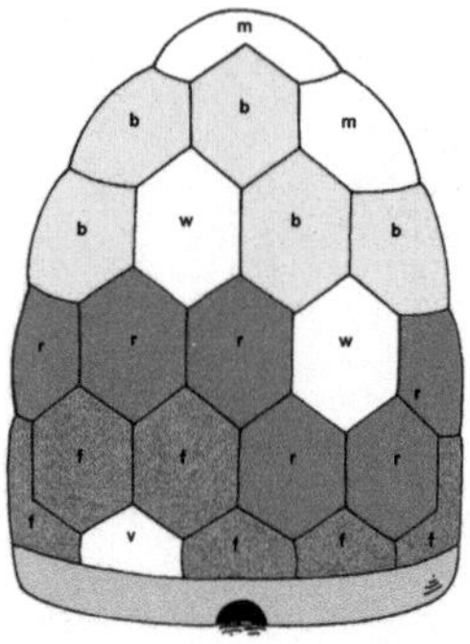

p. 186

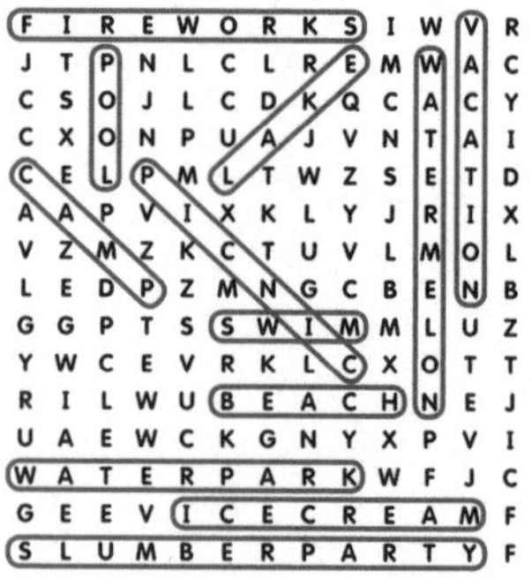

p. 187

The patterns are in the first row, left column and last row, right column.

p. 189

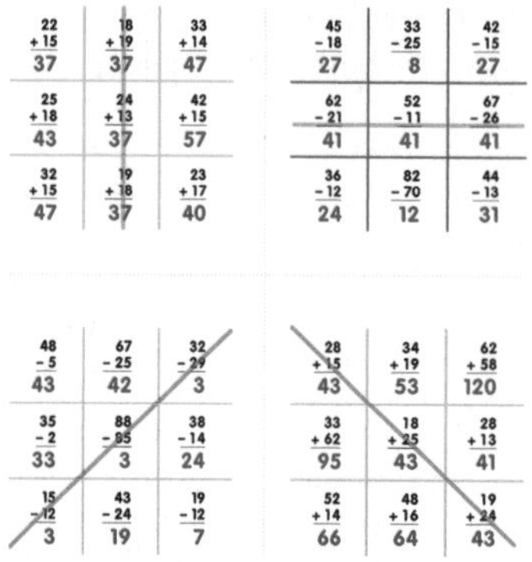

p. 190

24	19	28
15	16	23
18	19	22
25	28	25
18	27	18
19	16	29
18	15	28

p. 191

food, foot, boot, boat, goat

p. 193

p. 194

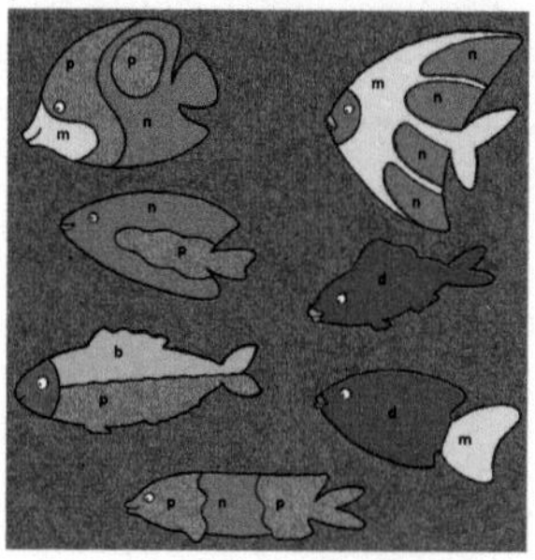

p. 195

p. 197

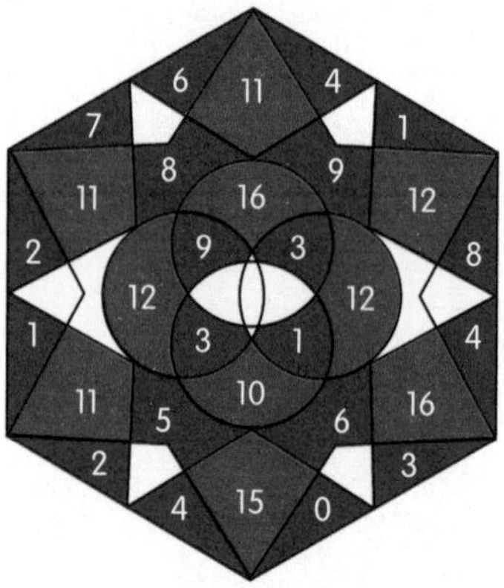

p. 199

Nothing, because he did not give a hoot!

p. 200

four, foul, fool, food, fond, find, fine, five

p. 201

p. 202

p. 204

Sample answers: ape, ash, happen, has, he, hen, hip, his, in, is, nap, pain, pan, pane, pass, peas, pen, pie, pin, pines, pipes, sap, sea, shape, she, shine, ship, sip, snap, spin

p. 205

p. 206

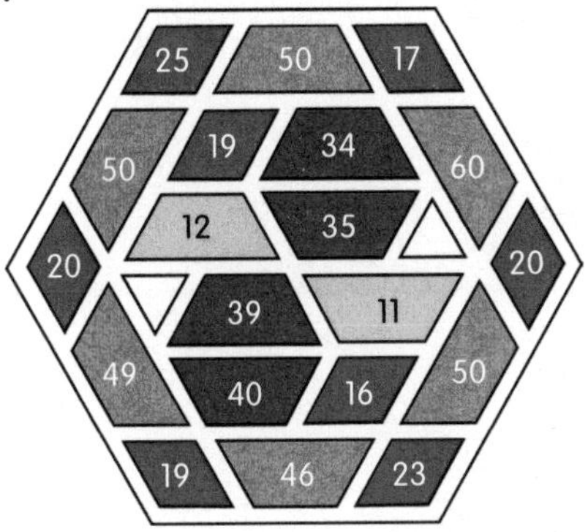

p. 207

duck, dump, jump, pump, bump

p. 208

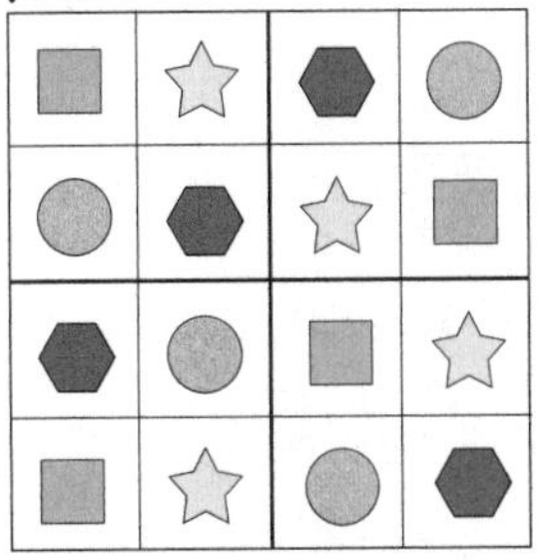

p. 209

He knew he had to do the right thing.

p. 213

1. CDE, EFG; 2. 26, 55; 3. ✖, ▲▲▲▲; 4. 66, 44; 5. k, o; 6. ➔, ⬆; 7. x, t, p; 8. B, W, F

p. 214

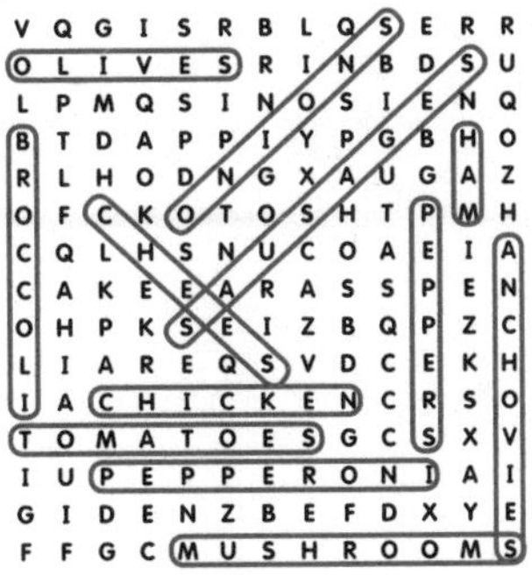

p. 215

p. 216

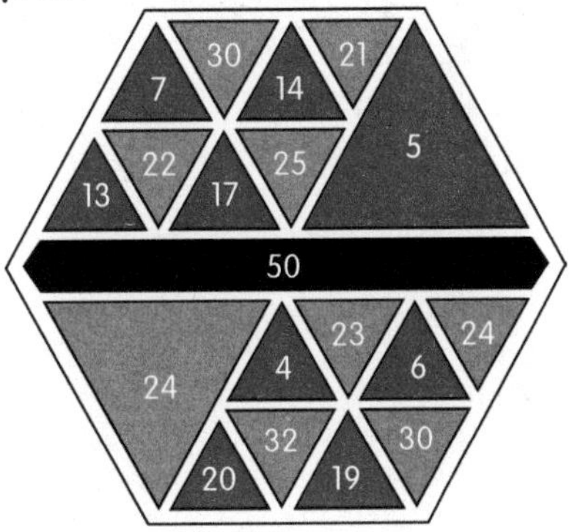

p. 217

fool, food, wood, word, wore, wire, wise

p. 218

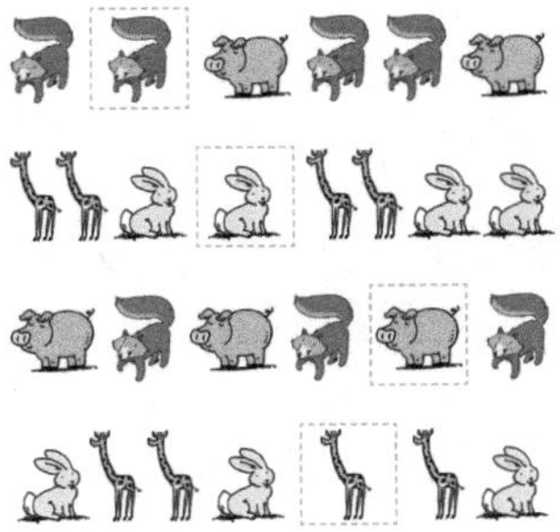

p. 220

p. 222

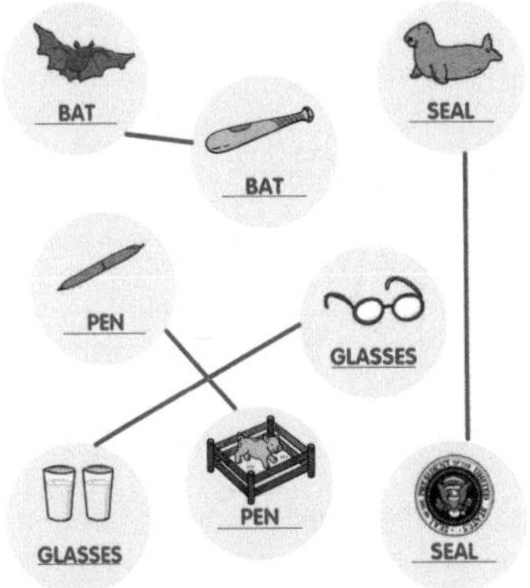
BAT
SEAL
BAT
PEN
GLASSES
GLASSES
PEN
SEAL

p. 223

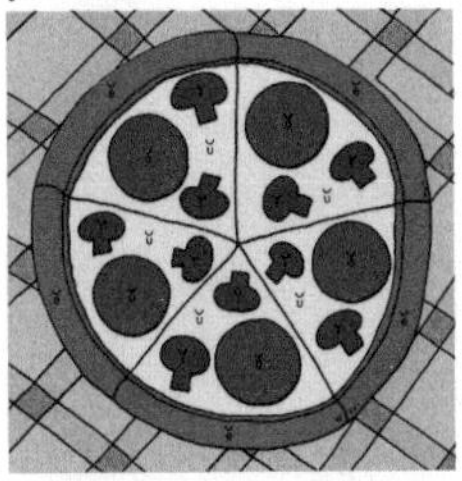

p. 225

p. 226

Even: 22, 46, 120, 234, 360, 346, 180, 18, 250, 48, 230, 194, 126, 150, 282, 24, 34; Odd: 315, 221, 63, 95, 243, 131, 153, 119

p. 227

Because it was squeaking!

p. 228

Arizona, New Mexico, Oklahoma, Texas; Grand Canyon

p. 230

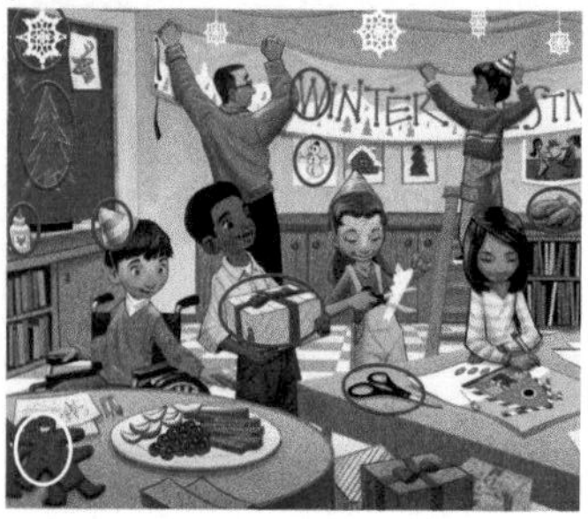

p. 231

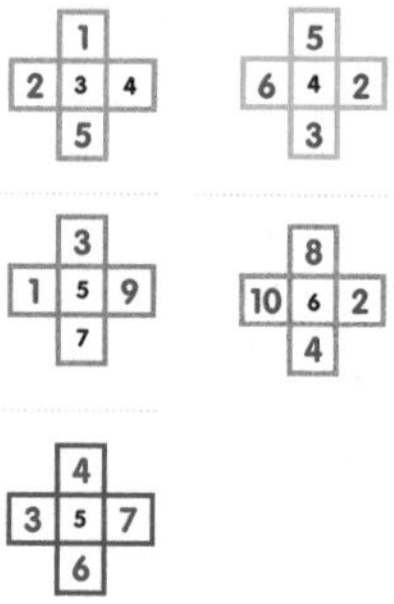
1
2 3 4
5
5
6 4 2
3
3
1 5 9
7
8
10 6 2
4
4
3 5 7
6

p. 232

Sample answers: decide, deep, deepen, den, depend, dependence, dice, did, died, dine, dined, dip, end, ended, ice, in, inn, need, needed, nice, niece, nine, nip, pen, penned, pie, piece, pin, pine, pinned

p. 233

BEETLE
BUTTERFLY
CATERPILLAR
ANT
GRASSHOPPER
FLY
LADYBUG

p. 235

p. 236

tack, sack, sock, lock, clock

p. 237

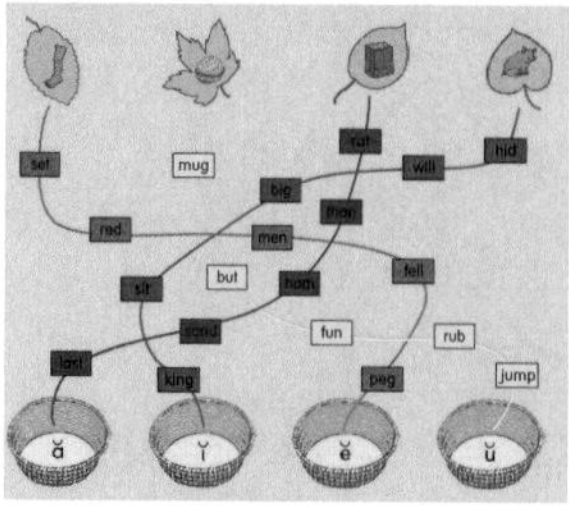
mug
but
fun
rub
jump

p. 238

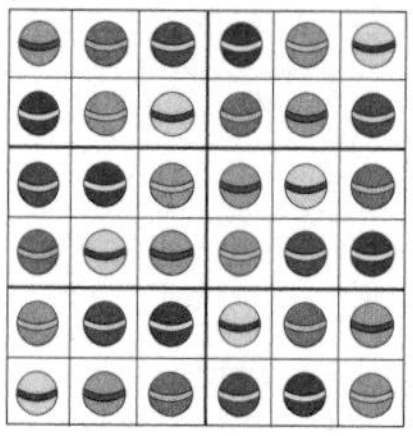

p. 239

p. 241

acorn, apple, school, corn, harvest, hay, pumpkin, scarecrow, sweater

p. 242

Sample answers: comet, cost, cot, eyes, me, meet, mess, messy, met, moss, mossy, most, my, sect, see, seems, set, so, some, soy, stem, system, teems, to, toe, toss, toys, yes, yet

p. 243

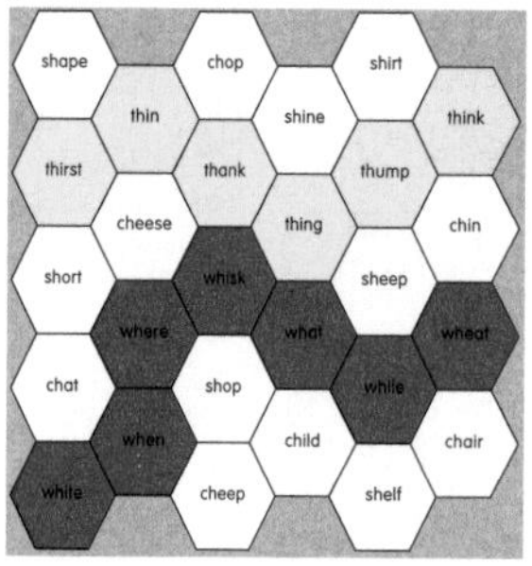
shape
chop
shirt
thin
shine
think
thirst
thank
thump
cheese
thing
chin
short
whisk
sheep
where
what
wheat
chat
shop
while
child
chair
when
white
cheep
shelf

p. 245

p. 246

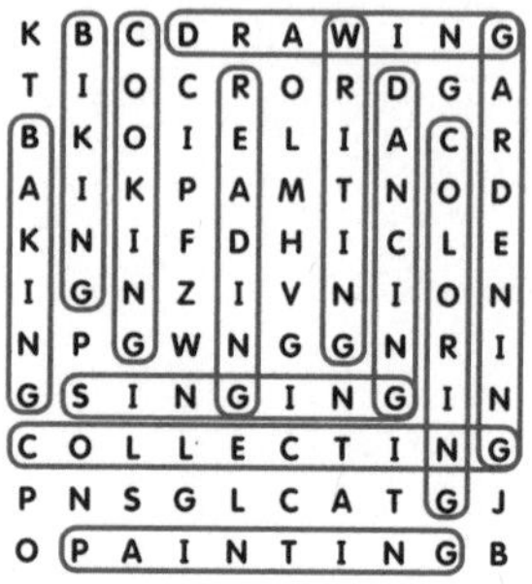
K B C D R A W I N G
T I O C R O R D G A
B K O I E L I A C R
A I K P A M T N O D
K N I F D H I C L E
I G N Z I V N I O N
N P G W N G G N R I
G S I N G I N G I N
C O L L E C T I N G
P N S G L C A T G J
O P A I N T I N G B

p. 249

tame, time, tile, mile, mild, wild

p. 250

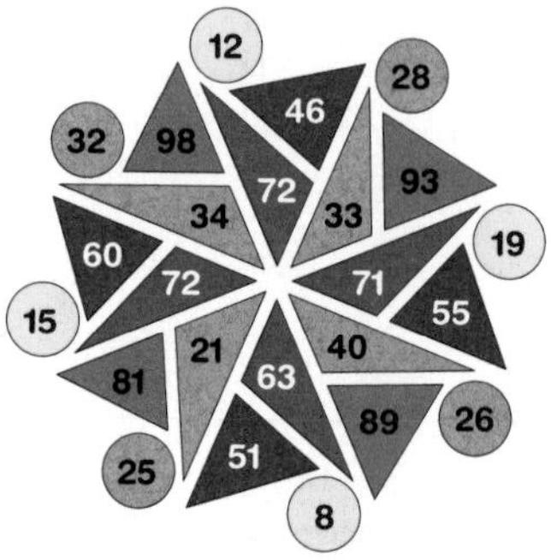
12
46
28
32
98
72
93
34
33
19
60
72
71
55
15
21
40
81
63
89
26
25
51
8

p. 251

2 Mia asked Mr. Carson for help.
3 Mr. Carson called his firefighter friends.
8 The firefighters laughed.
5 A firefighter climbed the ladder.
1 Mia begged Spooky to come down.
6 Spooky jumped to a tree and climbed down.
4 The fire truck came.
7 Mia scolded Spooky.

p. 252

pear, bear, bead, beak, beach

p. 253

There are 10 hidden items.

p. 256

TWO
TWENTY
TEN
THREE
FOUR
SIX
ZERO
FIVE
NINE
SEVEN
EIGHT
ONE

p. 258

The clocks are in the second row, first column and the last row, second column.

p. 259

cold, December, February, freezing, ice, January, snow, snowflake, snowman

p. 260

Sample answers: act, age, ant, can, cat, eat, face, fan, fang, fine, game, gate, get, giant, gift, ice, imagine, item, magic, magnet, main, mean, met, mice, mine, nice, nine, tea, team, time

p. 261

11
22
75
50
54
19
31
66
75
34
89
86
25
22
41
47
28
23

p. 263

THRILLING AND AMAZING TOURS OF BORING

p. 264

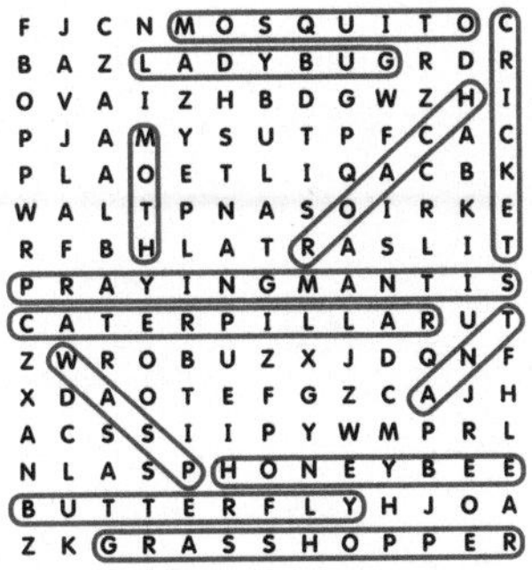

F J C N M O S Q U I T O C
B A Z L A D Y B U G R D R
O V A I Z H B D G W Z H I
P J A M Y S U T P F C A C
P L A O E T L I Q A C B K
W A L T P N A S O I R K E
R F B H L A T R A S L I T
P R A Y I N G M A N T I S
C A T E R P I L L A R U T
Z W R O B U Z X J D Q N F
X D A O T E F G Z C A J H
A C S S I I P Y W M P R L
N L A S P H O N E Y B E E
B U T T E R F L Y H J O A
Z K G R A S S H O P P E R

p. 265

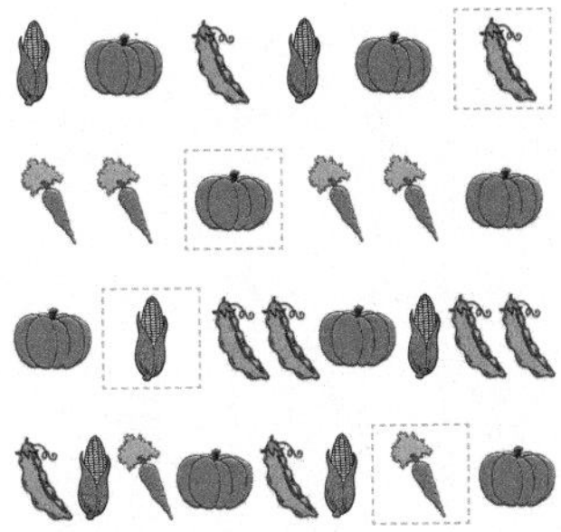

p. 266

p. 267

nap, cap, can, pan, pant, part, park

p. 268

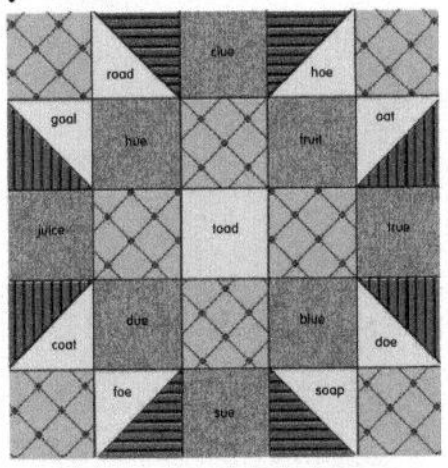

p. 270

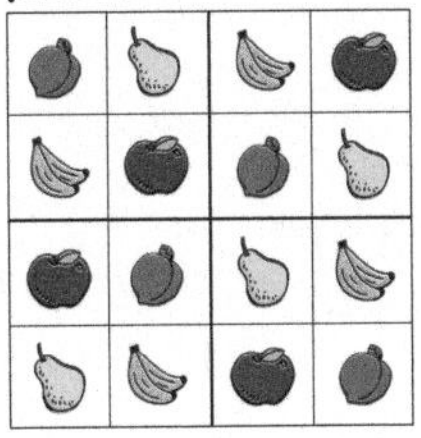

p. 271

Your great ant, of course!

p. 272

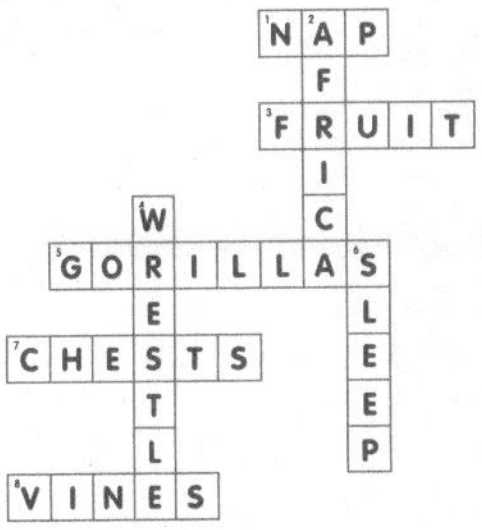

NAP
AFRICA
FRUIT
WRESTLE
GORILLAS
SLEEP
CHESTS
VINES

p. 273

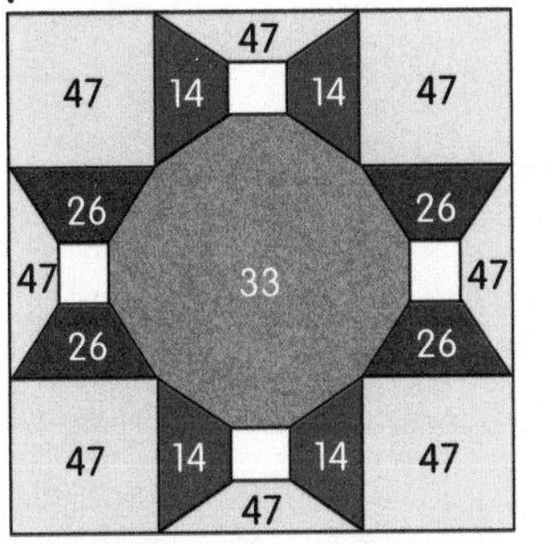

47
47 14 14 47
26 26
47 33 47
26 26
47 14 14 47
47

p. 275

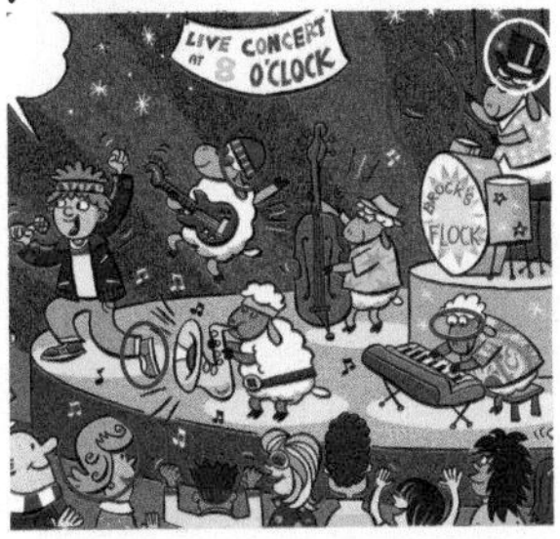

LIVE CONCERT AT 8 O'CLOCK

p. 277

1. TSR, NML; 2. ★, ❍; 3. 50, 140; 4. 72, 108; 5. ❍, ■; 6. df, pr; 7. 26, 68; 8. ✔✔, ✖✖

p. 279

4	1	2	3
3	2	1	4
1	4	3	2
2	3	4	1

1	3	2	4
4	2	3	1
3	1	4	2
2	4	1	3

2	1	4	3
4	3	1	2
1	2	3	4
3	4	2	1

1	2	4	3
3	4	2	1
2	1	3	4
4	3	1	2

p. 280

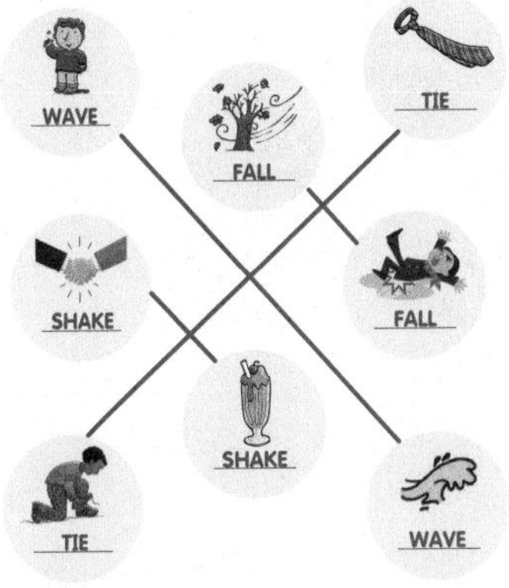

WAVE
FALL
TIE
SHAKE
FALL
SHAKE
TIE
WAVE

p. 281

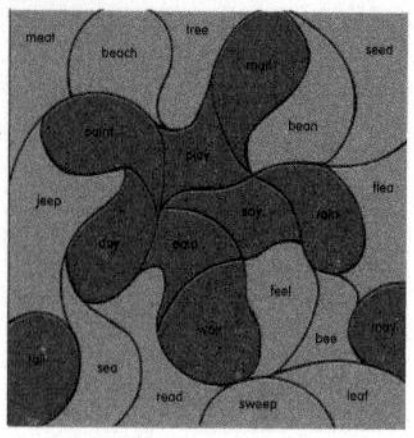

p. 282

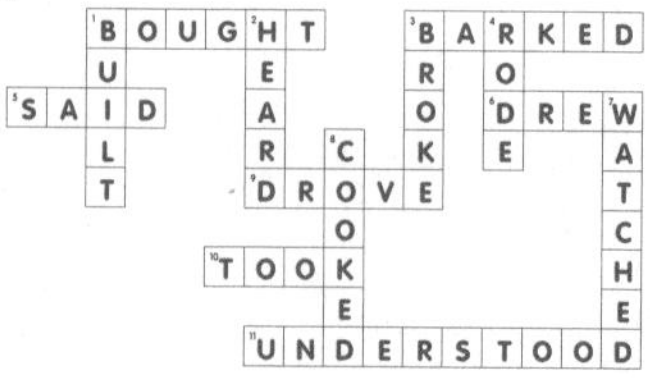

p. 283

rain, drain, stain, stair, hair

p. 285

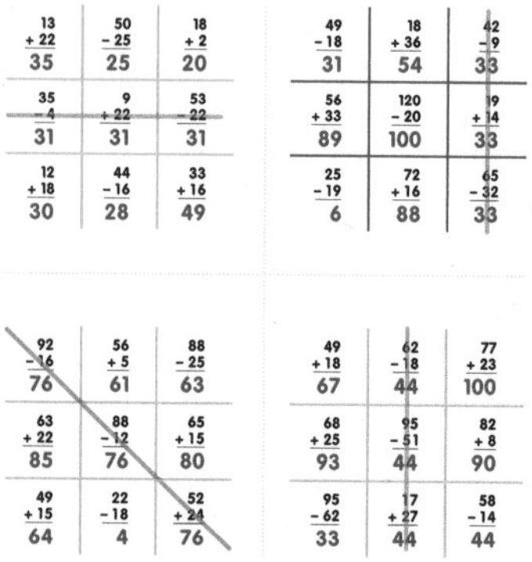

p. 286

p. 289

p. 290

book, boot, bolt, belt, best, test

p. 291

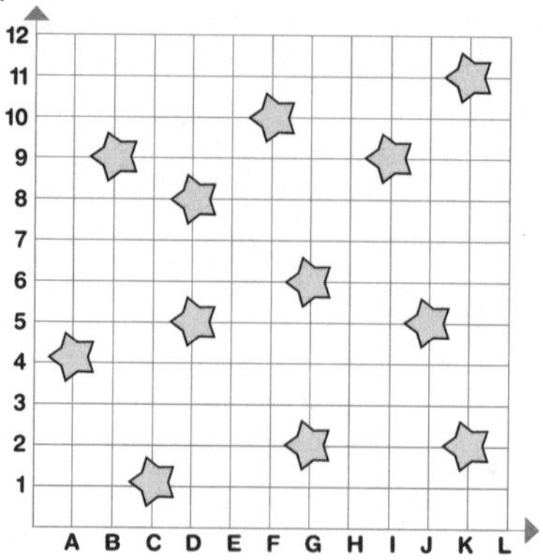

p. 292

A very embarrassed zebra!

p. 293

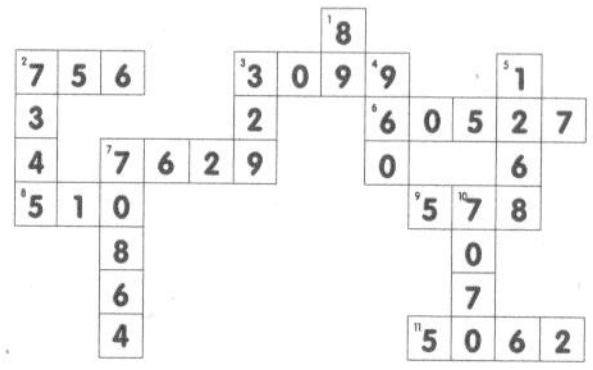

p. 294

p. 295

fast food; flower bed

p. 297

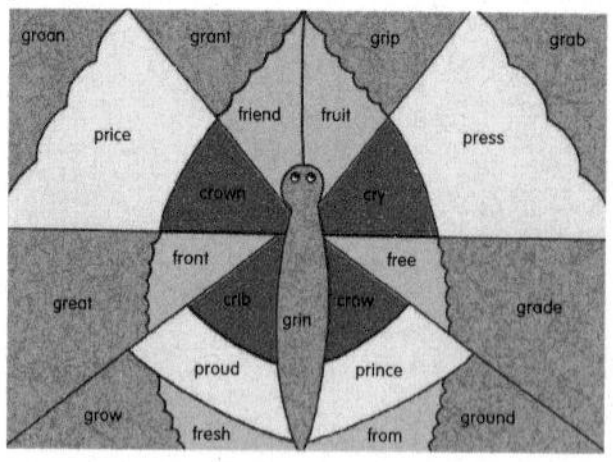

p. 298

Sample answers: air, art, hair, hamster, heart, hope, horse, map, pear, pet, poem, promise, room, rose, shampoo, sharp, ship, shirt, shoe, short, sit, smart, soap, some, star, stop, stripe, tape, teams, time

p. 300

Alaska, Colorado, California, Hawaii, Idaho, Montana, Nevada, Oregon, Utah, Washington, Wyoming; Yellowstone

p. 303

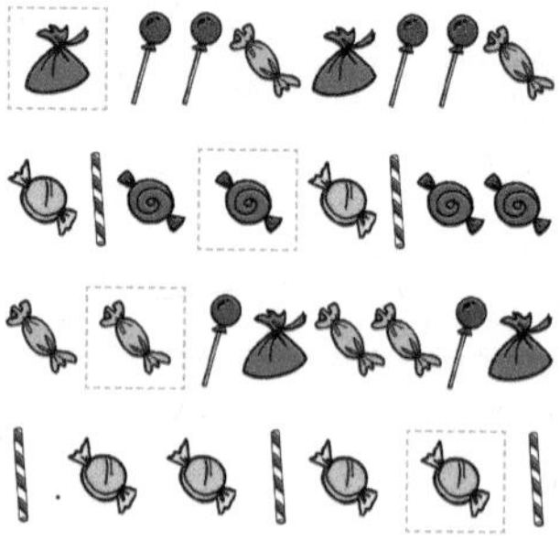

p. 304

p. 305

real, seal, sell, tell, tall, tale, take, fake

p. 306

The chairs are in the second row, fourth column, and the third row, second column.

p. 308

p. 309

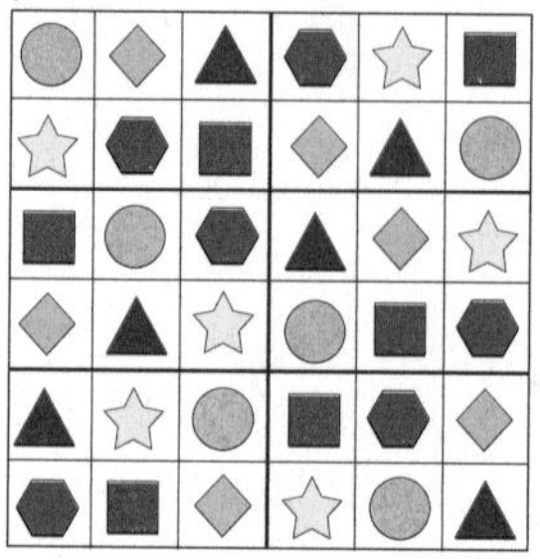